Truthfully, Yours

TRUTHFULLY, YOURS

THE BEGINNING

R. G. MYERS

iUniverse, Inc.
Bloomington

TRUTHFULLY, YOURS
The Beginning

iUniverse books may be ordered through booksellers or by contacting:

iUniverse
1663 Liberty Drive
Bloomington, IN 47403
www.iuniverse.com
1-800-Authors (1-800-288-4677)

ISBN: 978-1-4697-6699-7 (sc)
ISBN: 978-1-4697-6700-0 (ebk)

Printed in the United States of America

iUniverse rev. date: 02/11/2012

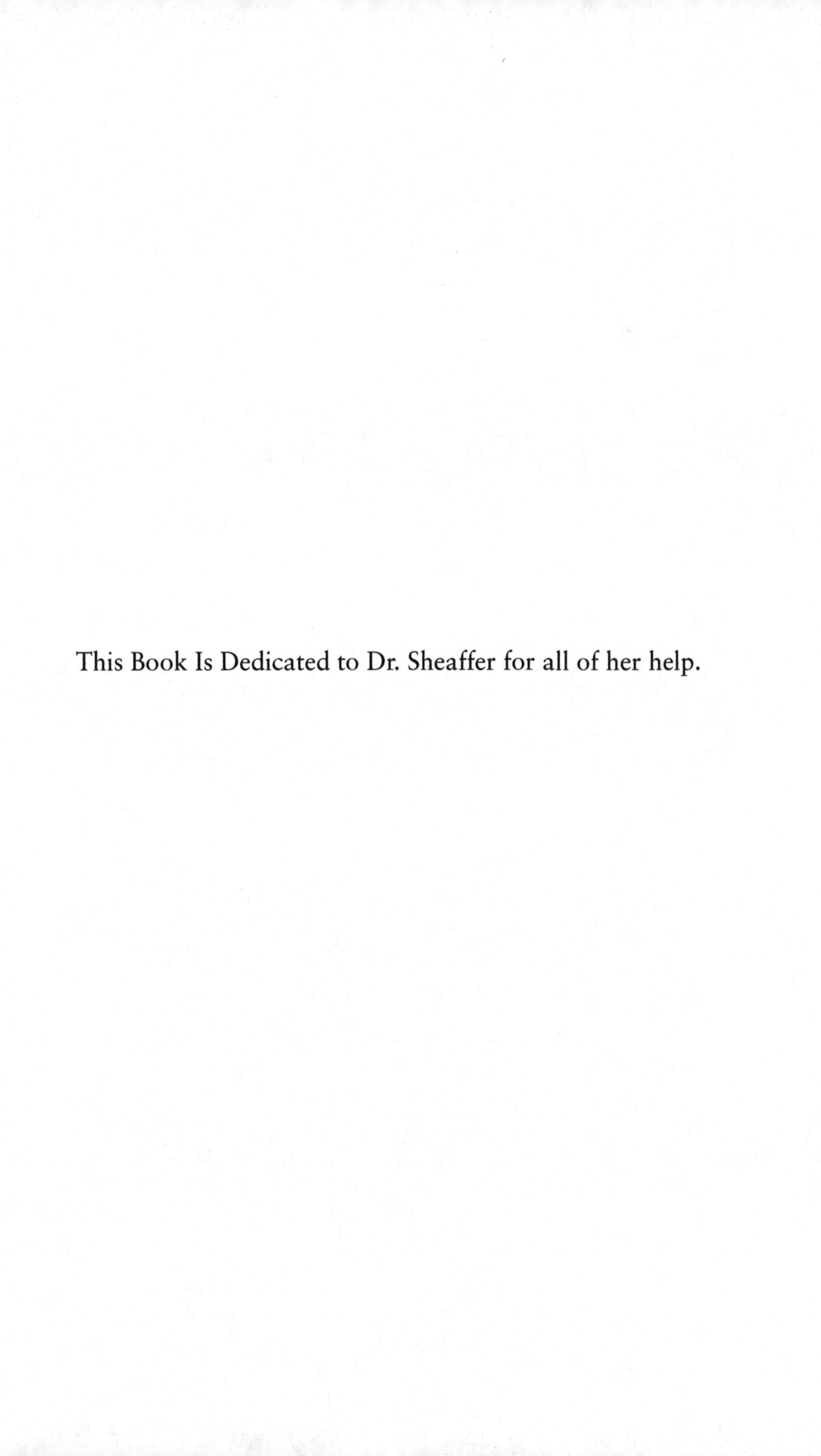

This Book Is Dedicated to Dr. Sheaffer for all of her help.

INTRODUCTION

I want to thank all of my readers who purchased this first sequel series. A message is provided in each chapter for you to relate your thoughts. Meet my main stars: Hans Schweitzer, Sasha Rebonwitz, and Mela. Their character represents bravery, love, and forgiveness; and the legacy of this book continues beyond that. You will witness their mistakes, their weaknesses, and their forgiveness to one another. Both Hans and I will tell you the story of how it all happened from the beginning. Listen to what both Hans and I say because this is a story of a young German officer, Hans Schweitzer, who refuses to hate and later on commits the most forbidden act in Germany. "Happy Truthfully, Yours."

INTRODUCTION

TRUTHFULLY, YOURS

I am Hans Schweitzer, Lt. Colonel Commander of Kassel Labor Camp in Germany of 1940. This is my story, a story that has been hidden that I can only tell. I was seventeen years old when I had to join Hitler's Youth group in which my parents never knew what it would be like for me when I joined. I had no choice because I had to join or else suffer the consequences for both my family. So being young and naive, I was on the proud kick where I thought I was the prime object, so I thought. I was a typical German, 5'11 with blue eyes and medium blond hair that fell on my face. I was muscular, mainly because I helped my father with building barns. I had no girlfriend or a future, especially during the war where nothing was certain. I only had my parents and my adopted family, Hitler's Youth. They promised me everything that I thought was perfect for me. Everything my parents could not give, they offered to give it to me. I had to go down to the Gestapo headquarters in Berlin. At that time, I met Frank Stomacher, Colonel of the First Division who spoke to me about my future. There he spoke to me about how excellent my grades were in school and conjectured that within a year I could become Commander. They needed good men who would stand up for what they believed. However, I thought that my own mind would be erased and programmed to what they wanted me to become. Anyway, I signed the papers, drank some soda, and went to say goodbye to my father. Before anything, I had to go to a large room for preparation. I noticed that this room was large with so many young men who were innocent to this nonsense. I myself sat in the front waiting to hear what I had missed in the newspapers. As I sat there waiting, a large stern looking man came in full uniform with medals plastered to his chest. I sat there looking at him picturing myself in that uniform. For once, I was getting excited about my future. The officer, Lt. Col Heinz Van Brueghel, was briefing us about our adventure in "Hitler's Youth" and how we will be prepared for the next step. He even went beyond in speaking about deserting the war and what would happen to us and any penalties. Actually it was death by shooting and no questions asked. We are not supposed to desert our mother country for nothing. I knew he wasn't talking about me because I sure didn't want to be a deserter to anyone, at least not now. The question was, would I pass their test for acceptance? The officer also told us of how we would be examined for any diseases and checked to see that we are from the pure German race with no mixes. I knew already that I passed that test and was ready to move on to the next stage of this training. The officer told us that we would also be examined for any diseases including any practice of homosexuality and the purity of our bloodline. Again, I had passed that test and now my training. The SS made it to the point we had to be in perfect health in order to complete the physical training. We couldn't have any defects, aliments or a disease: those were the rules, and rules had to be followed, so they said. Again, I passed that test. I next, went to another room in which I sat for two long hours, and I was getting hungry. I wanted a break, and it was around 1:00 PM that we finally ate. The officers took us to this cafeteria where we were all quiet and ate. However, before we could even eat, we had to say a short grace and were shown how to eat with our fork and knife. The officer told us we must eat like Germans and that is to eat with our fork in our left and cut with our right. I ate my meat the way they said we had to as I pushed more potatoes on my fork. While I was eating, I noticed an SS officer speaking as he sat with others in the corner. He had a stern looking face and talked without a smile. I began to wonder whether I could really adapt to this kind of life.

DEPARTURE

Mom and Dad were very proud of me, especially being the only child for them. I passed all of my tests, and my training was going well for me. I found out that we did not belong to our parents anymore but to Hitler, and I did not like that idea at all. I had to keep my mouth shut and not say anything. The SS officer told us that we had to respect Hitler because he was our father and leader of Germany. We were Germany's future, and I asked myself whether I was really Hitler's answer? The day was cold and raining, and I had to put my tan uniform on and go to class. My day was well prepared, and my mind was not my own. As I walked into my classroom, I noticed something strange written on the board. It read "Jew." I tried to think what Jews had to do with today's lesson. I did remember how Hitler kept saying it was for Germany, to strengthen our people and to have prosperity and pureness. We were Germany's eyes, future generation where we must succeed. Mother and Father never taught me to hate anyone, but to love. No matter who they were, we had to help everyone. Now I realized I would have to change all of that upbringing and live with Nazi thoughts. The question remained: will I? Still Nazis brings me to the great question, "what does this have to do with Jews?" I finally found out when the SS officer walked into the room, he had glasses that dipped below his eyes, making his eyes firm and not rising. None of us dared to speak or even laugh. I was serious from the beginning and wondered whether my face was turning stern. He told us that our first lesson is to know our enemy well, and that enemy was a Jew. Then he went on showing us what Jews look like and how they walk. The most ridiculous thing he said was that we are looking at their nose, eyes, and hair. He then pulled out an instrument that is used to measure heads to know if someone is Jewish. He also claimed that the Jews were a curse to Germany and that their life is nothing but money and sex. The SS officer also asserted that the Jews took jobs away from the German people and that had to be stopped immediately. He also disturbed me when he said that the Jews were perverted and that they encouraged homosexuality. Because of this "fact," they had to be destroyed. As the officer talked, my lips parted as I heard all of this nonsense. Yet I could do nothing about it, not just then, that is. While I sat there, the officer drew a picture of a Jew and told us that were not permitted to help a Jew, talk to one, or even eat with any. He said we were not allowed to feel sorry about what might happen to them in the future. My question was, "what is supposed to happen that we do not know about, now?" I thought we were to fight for Germany, nothing else. The lessons we had to study became harder, and I felt as though hate was our primary feeling. There wasn't any love here. In honesty, I could not really hate anyone, so I had to pretend. I realized my life was not my own anymore. I belong to Hitler's thoughts and wishes, and to Germany. Lives were about to change and I was afraid it was not for the best. My life was departing and everything my parents taught me was to be redirected. The old Hans will be dead and the new one will be living. "Will the old Hans really be dead? HAVE I REALLY DEPARTED FOR GOOD?"

ASSIGNMENT

We were trained for months, waited for our first assignment after the training period, slept in barracks, called home every week, ate good food. Class today at 9:00 AM would tell all of us where we would be going and for how long. Actually my heart was just beating with excitement ready to find out the mystery of my life. I could not wait to see where my life was going as young as I was. An SS officer came in, and I believe that his name was Lt. Weir, in which he was in charge of assignments. He had a stack of papers and there were fifty-six of us waiting to pass onto phrase three. This officer called each of us separately. When he came to my name, he told me that I should be quite proud of myself for achieving the rank of Company Lt. Colonel Commander.

But first he said, I must go to officer's school for training. After that training, I would then receive my assignment. My heart pumped for joy and beat for excitement this time with a different tune. Anyone who had an offer for officer's school had to report immediately to General Ludwig. We were released from class, after which we shook hands and were then led to another room to meet the General. I realized that not many made officer's school and the number was small. There were only fourteen of us. The rest went to field operations where they would be trained to fight the enemy. General Ludwig offered some chocolate for being good soldiers. We were then brief for about two hours. The worst was the paperwork, but the information became minor to me because soon we went to lunch. After eating, we went back to the briefing room where we heard that officer's school was eight weeks long.

After that, we will be receiving our assignments. I surely would be almost twenty years old before I would start my active duty. After this briefing, I had my first class and lots of paperwork and even a short test all in one day. When I saw the first topic on the test, my heart no longer wanted to beat, only to remain quiet. The quiz and assignment had to be at least one page long with the topic, "Why we must hate Jews?" I knew right there that the paper I would attempt to write would not be my writing, but the evil that is within me. I knew now what my future would be as a German officer.

PERMISSION APPROVED

In officer's school, I was taught nothing but pure hate. I did not enjoy hating anyone. Shortly thereafter, I received a telegram stating that my mother was very ill and asking whether I could possible come home to see her? I then went to Lt. Holster for permission to leave because he was the commander of the youth group for young adults. As I approached him, I asked him and then showed him the telegram I received from my father. Lt. Holster told me that I would be given leave for one week and then I would be picked up at my house for return.

Actually we sat and talked for quite some time. Then Lt. Holster gave me my final orders. I opened the letter and found myself in a very high position: Lt. Colonel Commander. I read on and found myself being Commander of a Slave Camp in Kassel, Germany. At this point I really didn't want that position, maybe Commander, yes, but not at a slave camp. A position like this one did not reflect who I was at all, and I wanted to tell him this. However, that if I would tell I him my true feelings I would be punished. I realized that no one disobeyed the Reich, not even me. I had to make myself believe in this; and I felt if I have faith in God, I could do the job, perhaps correctly. Immediately, I asked God for help and guidance knowing that someday this whole war would be over and the question was, "when?" As I continued to read the letter of acceptance, I had to sign that I accepted the position as Commandant. I asked the Lieutenant how and why I had received such a high position without any experience. He replied, "We have been watching you closely and we choose only the finest men without a doubt." I left the matter at that and signed the acceptance letter. Then I asked the Lieutenant a favor. I told him that my mother was very ill and that I had to go home to Cologne to see her. He then granted me the permission for one week off in which I thanked him and left. Headquarters assigned me a driver to assist me to my house and then reminded me that I had to return within one week. I agreed without a doubt and acknowledged that I had to wear my full uniform decorated with my awarded medals and honors and that I could wear nothing else outside. So I returned home only to find the unexpected waiting for me. As I approached my home in Cologne, I saw my father working in the backyard. I stepped out of the car with the help from the driver opening the door for me. He then saluted me and left. My father approached me and asked why I was saluted. I told him that I had graduated from officer's school as Lt. Colonel Commander. He was amazed and gave me a hug and told me to go inside to see my mother who had been waiting for me. I went into the house calling out to her, and there she was sipping soup. Mother dropped her spoon into the bowl when she saw me. "Hans, is that you? Oh my God, you look handsome my son!" I gave Mother a big hug and a kiss, took my hat off, and sat next to her as she ate. She asked me about the uniform, and I explain to her about being Commander. I would not dare tell her about the slave camp because she would object quickly. However, she loved the way I looked. As she was admiring me, Father came in to take a video of us together. When I asked Mother what was wrong with her she said that she was very ill with her heart and that soon she will be going home to the Lord. She also said that she was waiting for me to come home one more time before she died. For some reason, I believed her and tried not to think that my mother was leaving me behind. Father took my suitcase upstairs, and I explained that I could only stay one week and then I must return. He nodded and went upstairs to my room. Mother wanted to go upstairs and rest while we both helped her upstairs to her room. I kissed her on her forehead and told her that I loved her very much. Then I put on a warm blanket on her and watched her as she fell asleep.

GOOD-BYE TO LOVE

Mother passed away during that night on May 10, 1940; my heart was overwhelmed by her passing away. I never felt so much pain in my heart, where half of my life was torn away. Mother was so kind and true and her love to my father was rare. I remembered when I turned eight years old and we went for a family picnic over at the Rhine River. Mother had made my favorite dish, Sauerbraten and pork. Father was so hungry that he didn't wait for any of us to settle down; he just ate. Mother, of course, was upset with Father, they did not speak to one another for the entire day. Still, we had a wonderful day together. I did not have any brothers or sisters because Mother could not have any more children. I was never spoiled or neglected. I was loved from the moment I was born until now. I know that I would surely miss my mother and anything I would do in my life would be right, because of her. Mother was buried by the time I had to leave. It was a quiet and short funeral. I didn't want to wear my uniform, so I put on my regular clothes. Even though Mother had passed away, I felt glad to be home again. I enjoyed sleeping in my bed again, and I wondered when I could touch my pillow again. That night, Father and I ate some dinner and chatted about my training and my life. "Son, you need to find a wonderful woman now, you know to take care of you." I looked at Father and said, "Father, where at this time of war am I going to have time to find a woman?" He agreed and laughed. "To love and be loved is to feel the sun from both sides," I said to myself. I sat in the chair until my eyes grew tired and weary and had to go to sleep. I thought about what Father said about me finding a woman to date, but I also knew it was not the right time. I would enjoy someone in my life, perhaps to love and marry, but the war would separate love. Anyway, I said to myself, "Goodnight mother, I truly miss you."

PREPARATION

Her hair was dark brown and wavy and had the most beautiful dark brown eyes. Sasha was Jewish, born to Ira Rebonwitz and Sadie Mashov on March 18, 1922. She lived with her family, had no boyfriend nor an engagement to be married. She was only eighteen when the war finally broke out, and she knew she had no life to live. Sasha was discouraged by the war and especially the Germans, and yet she was taught to forgive her enemies. Maybe because her Father was a rabbi, who had taught her from her childhood that God wants her to forgive those who do wrong to her. Doing so was hard, but she did. Ira was not only a rabbi, but also a watchmaker who had his own business of making watches. He would always tell Sasha that someday she would learn to make the finest watch in the world and yet she was not sure whether she could ever do this kind of work. Yet the days were dark and the Gestapo were forming their army against the Jews in Berlin. All Jews were told that they had to move to the Ghetto in town because of losing their homes. I often wondered why people hate anyone as these people did. I became a victim of my own culture and watched so many Jews die on the street. Yet I couldn't believe that all these Germans would hate us and put us to death. I prayed to God to show me that there is one German who would not feel this way, and perhaps I would be able to understand this situation. My parents always told me that there was good and bad in everyone and that there was no one perfect except God. I tried to believe this and prayed I would find that person someday. We were a small family in which I only had one brother, Melvin. He was four years older than I, he was twenty-two years old. Melvin and I always read the newspapers to find that Hitler wanted war with Poland and to learn of his continued hatred for us. Every day we heard gunshots, screaming, yelling and crying. No more laughing or enjoying each others company, only despair. I couldn't remember when I last saw the sun shine on my lips. "My God," I asked, "what has happened and why has everything changed and we are being persecuted again?" Meanwhile, my Mother was baking four loaves of sweet bread because of the fear of no food, especially if we are taken away. The bread was so good with a touch of butter and jam. I watched mother roll out the dough, and as she did I saw the anguish in her face. Sometimes tears would roll down her pink cheeks. I knew in my heart that she sensed something was about to happen. At the same time, Father would always teach us never to fear death because it is the beginning for us. Morning passed by when we heard a knock at our door. My Father went to the door and asked who it was. It happened to be Boris, my Father's friend from work. He was upset but eager to tell us something very important. He told my Father that he was afraid to say that the Germans would be moving us into the town marked as the Ghetto, and right now they were gathering all Jews to this place. My Father fell down on the chair as we looked at one another in despair. We did not know what to do and how soon we were leaving. I was scared of losing my life and my family. I felt I was too young ever to leave this earth and I knew there would be a chance for me. God promised me life and he will do it. I remembered that love conquers all, and I was eager to find it. I knew that God could turn a bad thing into something good, and now I was waiting on Him. Boris left and quickly my father went to see if any newspapers were around to read. He found the latest paper and brought it home. There we were overwhelmed by what we read: "Hitler Orders Jews to Ghettos." Father then dropped into his chair and the newspaper dropped on the floor. I quickly picked it up only to read more about the news. I was surprised to see that the message continued, "All Jews were to wear a band over their arm with the Star of David." This was our identification. They even forbade us from cafes, public places, and any business. We were to bring our belongings and report to the nearest Ghetto and await any further instructions. Hatred had literally smashed our dreams, and I prayed while my family packed. We had to leave behind my Father's business and all our furniture. I was overwhelmed, for now I knew there were no good Germans, just evil ones.

HANS'S ORDERS

Hans received his orders to return to his headquarters in Berlin as soon as possible. He also read in the paper that Hitler had ordered Jews to report to the Ghetto in the area. His eyes were peeled on the newspaper as he read the next sentence: "All Jews are forbidden to go into cafes, public places." They must also wear a band around their arm identifying them as Jews." Hans was remorseful and devastated and admitted he was part of this conspiracy. He buried his head into his hands and wept. He asked God why he was part of such an ugly group. Silence remained. He had to leave and finish his training so he could receive his orders. If he didn't, Hans would die like the others; and his hopes and dreams would be forgotten. He remembered Paul's persecution during his days as Saul, a Zealot who had murdered Jews. That association with the Scriptures gave hope. Soon after, Hans's father escorted him to the door and gave him a hug and wished him the best. Hans was then picked up at the front door and escorted to Berlin. Before he went into headquarters, he saw thousands of people in the street walking. German soldiers were leading the Jews and others to their destinations. Hans had his uniform on and saw many Jews passing by looking at him with hatred and despair. His eyes were sympathizing, but he dared not to speak. His thoughts were simple, one thought crossed his mind: "If only I could save just one Jew, I would feel good about myself." Headquarters were very busy, Hans reported to Lt. Heinrich Faust known as "killer." There Heinrich briefed Hans and told him about his training and that they had to speed it up because of the war intensifying. He promised to have me trained by the end of the week and then issue my orders and payments. He also told me that my pureness and intelligence will gain me power, or so he said. I then had to report to Classroom A with several other men, and there I met Otto. He was about twenty-one and stood over six feet tall. Because he had nothing ugly about him either, we got along. Well there was no question in my mind, "Did Otto really want to be a Nazi?" "Nazis, I would rather live without them," Otto said to me. He repeated it twice in a low tone so no one would hear. We became good friends, trained and heard the word Jew just too many times. We were told at training to hate the Jews and kill them. We were brainwashed, and we had to accept that. How inhumane can one be and live with themselves? We knew that we would be despised years after the war and into the future of the world by the victims, and yet no one would know about us good Germans who had no choice in this matter. I felt a tug at my heart, my brain was racing with so many thoughts and I wanted to run far away. My question was where? No one knew how we felt and how we wanted to leave this army. Nothing could reverse this hatred. So many officers became victims of Hitler because of his hate in his heart and then had the pleasure of murdering innocent people. Because of this, it brought his hate and used it on everyone with no purpose, no reason, just murder. I still hung on to my beliefs; my heart knew I would change and that someday I would be able to love and to be forgiven by many. There is a little Saul in all of us and then converted to Paul.

GHETTO

Sasha and her family were ordered by the Gestapo to relocate to the ghetto as soon as possible. They wanted to know where they were going to live and how? Money wasn't an issue but living was the problem. Father knew how it was going to be for all of us especially under the regime of Hitler. Sasha pulled back her hair and put on a simple dress and left everything else behind. She knew what was to come and tears filled her dark eyes. She knew that in her heart those things could change, but how? She was only eighteen, and her life had not even begun. Again, she asked God why? Why did this all happen? I had faith that something good would come out of this hatred. Quickly, mother put some clothes into a small suitcase, gathered some bread and jam and gave it to Papa. Sasha gathered her belongings and met her family at the door. There they walked down the steps, looked at their home for the last time, wiped their tears and left. There they proceeded to the streets only to find instructions where to go from here. It was a cold day and soon the rain was going to fall from the sky into the people who sat in the streets. So many people were running and crying and even dead. The German Army was marching, directing and whipping so many people. Cries turned into torture, begging was quickly deteriorating. There wasn't anything to say; it was so horrible to describe. We then found several soldiers with rifles, and I looked at them. I could see that a lot of them were very young and bitter. I couldn't face looking anymore at their greenish color uniforms. It brought nothing but horror to my mind. Boots clicked, whips snapped, screaming was all I heard. Gunshots were heard, young and old were judged by these monsters. I looked upon my own people and I was so discouraged that I wanted my life to end. Yet I could do nothing. So many belongings clogged the streets, paper, food, garbage, and dead people. All were gathered. My heart was pounding, and my family was so distressed over this gathering. I could see it in Papa's eyes as he stood there with tears. Mama was clinging to Papa while my brother was walking behind us. Melvin never said anything, He was always so quiet, but yet he was my brother, and I loved him. We continued walking as the screaming and cries continued, and there we came to our rest stop until they decided where to put us. I put my belongings down, resting my body on my coat. Mama and Papa and my brother sat on a blanket they brought. We never thought or even believed we would be sitting in these streets. Here we waited, prayed, and believed. This was the beginning for darkness that came upon all of us.

TRAINING

Hans was up early and eager to go to his classes. Today was his last day of training, and the day that he would be going out to observe the way the Nazis work. Today also was something special where he would find out his complete orders to where he was going. It had to be confirmed before he left. I passed my courses from weapons to commanding with high grades. I was also issued my full uniform and weapons. Tomorrow I would have my picture taken and my assignment would start by next week. I was very eager to get this assignment underway. Classes were fine, but sometimes the officers would be boring and my mind was so intense and I felt the world was on my shoulders.

Wartime was never easy, especially this one that Hitler created for himself. So many men did not want this war, but we had no choice in saying anything and we couldn't resist or we would be shot. I went back to the barracks only to find my trainer Ludwig pointing his finger at me. He told me that I had to go down to the square in Berlin with Otto. We were supposed to be dressed in full gear and observe how the soldiers handle situations. He wanted us to see how the Jews were removed and treated. We left. Around 2:40 PM Tuesday, there was very little sun. I felt a knot in my throat in what I was seeing. Rows of old people were screaming with pain, garbage was all over, and I was part of this ugly conspiracy. I became something I did not want to become, and yet I was ordered to be it. My heart sank to see the pain and suffering of these innocent people, babies and children, and for what? What is this war about? I walked with Otto as he stood there looking in silence. I could almost read his thoughts as he was observing people. As we moved through the ghetto, I noticed a woman, no more than nineteen sitting on a curb with her dark hair pulled back. Her eyes were dark and she had a smile on her face. As I came closer, I slowed down in walking and I looked at her and there our eyes met. I was hoping that she would not find any evil in my eyes, but love. I gave her another smile, got closer and spoke to her. I asked if everything was all right as I spoke in German. I asked this beautiful woman if she knew where she was going? She hesitated to answer me, but kept her eyes locked on me. I asked her name and she said, "Sasha, Sasha Rebonwitz; and this is my family, Sir." I asked her not to call me "Sir," but Hans. She thanked me for asking. I had to grasp myself since I saw Sasha. Her beauty captured my heart that I could not move. I wanted to be part of her life right there. My heart had never felt this way before; yet I was a Nazi, an enemy to her, a German. I introduced myself as Hans and left it at that. I was afraid never to meet her again but wanted to thank her for that one-time feeling of love. I was that pure race that Hitler wanted mixed with no Jewish blood. I had to move on, and I took my hat off to her. I bade her farewell and told her that I hoped to see her again, someday. She looked at me with a puzzling look not knowing what to say to me. Love comes in many forms. Why couldn't it have come sooner for me? She is a Jew, and I am a German: a forbidden love. My feet were so weak that I could not move because of the way that I felt about Sasha. I was hopeless because I could do nothing. Yet a small voice told me to wait and trust. I did. Otto and I walked away and finished our observing and patrolling the Ghetto. We soon went back to headquarters where I received my full completed orders.

IS THIS FOR REAL?

Sasha stood there with her family in a very perplexed mood, shocked because of the way that a German soldier treated her. She could remember his name, Hans, who stood around 5'11, slender build with light to medium blond hair. He has eyes that were so blue that she thought she was looking into a blue ocean. She would never forget those eyes or him. She felt that there wasn't any evil in him, but love. She admitted that she felt love from Hans. "But how could we meet our desires that one time together?" Sasha thought. I dared not to tell my family about my feelings because they would reject Hans because he was a German. To herself Sasha asked, "Where are you, Hans, where did you go?" "Please Mama, don't let Papa read my heart or my eyes because they will tell you about how Sasha really feels, especially a forbidden love," said Sasha silently to herself. Quickly she remembered how she prayed she would find just one German who would be able to give her hope with her feelings. Could Hans be the German or someone else? My feelings became so mixed now, and yet I felt a sharp pain in my heart. I felt that I had lost something I knew and searched for, something that would never return. How tragic I felt, how brokenhearted; no one knew my feelings. I am not sure how I really feel at this moment. I shall hang onto hope that someday, maybe we will meet again. I believe if God wants me to find him again, He will find that way even if I have to go through suffering and pain just to find that happiness I have been searching. I remembered what Papa had said when I was young, "Sasha, joy comes in the morning."

DESPAIR

I came back to the barracks with Otto realizing that I had never felt love as I did that day. I felt that when I looked into Sasha's eyes, that contact changed me even more with hope and love. I wanted to give this hope to so many of these soldiers and tell them that hate does not have to be in their hearts but only love. I wanted to tell them that I was wrong in the way that I joined this party, and I knew nothing about how it was going to bring mass murders to all. After being in the classrooms and seeing pictures, and being taught that Jews were our enemies, I wanted to prove to the Nazis that they were wrong with hatred. I always felt that beauty was in our eyes, and yet so many miss that beauty. I've seen those who taught hate and wondered whether they must hate their own selves and then reflect that hatred to us. I felt certain that someday the world would judge us on what happened. I tried to remember one important thing: there is good and bad in everyone, and we must not look only to the bad but we must recognize good in someone. I realized that I cannot leave this party because I would risk my life and perhaps cause my father to be shot and then all of my dreams would be lost. I trust God for hope so I could be free from despair and Sasha would remain in my heart forever.

ORDERS

I received my orders from General Frank Franzholtzer that Friday, I came quietly to his door and I knocked twice. He said, "Come in." I then opened the door into a room of smoke. He saw who I was and welcomed me to sit down. Then he handed me papers and went over everything I needed to know. He kept praising my grades and my youth, telling me how special I was in the SS. He explained what the war the war was all about and described my position as Lt. Colonel Commander. He told me that the job would be stressful but worthwhile at the end. As I was sitting there, he offered me a cigar and whiskey because they would be part of my life as an officer. I refused his offer, and I told him perhaps another time. General Franzholtzer went on telling me more about my position. He said that I would be going to Kassel Camp, that my pay would be over 750 marks a month and it would increase each year that I stayed in the service. He then stood up and congratulated me as the new Company Commander of the Slave Camp at Kassel. He emphasized that I would be solely responsible for a slave camp, not a death camp. "If any should die, they would die from hard labor, not from you putting them to death," said the General. He told me that the prisoners would be politically involved and a lot would be Jews. "You will have prisoners from all over Germany, young and old, but mostly Jewish," he promised. My heart just died when I thought that these prisoners would be doing hard work for me. I went on in my thoughts, as he told me that the prisoners would be doing hard labor and whatever else I needed them to do. "It is your camp," he said. "Run it correctly, and let no one tell you what to do." "If by chance someone does not obey you," General Franzholtzer continued. "You have the right to shoot." Continuing his briefing, General Franzholtzer promised that I would have my own quarters or bunker and perhaps servants from the camp. "You will have the best food to eat and plenty of beer and wine for dinner parties," he promised. "Just do not drink much or you will be removed from the camp, so watch the drinking. You are entitled every other weekend to have off and you may leave the camp as long as you put your Second Commander in charge of the camp. So as today Hans, I congratulate you on your new post as Commander Hans F. Schweitzer of Kassel Camp. Your position will start this Monday and you will be transported with your Second Commander." He asked whether I had any questions, and of course I said that I had none. I sat there telling myself that I should be pleased with myself, but in honesty I wasn't. I felt as if I had a knife in my throat that cut through my heart after hearing all of these details. General Franzholter kept going on with more details and kept asking me whether I had any questions. When I shook my head, he told me that I was relieved, so I left the General's quarters. I had to go over to the photographer to have my military picture taken; so I went back to my barracks to put on my full uniform that I would be wearing in the camp. As I arrived in the room where pictures were being taken, I found myself being saluted by everyone I met. The photographer told me to sit down and smile if I wished for my picture. Then they propped my arm on some decorated box and suddenly the process had ended. The pictures would be ready on Sunday morning they said, and I could pick them up before 12:00 noon. I then went back to my room where I ran into Otto. He was the only one who respected my ideas. He told me about his orders and how he made it to Lt. Major at Camp Kassel. I was shocked. I asked him whether he was going to be my second commander; he shook his head, "Yes." Now I knew that God was on my side. As we went to have some lunch, I told him that I was somewhat pleased about being commander at Kassel. Otto promised me that he would help me the best he could and would do anything to please me. He said he would be there to serve me as part of the team. I told him that he did not have to call me "sir," unless we were among others. He agreed, and we ate lunch together talking about our journey together in this war.

THE JOURNEY

Sasha and her family were directed by the SS to walk quickly over to the train station without stopping. It was harder for Sasha's Mother to walk, yet she kept up with them as Sasha helped her. As we arrived at the station, some officer was telling us that we would be staying together as a family and live together there. Sasha's eyed welted up with so many tears that she forgot what it felt to smile. A guard pushed her family to the side and her hope was tucked away in her heart. She knew that God would not let her down. Papa and Mama were very quiet and they looked for hope, but they saw none. My brother Melvin was quiet. I saw how upset he was, and yet he could do nothing. I knew that my brother had lost his hope to live, and I didn't know what to say to any of my family. I sat there hoping and praying that Hans would pass by so I could see him one more time before I had to leave Berlin. I wasn't sure where I was going with my family, but all I knew was that I didn't like what I heard or saw. The shinny day seemed to be a sign from God that my wish would happen. We proceeded to the train station where so many people were gathered with all their bags waiting for the train. No one had any idea where we were going, and we could not ask. While we were waiting, I heard gunshots go off and saw many soldiers standing near the platform. I was looking to see if any of them were Hans so I could speak to him. As we were standing there we were told in German to wait for the train, and then hurried on. I wanted to know where we were going, but Papa said it didn't matter anymore. Five minutes later, we heard the train whistle and there we stepped back to get on board. We were like cattle packed in with a small window and nothing else. I noticed that the train was decorated with Nazi flags and had many soldiers guarding the train. Again, I looked for Hans. The soldiers continued to yell as they crowded people in, and so many fell into the train. Those who did fall were ordered to get up or be shot and many were. The soldiers closed the doors as though we were cattle. In fact, we actually was in cattle cars. Our car had a strong urine odor, and hay covered most of the floor. We still did not know where we were going, and many people were upset and crying. I saw so many people sick and crying, wishing death upon them. Many were yelling out that would rather have death than to be shot by a Gestapo Nazi. We had very little water and no food. It felt like hours in that car, which had only one window, and people were looking out hoping they could find out where we were. Hours passed before we stopped, but that stop was not our final one. We were not even permitted to get out, so we stood there wiping the sweat off our faces. Many of us were thirsty and hungry and very hot. Those who were looking out the window were telling us that the German soldiers were sitting on the grass taking a break and eating. Some were smoking and laughing. Still my heart wanted to despise all the Germans, but hope was still in my heart. Finally the train started back up and we moved forward, still without food and water. Babies were crying and many died from having no water or milk. Mothers were crying over their dead babies and their tears cried out for death. Mama looked weak and asked Papa for encouragement. He prayed for strength and remembered what God did for the Israelite. My brother prayed also. His lips were moving, but no words were coming out. Now we were all family and needed to believe that because we had nothing else, and perhaps all we needed was God. I reached into my purse and pulled out an old crusty handkerchief to wipe sweat from my face. I thought about Hans for a moment wondering where he would be. Was he still in Berlin or in Germany? I thought again that maybe Hans was a put on or just a dirty Nazi wanting to take advantage of me. I could only hope I was wrong. I looked at my watch and counted the hours to six. Finally the train was slowed down. The people were still trying to see where we were, but we still had no clue. They did say that we were coming into a station with many German soldiers and officers. Suddenly the train gave a quick halt and we waited for the next step. A voice speaking German announced that everyone should get out when the doors opened. Then a soldier appeared and ordered us to get out immediately. Many made it out but some were dead. Papa grabbed Mama by the arm. I looked around to find some answer to where we were and suddenly I saw it. I found out the mystery. We were in Camp Kassel in Kassel, Germany. I knew very little about this camp only that it was a slave camp for Jews and others. We stood there with our belongings as the German officer directed us with a fog horn to move to the side as we approached the camp. A head Jew took orders from the Germans to get us moving faster. While we were moving, I heard screaming, yelling and gunshots. I dared not to turn around as I passed and saw prisoners dressed in stripe outfits with very short hair and sickly faces. Soldiers in black uniforms were walking with dogs while others were guarding the gates. Barbed wire surrounded us. As we approached, a horrible smell filled the air. By now I was sick and Mama worried me. I prayed to God to take Mama home or get us out of here before she would die. Several minutes later Mama passed out and died. I cried so much that I had to stop myself before one of the soldiers would whip me. The fact that we had to leave her body upset me so much. However, I knew that God answered my prayer and had given me a sign for me to believe in what would come therefore.

DEPARTURE

I picked up my pictures on Sunday afternoon, quite impressed in how I looked but ashamed of what uniform I had to wear. I had carried an identification card but we had also been branded under our left arm for identification. I had to stop at weapon control to pick up all my weapons for camp. There the supply soldier issued me a Walther P38 and a Gewehr rifle and ammunition. I then went to lunch with Otto and took the day off. We talked all day long about camp. We had some cold drinks and sat on the huge patio as we heard weapons being launched in the background. I was sure we would be hearing more of those weapons. I asked Otto about his hopes and dreams. He said that he wanted to leave the SS so badly but knew the consequences. He actually poured out his feelings and told me how he had lost his family in the war. He admitted that he had no one left; everyone had been shot. So where was my hope and dreams in a country like this? So far I could see no freedom, no changes, and just mass murders. It is not what Germany wanted, but about one person who wanted murders and involved everyone. I feared that my eyes would see the worst as days and months passed by. I agreed with Otto, and said we will all stick together. Dreams can only come true if we start them and carry them out. The rest of the day I polished my boots and packed. I received all of my paperwork this morning and ready to leave. We both left at 6:00 AM Monday morning after breakfast, and we had a long trip ahead of us, perhaps five hours. We did pack some drinks and sandwiches in case we were hungry or wanted to feed the driver. The journey was long and as we rode, we have seen many injured soldiers on the road. We even saw gunfire, clouds of smoke, and dead men. At one point we had to stop due to massive fighting. There were so many fighting against useless thoughts. We continued, and at one point we spoke to the man who was driving. His name was Luther and he was only eighteen years old. He told us that he rode everyone around, which was his job. He didn't enjoy the war either because many of his friends were killed. He wanted to go home to his family but didn't see that yet happening. Luther smoked a lot of cigarettes for his age and I think it was his nerves. I only smoked one and Otto too. He said the only thing he feared was being shot while driving. I agreed on that. I asked him how long it would be for us arriving in Kassel, and he estimated it at about an hour.

ARRIVAL

We arrived in Kassel prison camp at around 12:00 PM at the front gate of the security where we had to show our identification cards and orders. The two guards welcomed us with salutes and directions to where we had to go. When I arrived with Otto at this building, I said goodbye with and best wishes to Luther. We could see very little activity but did notice a stench of something burning. I knew that sooner or later I would find out what that smell was. I saw dead bodies practically all over with so many prisoners in pain. I asked myself, "is this where I want to be?" The guards constantly saluted Otto and me when I found my place of residence. I found a soldier standing guard at the front door, I asked his name, and he said PFC. Fritz Hausdorff. There we were also greeted by my mentor, Lt. Josef Steinmetz. He welcomed us and showed us around the camp, introducing both of us to all my officers and guards. He showed me all the blocks in which the prisoners lived. Lt. Josef did told me that they just received new prisoners and that they were supposed to receive their jobs. He also explained to me that in this labor camp most of the prisoners die from weakness. I asked him to give me all of the reports by morning and he said he would. He then showed me where I would be living from the blocks and there we met Fritz. My residence was a little further out from the blocks which I could see from my window. The house was big, two floors and quite cozy. It seemed too cozy for a war. I had a huge meeting room with a big kitchen and plenty of food. I sat down for a minute as Lt. Josef left. Otto lived in one of the bunkers next to mine but not as big as the one I had. I was afraid to walk through the camp, but I knew I had to do it sooner or later. I took off my jacket because it was very hot outside. I pushed back my hair and sat down feeling the cool breeze going past. I dozed off for a while, and then awake, pleasantly surprised by Otto. "Hans," he said, "I went through the camp and it is very sad to see what I saw." I reached for my jacket and also my side hat. After I started to walk toward the camp, Lt. Josef greeted me and gave me all the necessary paperwork that I needed. I thanked him and moved on. I saw several soldiers walking with dogs and guards sitting in the towers, watching and ready to shoot. Everyone saluted me not knowing who I really was. The foul stench came from a stack chimney, and I felt my stomach churning. Several barracks were on the side of the chimney and there I met a lot of the prisoners all in stripe uniforms. Many were weak while others were doing heavy work. I noticed they were putting huge pipes into the ground. I came across the woman's block and saw many doing some sort of garden work. However, I noticed many were were lying dead on the ground and no one seems to care about this. I needed to address this issue of dead bodies on the ground as soon as possible. I knew that I had not seen everything that I wanted to see. I went back to my office to read the schedule and list so I could study it to see how I could bring changes to it. At my desk, I became so hot that I took my jacket off. As I was writing, I heard a knock and told whoever to come inside. A tall soldier entered, saluted me, and said that he was my door guard. He said that his name was Wolfgang; I thanked him and told him to continue. I looked at my schedule and I was not pleased at all with how it looked, so I knew I had to work on it immediately.

DISCOVERY

I had roll call at around 5:00 PM. The sun was only just up, and the camp was already burning from the heat. I asked the one prisoner to blow the horn to gather the prisoners and to signal my officers to line up. When he did blow the horn, everyone came running at a tremendous speed, coming to full attention. I stood there observing everyone and I noticed the men were on one side while the women and children were on the other. The women wore a skirt-like gown and their hair was very short to the scalp. My eyes quietly became so tired in what I was seeing. As I was standing there, Otto came to my side and handed me a microphone to speak through. I told them that my name was Hans Franz Schweitzer, Company Commander of Camp Kassel and that I would be doing inspections on the entire camp the next day. I said that I would be asking many of them if they could perform certain duties for the camp. "I do expect all of you to follow my rules and regulations and not to try to escape. If anyone does, two things could happen: either you will be severely punished or shot on the spot." I told them that I would be watching everyone's performance in this camp. Then I released them from roll call and directed them to proceed to the food line for their meal. As I watched everyone leaving to get their food, I noticed a woman whom I believed I knew. I walked up to her only to discover it was my lost love, "Sasha." When I stood there, she looked at me and yet spoke nothing because she was afraid I would do something. I believe she was in shock and not believing that I was actually standing before her. I noticed those dark eyes that I had fallen in love with and saw again how beautiful she was. I had missed seeing her beauty, and I could not believe that I had finally found her again. I thought surely that I had lost her when she disappeared somewhere in the Ghetto. I was so overwhelmed that I could not think straight. I felt my body tremble with excitement that now I was reunited with my love whom I left behind in Berlin. I thanked God for this discovery and I felt that God would help us all to get out of here and to lead me to the truth in order to help others sitting in this camp. I realized that God was on my side and that He was here directing my plans to unfold.

HOPE

Sasha looked at Hans and knew he was the gentle officer that she met in Berlin. She was praying that he would come up to her and speak to her. When Sasha got to the food line, she had to be told twice to receive her food. A Jew leader pushed her and said, "Move it," he said. She received her broth with vegetables and old bread. Her eyes watched every move that Hans made. She admired him in how he looked. Out of all the men she thought that he was the most handsome of all. She sipped her soup and went back to the stalls to clean her utensils. Sasha was quite tired from all the labor but her hope was now stronger. As she laid on a bed filled with dirty hay, she prayed to God and thanked Him with all of her strength. His will was now being shown to her. She told God that she loved Hans and this relationship was all in His hands. God reminded her that good will come out of this imprisonment. She told God that she was ready for His goodness. Sasha had never felt as happy as she was this very moment. She believed in her heart that if Hans really loved her, then he would save her. She had faith that he would help her.

MEETING

Hans arranged a meeting with all of his officers at his house and treated them to drinks with fresh bread and meats. Hans did not want to waste time but just get into the meeting since he had other important things to do. He asked everyone to sit down while he spoke and they did. Hans told his men that he wanted clean-up immediately and that "clean up" meant to have all dead bodies buried or burned so they would not be in the way of others. Hans also told them that the food had to be changed or upgraded because the soup was made of rotten vegetables and the bread was moldy. "I need my prisoners to have strength so they could perform the hard work that they are here for," Hans said. No one said anything and I left them with not much to say. Hans mention one other rule that he wanted to go in effect immediately. "Our soldiers need to be drilled each day no matter of the weather conditions," Hans reminded his men. "They are to be trained for one hour each day with formation and marching. They are to be fully dressed and their uniforms inspected." I want strong men. He also mentioned that he wanted to hear them drill from his quarters, for he would be watching. "I want to hear their boots hitting the ground," Hans said. He then assigned Otto to be the officer in charge and told him that tomorrow he would be starting this drill. "If we have 300 men in this camp, we have enough to cover the gates and towers," Hans told him. Hans told Otto to take Lt. Sweitzhauder with him tomorrow riding his horse as he followed the men. "Observed them," said Hans, and then we will make necessary changes. Drill them heavily and do not let them have a break no matter what. "Do you understand Otto?" He rose and said, "Yes sir." Hans asked all of the officers in his den whether they had any questions concerning these changes. No one said anything to Hans because he dared them not to; he would override their opinions. As Hans was finishing up with his speech, they all stood up and clapped. Hans was completely overwhelmed. His meeting lasted no more than an hour and everyone shook hands before leaving. Hans stood there alone mulling over his next important plan: how to save Sasha.

SAVING SASHA

The next day Hans walked around the bunker looking to see how he could make his house more comfortable for himself. He knew there had to be cleaning done, perhaps the garden and his wash. He knew that he wouldn't have the time for any work, not with his schedule, for he had to keep his eyes on the camp and to watch that everything was being obeyed. He decided to go over to Sasha's block and bring her in to assist him. As that he could save her from hard labor. Hans now felt convinced that God had given him the opportunity to save this one prisoner. Hans knew that he had to save Sasha from this camp, and that he had to do it right away because he did not know what would happen to any of those in the camp. "If I could save more prisoners, I would be pleased, so would God," Hans told himself. Hans quickly went over with Fritz to Sasha's block to save her from the agony of prison life. I realized that as company commander, I could do anything and not lose the respect from others. I walked into block C, and which Fritz announced to everyone in German, "Attention." All the women who had the strength came to a halt and stood in front of their bunk beds. Hans told them to be at ease while he looked for Sasha. Hans looked from front to back and he found her in the back standing. Hans went up to her and ordered her to follow him with a stern face, because he didn't want anyone to suspect his feelings. Hans then took her to his bunker as Fritz went back to guarding the entrance when Hans took Sasha inside. He knew that she was safe now. Sasha stood before Hans and as he looked at her he couldn't believe her appearance. Her hair was cut to her scalp, her eyes were very tired, and her clothes were dirty. She told Hans she had been doing very hard work and for that reason she looked the way that he was now seeing her. Hans assured Sasha not to worry about her appearance anymore and promised to nurse her back to good health. She gave Hans the biggest smile and embraced him with love. She buried her head in his shoulders, and they both stood there feeling the warmth of their bodies together. Hans gently picked up her head and drew her lips to his. Hans felt her warm lips pressed against his and he held her close to his heart. He had never felt love as he did with her in that moment. Hans wiped her tears with his hand and told her how much he really loved her. Sasha agreed and told him that she had fallen in love with him when she had first met him. Hans asked her about her family so that he could save them too, but she said they were all dead. Hans was so overwhelmed that he just wanted to blame himself for their death. Hans looked at her, held her hands in his and asked her to marry him when they finally left out of this camp. Hans told Sasha that he wanted to be with her for the rest of his life, to love and cherish her. He promised to take good care of her and make her very happy and declared that he wanted her to be the mother of his children because he loved her so much. Hans didn't care that she was a Jew and he was German, for to love was love without any restrictions. So they decided to make their plans little by little until the time to leave. I whispered, "Take care of me, Sasha," "Hans, take care of me too."

THE MARCH

The men started their one-hour march with Otto directing every step they moved. Hans watched from the bunker as they formed and all stood still as statues. Otto had his whistle; and Sweitzhauder followed on his horse. Hans heard Otto giving the command to start marching. Hans reminded Otto that he wanted to hear their boots hitting the ground as though they were marching to battle. The men started at the spot where roll call usually started. Everyone delighted to see the drill as men moved to each beat that they heard commanded. Everyone could hear them coming, and Hans made sure that they did. Around 150 soldiers were marching for one hour. Then they would come back and replace the next group for duty, and there they would stay for eight hours. Sasha and I watched from the bunker as the men drilled and got louder. Hans told her that he had learned in the same way. "The soldiers must learn just like any of us because they cannot stand idle." Hans told Sasha in case they come under attack, these men will be ready to fight. Sasha looked at Hans and saw that he was proud of some of the ways. But Hans knew that he disliked a lot of other ways. Hans went over to his office to do some work until the soldiers returned; and when they did, he was there to greet them. Hans could hear them drilling in the background. As they approached the camp, I heard shouting from Otto and his whistle blowing. Every head seemed to turn in the camp as they watched the soldiers approach the camp. When they returned, Otto had the men stand in formation until Hans gave orders. Hans looked at every soldier and commented that he was pleased in what he saw. Hans also promised them that they would drill every day, even in bad weather. Hans reminded drilling was part of being a soldier and it had to be kept up no matter what the situation was; rules had to be followed. Hans told the men that they were to replace the next group for drilling for the next eight hours. They were released, and Hans commended Otto for doing a fine job and told Otto that he was pleased about his first command as an officer.

DUTIES

Sasha had several duties in which Hans had to keep her busy during the day. She cooked three meals a day, she also cleaned, washed clothes and gardened. Sasha took care of his uniforms. She also ironed and shined his boots. Sasha was more than happy to do all of these jobs. Hans spent many hours at his office doing work and a lot of time around the camp watching the prisoners and his officers. He tried to stop at the bunker around 1:00PM to get a quick lunch to see Sasha. When he arrived, Hans found her scrubbing the floors and preparing meals. On the table, Hans saw a plate of cheese with fresh baked bread and soup. He grabbed a glass of wine and sat down with Sasha. He wanted her to sit down with him and have something to eat as a break from work. As Sasha sat down, her eyes met his. She grabbed his neck and kissed him softly; he didn't refuse. Hans asked whether she was feeling any better. She did feel better, and said that she slept very well. Hans told her to keep busy during the day. "If anyone comes around," he said, "just keep on with your work and look busy." Hans also told her that the only one around the bunker would be Fritz. "If he needs a drink or something to eat, it would be all right to feed him," Hans said. Lunch was wonderful, and Hans told Sasha that he had to return to his office and then make his rounds around the camp. He gave her a quick kiss, said goodbye until later, and left.

LOVE

Sasha never thought in her heart that she would fall in love with a German who happened to be a commander of a slave camp. Hans was a gentleman; he was gentle and sincere. Although he was a German, but in her heart she saw love for who he was regardless of his nationality. Sasha felt that too many people look at what a person is and forget what the person actually feels. "I couldn't believe I fell in love with him, but I did." Sasha told herself that she realized that Hans was an answer to her prayers, and she thanked God for him. "Hans saved my life, and God used Hans to do that," Sasha whispered. Sasha saw Hans as the German to be trusted. "He is my angel and my friend," she said half aloud. I wish so much that Mama, Papa and Melvin were alive today; but they died, and out of all of this suffering I received my blessing. Sasha loved Hans. When he came home, she couldn't wait to be with him again. Sasha felt as though she was a young child in love for the first time. She was so surprised that he asked her to marry him. "I know that day will come and we will get through this hatred that others try to push onto us," she exclaimed.

CHANGES

Hans gathered several of the cooks from the kitchen and asked them the recipe they were using for the soup. They told him that it was nasty and that they made the soup mostly from rotten vegetables and potatoes. Hans told them they would be receiving fresh vegetables and potatoes and ordered the cooks to make the soup with some taste. After he had finished that detail, he moved on to his main project: the roads. Hans knew that so much had to be done at a short time and that he needed Lt. Goetz to make his men help with this work. Lt. Goetz told Hans that most of his prisoners were weak from lack of food, sleep, and diseases. Hans had to tackle this problem first or else he would not have anyone to do this work. Hans had to see that these prisoners had proper food and proper treatment at the hospital. Hans knew that he could not function without these men because the work had to be finished. Lt. Goetz said that he would work on this problem immediately today so that they could make some progress by the end of that week. Hans also mentioned to him that there was not to be any attempted escape from any of them or else the prisoners would be punished. This situation left me with no choice because I had to obey some of the rules from headquarters. Hans told Lt. Goetz before he left that his prisoners had to work hard and that in return they would have better food to eat. Hans spoke to one of the officers who did not like any particular changes. This officer told Hans that all Jews should be treated like pigs. Hans told him that the camp could not continue to keep different men and women out to work if they were dying one by one. Hans also told the officer that he had no information that the camp would be receiving new prisoners. The officers must deal with what they have and keep those prisoners alive. Hans made it clear to the officer of the prisoners that they must be kept alive or else every officer would be doing their work instead. The officer kept quiet and walked away after a salute. Hans then wiped the sweat off his forehead and decided to have a roll call. The Jew camp leader blew the horn, and everyone came running. Hans saw his chance to prove who he really was to them. Hans told everyone that the food starting today would change for the better and that after 6:00PM everyone would have showers. All of the prisoners began to cheer for Hans and this announcement. Hans was "the good guy" to them but bad to some of his officers. Yet they never said anything to Hans because they knew the work would proceed as required. This day was one for Hans to remember and happily, for he recognized it as the beginning of leadership.

DINNER

Sasha had dressed in a clean uniform, and her face was shining with so much love. She was preparing dinner for all of the officers, and she always made extra for Fritz and anyone else. Fritz was quiet and shy, and when someone did something for him, his face would turn bright red. So Sasha gave him a plate of potatoes and beans with fresh-baked sweet bread. When Hans came home, he could smell the aroma of sweet bread, which reminded him of his mother's baking when he was younger. His mother always baked fresh bread each day for him and he truly cherished those memories. Hans went to Sasha and kissed her. She asked him about his day. Her dark eyes met his and told him that she had been busy with her chores. Hans told her that he was busy by making great changes for the prisoners including the food. Hans assured Sasha that the prisoners would be having better soup with fresh vegetables from now on. Fresh bread would be distributed and also clean fresh water to drink. Hans also told Sasha that all prisoners could have showers at 6:00PM each day to avoid any diseases. Hans also mentioned to Sasha that the prisoners all clapped for what he has suggested. He acknowledged that a few were not pleased with these actions but that he really did not care. Hans told Sasha that he was really pleased about the day's work. Hans had Sasha sit down and relax for the rest of the day without doing any work, he looked at her and realized how beautiful she was with her long dark hair. He knew again that he loved her. Hans did not care for his involvement with the Nazi, and yet he continued to serve his country. Hans knew that he must make the choice in what he truly wanted and he already knew that he wanted Sasha. Hans wanted to buy her a nice dress, and promised himself that after the war and he could make good his promise. Sasha's eyes looked very tired, so Hans suggested that she go to shower and get to bed earlier. Hans told her that he would not mind because it was 8:00PM already. Sasha then went upstairs and took a shower and went to sleep. Hans put on his night clothes after a long day and sat in his chair thinking about this day, tomorrow, and next month. Hans had been at this camp for only a few weeks and already he wanted to leave. His eyes felt tired and his legs were aching from all the walking that he had done. He went to his room, closed the door, and fell fast asleep.

ESCAPE

The bell rang outside. Hans woke up suddenly, alarmed that something was wrong within the camp. He looked at the clock. It was only 2:21 AM. He had this feeling within that someone was trying to escape. Hans quickly went to put on his jacket and ran outside. He saw the entire camp standing with all of his officers and guards running around with their dogs. Hans asked what the problem was, and they showed him the prisoner. "Sir, this prisoner decided to escape this morning." I asked the guard who he was. They grabbed the man's head and asked his name for me. "What is your name, pig?" He replied to the guard, "David Kohl." The guard at this time had a loaded pointed rifle to his head waiting for me to give the order to shoot him. I stood there asking myself what I should do because I had to follow some of the rules. I did not want any of my men to become suspicious of my actions. I looked at the guard and nodded my head, he fired the shot. The prisoner died instantly and the guards removed the body for burial. Hans's heart stood still. He went back to his quarters and tried without success to go back to sleep. Hans asked God's forgiveness for what he had done. He knew that the party had made the rules and if anyone tried to escape, that person would suffer instant death. Hans tried to convince himself of the rules.

CHORES

Sasha was again alone and this time she had the chance to do some thinking on her own. She first thought of Hans and how much she loved him. She also knew that she had to act and look like a prisoner so Hans would not be in any trouble. Sometimes she wanted to put on a beautiful dress with nice perfume and go to an expensive restaurant with him. She still couldn't believe that her heart was in love with a German officer, an enemy of her people. But she knew that good and bad was in all humanity and not just the Germans. For this reason, she made Hans her dream, someone that she had hoped for all these years. He truly was handsome with beautiful blue eyes and a perfect gentleman. She understood how he was in such a triangle in which he had to do his job as commander, but remained her love. Sasha wished that her family were alive and that she had more family. Unfortunately, all of them had gone to different camps. Sasha remembered some of her extended family in America. Someday she hoped to visit them because she had not seen them for a long time. How lucky they were to be free! Sasha wanted to marry Hans. She wondered where they would go after the war. Sasha thought of Hans often when he was not with her. Sometimes he would stop by a few minutes and make sure that she was doing all right and have some lunch. She would not usually see him until late at night when he was finished with all of his work. Sometimes when he came home, she would hear his sigh as he sat in his chair knowing that his job was finished for the day. She knew what a tough job he had. Sasha would cleaned for Hans each day from early morning to late at night. She scrubbed the floors and polished the furniture. She also prepared the meals, ironed his shirts and even polished his boots. Sasha took care of the garden, planting and digging. She prepared herself with these chores, knowing that someday she would be doing the same things when married to Hans. He was kind and never called her a Jew in front of any of his officers. He said very little about her; and Sasha knew that if he did, he would suffer the consequences. Sasha reflected upon how much she loved this man of God very much. She vowed to make him homemade chicken soup with fresh sweet bread for supper. "I love you Hans, I really love you," she whispered happily.

OFFICER'S MEETING

The meeting was scheduled for 2:00PM at his quarters where the officers would be having lunch. Sasha would be serving sandwiches, fruit, and wine. Hans had to go over the papers from headquarters with the new orders. He had to follow these orders no matter how he felt about the party. The one order he did receive concerned a train that was carrying Jews, and other trains would soon follow. This move would allow over 1000 prisoners to come into this camp. Hard labor had to be induced and possible death. The rumors was that headquarters was still suggesting death to the Jews, but nothing of this sort had yet to be confirmed. Hans felt utterly disgusted because he tried to appear liberal about these discussions. Lt. Freidhauser from headquarters asked how the officers would murder these prisoners? Hans told him that he did not know as yet. Freidhauser promised to ask Hans again. Hans left the matter. Now Hans knew that all the Jews would be killed in this camp and that his superiors had lied, telling him how this camp was only for slaves. Hans's superiors had assured him that death would come to the prisoners by hard labor, not by taking their lives. "Liars," said Hans to himself. Now he knew that he now had to position himself to look for an exit out of this camp. The meeting lasted two hours, and most of it was eating and drinking. Hans served the finest wine from France and the meats from Germany. Sasha of course, had baked the bread. Hans told all of his officers to remain on standby for any further orders and to proceed in what they had already been doing.

OBSERVATION

Hans walked through the camp and felt it as though he was walking through the "valley of death." He saw so much pain and suffering, and most of the prisoners were dying. He asked himself that question again, "Why?" The prisoners looked at him with begging eyes that needed help so desperately. How could a German assist them when his own people are putting them to death? Hans knew that he was a traitor in their eyes and yet they knew nothing about his feelings. "Someday they will know," Hans told himself. "For now, they see me as a possible monster, someone who murders and hates Jews and anyone else." Little the prisoners knew in how he truly felt. Just because he was wearing that particular uniform did not mean that he enjoyed murdering anyone. Hans said to himself, "It is not the uniform that makes the person, but the person that makes the uniform. Do I really believe in what I am told to do?" Again, Hans reminded himself that the prisoners knew little about him and who he was. Hans went over to several of the blocks and saw many sick people; many of them were men. They were so skinny and undernourished. "Am I to blame for this?" he asked himself. Their bones were sticking out while others were becoming that model. Hans took off his hat as he walked through and went over to one of the men. He looked around in his early twenties, not talking. Hans knew that he could not talk because he was weak. Hans also felt that the prisoner feared to speak with him because of his uniform and being German. Most of the Nazi would have hit the prisoner on the head or shot him dead. Hans had seen that kind of behavior before. He had watched his own people be ruthless and inhumane and led him to believe that such behavior was the right way. Hans went over to the prisoner to speak to him. Hans spoke German and told the man not to worry, that he was not answering him not like most officers in this camp or anywhere else. Hans held back tears as he spoke to the prisoner and asked what his name was. The prisoner replied, "Isaac." Hans walked further and found more sick in their beds. As he stood there, Hans told everyone that he was would get them to the camp's hospital the next day. Hans believed that treatment was necessary and not death. "How could I run a labor camp with everyone dead?" Hans asked himself. He knew that he must devise a plan and help the prisoners regardless of the Third Reich. These are people, humans with feelings and we are not to judge anyone. Hans reminded himself knowing that he was risking his life, rank, and his family even in speaking to prisoners. Hans knew that he just wanted to do what he needed to do. One prisoner come up to Hans and thanked him for helping them. Hans replied, "You are welcome, my friend." Hans then proceeded to the woman's block. As he walked in, he took his hat off and told everyone to stand up so that he could speak to them. Most of the women were young, innocent and very pretty. They kept their eyes peeled on Hans as he walked around. Hans saw only a few who were sick and told them the same thing that he had told the men. They nodded and gave him a smile which also put hope in their hearts. One woman came up to Hans thanked him, and kissed his hand. Suddenly, Hans's heart broke down, and had to leave. Hans recognized that many prisoners were sick and undernourished and not because of him. He had not begun this sick cycle; the party did. Just because the party had said that the camp officers must kill the prisoners or starve them and let them die as dirt. Hans resolved not to stand by the party's decision, for the prisoner deserved to breathe too. Hans pushed his hair our of his face and walked over to the hospital.

HOSPITAL

Hans went over to the hospital to see who was in charge of this nonsense and found Major Heinrich Hefner. Hans knew Hefner was part of this conspiracy. Hefner looked as if his face was made of rock; he was bald and heavy. Hans approached Hefner by asking whether he could assist the prisoners who are quite ill. Hefner nodded and said he could help some but not all. Hans asked him, "Why?" "They are Jews, and if I help them, I am labeled as their friends," Hefner replied. Hans was furious and looked at him. This time Hans wanted to take his pistol out and shoot Hefner because of what he had said. Hans told Hefner that he needed the roads fixed and built properly and have not dead bodies falling all over the job. Hans emphasized the need to have people to build and fix because he would not receive any more prisoners until further notice. Hans then told Hefner either help the prisoners or get out there with them and build. "I can arrange that easily," said Hans. "This is a labor camp and if the prisoners die, they die from working, not by killing them on purpose. My orders are to keep this camp running, we work and we live." Hans then commanded Hefner to go over to the prisoners first thing in the morning and help them or else he would have Hefner severely punished. Hefner protested that he felt he will be going against the Reich. Hans told him that he was fully responsible for this order, not Hefner. Hefner then went over to his medicine cabinet, gathered pills and anything else he needed, and said, "not to worry about tomorrow, I will do it now as you asked, Sir." As Hans went to the blocks, sickly prisoners greeted him. They had lost so much weight and now suffered in great pain. Hefner gave numerous shots to each prisoner and told them they can rest. Good food and rest will do it and that he would be back tomorrow to check them. Hans thanked him and he left. Hans then looked at the Jew who was in charge and told him to take care of his friends. The Jew looked at Hans with eyes that could not realize who he was; all the prisoner could do was nod his head. Hans felt better because both the men and women were taken care of for the night and if they died, they would die with the feeling that someone had tried to help them. As Hans was leaving, a woman who was around her forties came up to him, and hugged him, and put her head on his chest. Hans told her that everything would be fine. Then Hans went back to his quarters for the night.

THOUGHTS

Sasha thought about her family and remembered how she had lost them in this camp. She wished that Hans had been the commander then so they would be alive. Sasha's family were her heart, and memories linger in the present. Sasha believed that she loved Hans because of her love for God. "My trust and my faith brought us together," she assured herself. Right now Hans was her family, the only one close to her left in her life. "I cannot turn his love away because it covers all of my wounds," as she told herself. "I knew this war was not intended by every German; someone surely has objected!" She remembered what Papa had told her: "There is good and bad in all people no matter who they are. We cannot judge anyone or we will be judged by God." Remembering these words, Sasha thanked God for faith and for bringing her here with Hans, into safety. Suddenly Sasha had an idea. "Today is my Mama's birthday July 10, 1943 and I want to celebrate with Hans, Otto and my friend Fritz." Because Otto was Hans best friend, Sasha trusted him for his sincerity and honesty. Fritz, Hans's door guard, made Sasha feel each day that his mannerly personality was genuine. She reflected that Fritz was always very kind and does not seem to favor the war. He stays quiet and does his work as he is told to do. "Tonight I shall prepare a special dinner made to celebrate Mama's birthday with sweet bread, baked pork with some stuffing, beans, and a cake. I will also make sure Hans will have wine so we can make a toast for Mama," Sasha exclaimed. She knew that she would spend many hours preparing this event, and she could hardly wait to see Hans's face when he came home. As she was preparing the food, she wondered when she would become Mrs. Hans Schweitzer. Sasha had never felt so special, so loved. She thought about writing to her family in America telling them about Hans; I am not able to tell them now but later. I did not want to jeopardize Hans's life. Sasha could tell them at least she had found a wonderful, handsome man that she loves and could someday marry. Sasha speculated their lives as husband and wife. Though Hans rejects what he represents, still Sasha found him handsome in his black uniform garnished with his medals. I can't wait to grow my hair again and put on a beautiful white dress and nice high heels. Perfume would put a touch on me making me smell so lovely for him. "That day can't come to soon," Sasha exclaimed to herself. She knew that she must carry on as the only survivor of her immediate family. She wanted to have children and perhaps name at least one of them after her parents. "It's funny, because I never knew how life was so short until I came to this camp," Sasha said to herself. I must go now because I must bake a cake in memory of Mama. Sasha then decided to bake coconut on it, her Mother's favorite. Almost prayerfully, Sasha whispered, "Thank you, Mama. Happy Birthday and Shalom."

MAMA'S PARTY

It was past six and roll call was going on, so was the visitation to the blocks. When Hans had finished, he went over to the line checking out the soup and bread. When he took a small sip of soup and ate a piece of the bread, he found them much better than before. He also observed that Sasha must have made extra sweet bread for them for which Hans was grateful, and so were the prisoners. Everyone lined up for the meal, and the officers went to their bunker to retire for the night. So Hans went into his bunker. Fritz greeted Hans with a click of his heels, and there Hans disappeared into his bunker. Sasha and Otto greeted Hans. Sasha put her arms around Hans and gave him a soft kiss on his cheek. Hans blushed and wiped the sweat from her brow. "You look tired and I am telling you to slow down," Hans said. But she knew that she couldn't. Anyway, he didn't know about the special dinner. Hans went to wash up, took his jacket and boots off and went into the living room where everyone was. As soon as he sat down, Sasha called for everyone for dinner including Fritz. He looked at Hans asking silently if it was all right to sit down and eat. Hans told Fritz to have something to eat. They all looked surprised at what was happening. Sasha carried out fresh fruit bowls topped with cream. All of the men were smiling and waited for Sasha to become part of the group. So she sat down and told everyone that the meal was for her mama's birthday today. They all knew that she passed away at the camp. Everyone bowed their heads, thanked God, and most of all wished Sasha's mother, "A Happy Birthday with God." It was amazing. Cream was all over their lips and face and the fruit was so tasty. Sasha knew this meal was only the beginning. So she gathered all their bowls and took them into the kitchen where she gathered their plates. She put their meal on the plates and served them. The men again were astonished about the meal and all the food they were eating. Otto and Hans were starving because they had skipped lunch. Everyone enjoyed the pork they had. The soldiers felt so full that they could not even move from their chairs so Sasha cleared the table and announced that the dessert would be in an hour. She then disappeared into the kitchen while the men gathered in the studio for some wine. She cleared the dishes, washed every pot and took out four cake plates to serve her "special birthday cake." She went into the study and gave each of them a dish of coconut cake. No one said anything while eating, because they knew this was the best part of the meal. Each one of them raised their plate and said "Happy Birthday to Sasha's mother, Natalia." A tear appeared in her eye, and Sasha was happy that her mother enjoyed her birthday with everyone.

PRISONERS SPEAKING

My name is Ira Lebensraum and I am from Poland. I am here because I am a Polish Jew and my heart aches with pain and so much sorrow. I had not believed in God before I was captured, but now I do. I never thought something like this would happen to me or to others, but it did. I am here at this camp because I am destined to die and because of this I am finding myself loving and not hating anyone. When someone has nothing to live for, he finds every possible way to to forgive. I know God in a way I have never known Him and that is because I am here. So many here are bitter, and those who are left behind and future families of these prisoners will later hate the Germans. But my words are to forgive and know that there are good in many and we should not live our lives like those who hate us. I must be an example to show how to forgive. If we do not forgive, we will be torn and allow hate to grow within us. I know that there is good and bad in every one of us, and I realize what as a prisoner that there are some good people in this war. I saw a few officers here at Camp Kassel who have been somewhat kind and have sneaked behind the backs of those who are committed to these crimes. I must go now. Forgive as my soul departs to God so I may rest in peace. Be strong and forgive.

My name is Jacob Liber and I am a Hungarian Jew. I lived in the Jewish Ghetto with my family in Berlin. We were told to go to the trains where we would be transported to one of the camps. I am so tired, my body aches, and I am so bitter to everyone I see. My friend, Hymen Bachman, has been encouraging me to have faith and not to hate anyone. He also told me that all humanity is sinful and has sinned against God. So I ask the question, "Who am I to condemn these murderers?" I have bitter feelings against these Germans because they treated my family with misery, cruelty, and murder. However, I see the commander of this camp, and he is a German, yet he shows mercy to us. He even changed the food and allow us to shower. Does this tell me that God has good Germans to help us? Yes, I can believe this now. I will forgive everyone who has wronged me, and I do pray for my family that they will do the same. I want them just like me to live in peace after I am gone. Please pass the peace to others as I speak.

FUTURE PLANS

Wednesday came fast and so did the weekly inspection from General Strauss. The officials come often but only every two months to see how we are keeping the camp and prisoners. Hans was told that they would inspect all his officers including the soldiers. The General arrived early in the morning and had breakfast with Hans and Otto. They wanted to see all of Hans's paperwork on the money that was spent including the food. Hans showed them the records of everything and told them that he cut down the waste by improving the soups and giving more to the prisoners to eat. Hans also told the General that he has had the prisoners making the bread so that the camp does not need to have bread shipped to us. Hans emphasized that his changes saved time and money because the prisoners eat leftovers from cooked food and preparing with left overs takes less time. The General was well pleased with Hans's plan and checked all of the camp's supplies and everything else. He didn't stay long because he had a meeting early afternoon. He bid Hans farewell and told him to keep up whatever he was doing. The General was pleased and so was Hans. He went over to his office, took off his jacket because the heat was bad. Hans looked out his window and saw Sasha hanging their clothes on the line. Hans could not see any fault in Sasha. Love has a purpose; hate has nothing. I remembered in youth school when I was trained by my superiors that I was to hate Jews. How foolish they were and how much they wanted me to believe their dirty lies. What strikes me funny is that Sasha does not look like the way they described a Jew. So why bother with their philosophy? Hans saw that it took one person, Hitler to invite all others who had the same hate in their hearts. Hitler even promised everyone in Germany that they would be the superior race no matter what, and we will rule. “I, Hans, will never approve it or follow, and I declare this in silence,” Hans vowed to himself to let the prisoners do some sports. Many just stand around doing nothing. They have to be in shape in order to do the camp’s work. Hans knew that he was not in the position at this moment to receive new prisoners. The General had told him that he would receive notice “when and if.” Hans had a road to be laid out and hot tar to cover those roads. Hans had to keep the prisoners fit until we proceed to the next process. At this time, Hans was reluctant to say that he knew very little. Hans had changed the food to give and save more. He wanted to keep these changes that he had already made and put them into his future plans. Some of Hans’s officers had home leave each weekend for Hans always felt that they should stay in contact with their families. Hans could permit two officers to go home every two weeks. The leave system was Hans’s next project to work on so he can get two officers home by next weekend. Hans learned that the several large houses from the camp were used for the families of his officers. They were not close to the camp but yet not too far away, and that was fine with Hans. Everything he did was for the best of everyone and not just for himself. I even gave the family permission to have some of the prisoners help them with their chores. At least four families could stay at the house. Hans went outside to observe everything, and he saw that the train tracks ran into the camp. The train came from Berlin, and Hans was told that the train would be in use again, soon. No date has been set but the idea has. Hans heard in Auschwitz that “death trains” started a while ago and many have been put to death each day. Hans despised this thought and felt ashamed of the uniform that he wore. My question is, what would I do when this “death train” faces me? Do I run or agree? He knew he had to do what his Mother taught him, “to pray.” Hans’s plans included Sasha, and we had to come up with more future plans that included us and what we should do. This was Hans’s main plan but he was not sure what he needed to do. “I have been here for twelve weeks and in those weeks I have seen nothing but horror,” said Hans. Death, sickness and suicide are what he saw. He was not pleased about what he had seen. Many of his officers whipped the prisoners even though he had ordered none should be whipped. Hans needed every man to fix the road and layout the foundation. Hans ordered the officers to whip only if necessary and that meant only if the prisoners were trying to escape. Many were not pleased and dared not to say anything to Hans. If any of Hans's officers were to disobey his orders, he would have to put them into his own prison for two weeks. Hans had the authority and was not afraid to use it against them. "Yes, the camp was changing and Kassel is my toy, my playground," said Hans. Where I made the rules. Hans had to make his plans because the war would continue, lives will be lost and decisions will fail. He realized that he must contact his friend with whom he had grown up with in Cologne, Peter Ott. Peter was Hans's best friend since school and when they graduated together he was scheduled to go and fight at the front line. Hans wasn't sure where at this point. Hans needed to contact headquarters and find out the status of Peter and whether he is doing well. Hans remembered that he and Peter had vowed that when we would be out of this war, they would drink so much beer that they would swim in the Rhine River.

HEADQUARTERS

Hans made a call to headquarters and I spoke to Major George Mueller, who happened to be an old friend of mine. I told him that my friend Peter Ott was at the front, somewhere in Germany. He asked other questions because there might be duplicate names as his. Hans gave Major Mueller all the information and Major Mueller said that he would take care of this for me, today. Hans asked Major Mueller if Peter could be transferred from his company and be under his command at the camp. Major Mueller assured me that he would do what he can. He said that Hans would hear from him in a few days. Hans agreed, and thanked him and hung up hoping he will hear from him sooner. Time passed by, and Hans finally heard from Major Mueller. He told me that he had finally located Peter and put in a transfer to Hans's camp. Peter would be coming here by the end of the week for his new assignment with Hans. Hans was relieved because he needed more men like Peter. Hans waited.

FIGHT

It was a warm day and Hans was in his office doing some paperwork and he looked out his window and saw his officers. A fight broke out in block ten where the women were living. Sirens were going off, guns were being shot in the air, and almost all the dogs were ordered to kill. Hans ran to where the fight was and saw two women on the ground rolling in dirt with blood on their faces. Hans ordered them to get up and told them that he was against these fights, especially with the women. He looked at them and knew he had to find out the purpose and reason. When Hans did found out, he had to come up with a reasonable punishment for both of them. Hans spoke to both of them in German and ordered them to come to his office immediately. There he met them both with Otto ready to hear their story. As they were escorted by two soldiers, Hans looked at them wondering why they would turn against one another. "Shouldn't they help each other?" Hans asked himself. One woman had her nose broken, and the other was cut badly on her face. Hans came to the most difficult question, "Why?"

The one woman told me that the other called her mother a very bad name. Hans said, "so does that justify it by your actions?" They didn't say anything and just went on in telling me the story. The woman who was hit in her face said the other woman knocked her down before she could do anything. I stood up and said that was enough and declared their punishment. Hans told them that both of them were wrong in what they have did. Hans answered that the women would be confined in separate cells for one day and would also do hard labor, scrubbing the entire barracks until they learned about this nonsense they had committed. Hans looked at them sternly and dismissed them directing his guard to take them to their cells. Hans sat down alone to consider how he could prevent any future disasters like this one today? "The prisoners are causing death for each other and they could have been shot if I did not intercede for them," Hans told himself

He decided that he needed two women officers to watch over the women and control them. Again, I made a call to headquarters for help. Once again, Major Mueller came to Hans's aid and sent two women named Ida Holster and Hilda Housman.

RECRUITS

It was half past seven when Hans received the good news about Peter and his arrival; he was being transported to the camp. Hans was sure that Peter would be surprised to see me as him as company commander. So now all Hans had to do was wait for Peter's arrival. It was raining very heavily outside, and the mud was knee deep. Hans had to relieve his guards outside and put new guards to watch. Hans told them that he wanted a change of guards every four hours until this rain stopped. Hans then went back into his office covered with mud and soaking wet.

As he was drying off, a car pulled up outside his office. It was almost 8:00 PM, and I realized that this was my late night. Hans heard a knock at the door and as he gave them permission to enter, there stood two women. Hans knew right there they were the two women he asked for the other day. "Sit down and please take off your wet coats," Hans said. They were very tall women, perhaps 30 years old and very stern. Hans offered them a cup of tea and told them what I needed from them concerning the women here at the camp. I also mention that hitting and beating was permitted only if a prisoner tries to escape. Hans told them that he did not want to see any more fights like the one the other day. They agreed and assured me that no disturbances of this would occur again. Hans took them to their quarters, bade them goodnight, and finally went to his bunker. There he met Sasha, upset and crying.

CONFESSION

Sasha was crying and her deep brown eyes were so red with tears. Hans grabbed her and drew her close to his heart where he comforted her sorrow. She was upset about the fights, the camp, and the war. She told Hans that before she ever met him, she prayed a prayer and said it every day: "Dear God, keep me quiet so that I don't end up in any camp." But she did." May God help me as time passes me by." Sasha cried. "Day after day my tears are silent, my heart is so broken, and here I remain. Why is there so much hate in the world? Please help me, please?" Hans's feelings for Sasha just dug at his heart, and he wished that they were out of this camp where lives would be different. "Do you hear God, do you?" Hans prayed silently. "Take these tears, put them away and help me through this. I disliked the war and I felt these feelings along with others that it was all useless. How long will this war go on?" He could see this war coming to an end with us all losing. He asked the question again: "What would we accomplish besides murder?"

PETER OTT

Sasha and Hans were in the dining room eating breakfast when Fritz marched into the room. "Sir, you have someone here to see you." Hans told Fritz it was all right to let him in. Hans was finishing his last sip of coffee when the new soldier came before him and saluted him with a hard kick to his boots. Hans looked at him, and sure enough it was Peter Ott. Hans saluted him back, and Peter looked at him with shock in his eyes. "Hans, Hans is that you?" Hans looked straight at him and got up to give him a huge hug and a handshake. Peter couldn't believe that Hans was the company commander and just stood at his best pose. "Relax," Hans told him. "I know you; and how are you, friend?" Peter sat in the chair and told Hans that he was doing well. Hans then told him to have some breakfast, and he had some eggs and sweet bread. Peter looked at Sasha and asked who she was. Hans told him that it was a long story, that Sasha was his sweetheart, and that she is a prisoner of war at this camp. Peter shook his head and was very surprised but yet he respected Hans's wishes. Hans told Peter that he loved Sasha, and that she was a Jew, and that they wanted to be married after the war. Peter looked at Hans again and then at Sasha and agreed that she was pretty and her eyes were especially beautiful. He said that he hoped everything would work out for both of them. Hans took Peter's bags upstairs to his room. Hans needed to speak to Peter as soon as possible because Hans wanted to get things moving fast as possible. Hans explained that he would be the overseer in the kitchen and the hospital and that he would be in charge. Hans mentioned to Peter that food was mysteriously disappearing. He told Peter that he needed to find out why this was happening and by whom. Hans did not want the General to find out about this lost food because he did not want his visit here. Peter's job was hard, but not complicated, but Hans trusted Peter to accomplish this goal for the camp. We must find out who is responsible for the food disappearing, and if that person is found, he will be punished to the fullest. Peter promised to get down to business and start his work with the assignment that Hans had given to him. Hans assured Peter that all would turn out well.

"ARBEIT MACHT FREI"

The prisoners were assigned to build a bridge that would extend out and around the camp. Hans knew that hard work and plenty of sweat would help build the bridge that would be needed as time moved on. Hans saw that "Arbeit Mach Frei" was posted at the front gate. He always questioned whether work could really make one free. Hans did not know where and who had given that slogan to be used in the camps, but surely it was false. The prisoners started to work. They were mostly men digging deep down using only shovels and removing large rocks. The ground was steaming due to the hot weather. Hans saw the men sweating from the heat and the burning sun. Hans went over to the labor field to see the men working; but as he approached the field, he heard cries of suffering. Shovels hit the ground while the officers were yelling at them to go faster. Hans went over to Captain Goetz, a very tall insecure man. Hans asked the reason that Goetz was yelling so much at them. Goetz told Hans that he was doing what the Fuhrer wanted him to do: inflict suffering and pain. Hans knew this man was from the old school and typically brainwashed. Goetz even announced to Hans that the German race was superior and that superior is the way that the Germans were to remain. Hans saw Goetz also hitting several of the prisoners with his whip, and he hit one prisoner so hard that his shirt was ripped open. When Hans saw blood splattering, he approached Goetz and grabbed his whip right out of his hand. Hans ordered him to stop. "I need the bridge built and by whipping these men who are stronger I will lose them to death," Hans told Goetz. Goetz stopped, and caught his breath, and walked over to another area. The prisoner remained hurt, so Hans ordered two of the Jewish leaders to carry him over to the hospital. Hans told them to let the doctor know that Commander Hans said to treat the injured man immediately without questions. They agreed and took him over to the hospital. Everyone had their eyes peeled on Hans wondering what he had said. Hans turned to everyone and told them to carry on with their work. Before Hans left, he told Captain Goetz that work was to end at 5:00PM, that the prisoner's food would be ready to distribute, and that no one should wait. Goetz saluted Hans and carried on with his work. "The bridge will be built for us; I hope there will be no more interruptions!" Hans said to himself.

AIR RAID

It was another hot day. Everyone was working on the bridge site, and the fact that deep holes were showing pleased Hans. It was a normal day for most, and news came to me that the British allies were being attacked by us. Our team spotted several bombers, and we were warned of a possible air strike. The British were bombing parts of Germany and we were not exempt. Our first warning came at 11:27 AM. Hans had the siren ring around the camp warning that the British were nearby and possible attack. Hans's soldiers got their weapons together and were ready to defend. At 12:01 PM, the alarms went off again and a call from headquarters came with warnings. The British bombers were at least ten miles north approaching at a rapid speed towards Kassel. Hans sounded the sirens and everyone took their positions. Everyone was cleared from the fields, and the camp's soldiers were ready with all their weapons. Everyone was on high alert, and soon we heard the planes approaching. Hans ran into the bunker to get Sasha and Fritz into the basement. As he did, he heard the bombs going off and his men firing. Hans left Sasha and Fritz in the basement, and Sasha begged Hans to stay, but he couldn't. He had a camp to watch and had the responsibility for everyone including himself. Hans then ran outside; and as he did, one of the bullets from the plane struck Hans in his leg. There Hans felt the worst pain that he could ever experience. Hans lay there for a few seconds and then tried to pull himself to shelter behind one of the buildings. He noticed a lot of blood coming from his leg. Then the raid was over at 12:33 PM. Hans saw blue smoke filling the air of the camp and cries of people. Hans lay on the ground. His glasses fell off his face and his hair was hanging down into his eyes. He was full of dirt and dust and his uniform was no longer black but dusty. His leg was bleeding very badly, and the blood seeped through his trousers. Hans was crying for help when several officers with his guards came running to assist him. As they approached Hans they saw that his leg was hurt badly. He couldn't stand up, so they carried him quickly to the hospital. There Hans met the doctor, who directed the officers to carry him to the bed. As they did, I told Otto to take inspection at once and report back to me with any causalities. As Otto left, the doctor was ripping Hans's boot off and cutting his trousers. At that point Hans didn't care because his leg was painful. As the doctor looked at Hans's leg, he told him that he had a bullet lodged and he had to get it out. So the doctor took a big knife, poured some antiseptic on Hans's leg and dug into the wound. Hans was biting on his sleeve and couldn't take the pain as the doctor removed the bullet. Hans was relieved. The doctor then cleaned out the wound and wrapped Hans's leg in a bandage. Hans was lucky that he had received only that wound. The doctor ordered him off his feet for at least a week and then to report back to him. He gave Hans morphine and told him to take one pill every twelve hours for pain. The doctor warned Hans that those pills would put him to sleep, so Hans had to rest. As Hans was leaving with the assistance of soldiers, the doctor told Hans either to keep off the leg or get a horse. When Hans went outside he saw several of the buildings burning and smoke coming from the fields. He asked the soldier who was helping him to put him on the bench across where they were standing. Hans ordered the soldier to have roll call immediately. Hans stood in great pain as the whistles blew and the horn went off. Everyone ran and settled in. Everyone stood at attention and waited for me. As Hans was wobbling, he saw Sasha looking out the window crying. He nodded to her that all was all right. She didn't believe him. Hans asked for a report to see if everyone was all right and the number of the dead. Lt. Schopenhauer reported to me that three prisoners were dead, twelve of our men were hurt and one soldier dead. Two buildings were on fire, but they had managed to put it out. Hans thanked the soldier and spoke to everyone about what just happened. Hans told them that the camp had just had a raid by the British and that he was injured in the raid. Hans then told everyone to go back to their blocks and prepare for their meals. As Hans was helped to his bunker, he met Sasha and Fritz. Fritz helped him up the stairs and laid him on the sofa. Sasha ran over to him and hugged his neck. She was happy that he was still alive and so was Hans.

ASSISTANCE

Hans had to go back to the doctor to have the bandage changed, the doctor told me that I needed crutches and a horse. Hans couldn't walk alone with this injury. So he asked one of the prisoners to make him a set of crutches. He was an older man named Hymen who showed a very kind heart to Hans. He went to the work area to pick up some wood and made the crutches for him. Hymen sized the crutches to his height so Hans would be comfortable using them. Hans's leg was in such pain and for a minute he was experiencing pain that these prisoners perhaps were also feeling. Hans had to wipe his tears as he saw this man before him helping him without prejudice. What Hans saw was a gift from God and his heart sank as Hymen made those crutches for him. Hans was so ashamed of himself and yet his uniform represented hate. However, Hymen didn't care about what his uniform represented. Hymen saved the agony of Hans's leg, for the pain to walk unaided was worse. Still Hans wanted to find a way to reward this man who helped him. Hans thought for a minute that he could save Hymen's life but he had to figure out how to do it. Hans thanked Hymen and told him to follow me to his bunker. Hymen helped Hans with the crutches and to the bunker. Usually it would take Hans only five minutes, but now the trip took twenty minutes. Hymen was kind to hold Hans, who never was so grateful for the man's kindness. Hans realized that there was love in this man, and who didn't care who the German was. That realization meant a lot to Hans. Reaching to the bunker, Hans used the crutch while Hymen pulled him up the stairs. As Hans reached the top of the steps, Hymen held out his hands out for Hans to grab them. Hymen actually showed Hans much mercy that at that point Hans forgot that he was even a German and Hymen a Jew. Hans knew without help he was useless. Tears were flowing as Hans reached to grab Hymen's hand and he pulled Hans to that last step. Before Hans's eyes met his, Hymen told Hans to hang onto him. Together, they closed the last distance. Hans's heart broke, and Hans knew that he had to repay Hymen, now his friend.

THE ENCOUNTER

Fritz was at the door guarding since the camp had this attack. Hans nodded to Hymen to escort me to the chair. There Sasha met Hans helping him to sit down while Hymen's job was finished. Hans felt so much gratitude to Hymen and knew that he owed this older man a lot. Hans asked Hymen to sit down and have something to eat, then asked Sasha to fix Hymen something before he would leave. She prepared him a bowl of chicken soup with fresh sweet bread and a glass of wine. Hymen ate quickly, and he just sat there until he finished. Sasha offered Hans some food and a drink, but he did not want anything. Hans just lay there with his leg up on the table fighting pain. Hans asked Hymen to sit down, and Hans spoke to him about his family. He told Hans that they had died because of being weak and sick from diseases. Hans saw Hymen's tears, and just sat there trying to comfort Hymen through his sorrow. Hans offered him the best reward he could ever ask because he had taken care of him. Hans told Hymen that he would release him from this camp so that he would be away from this hell. Hymen broke down and cried. So Hans signed the papers for Hymen to be released as his gratitude continued for Hymen's help. Hans asked Otto to bring Hymen to his office. Hans told Hymen that he was immediately released from Camp Kassel and that he would be transported to Hans's father's house for protection. Hymen started to cry so hard that Hans filled up with tears too. Hymen wanted to go but couldn't leave. He was scared, but Hans assured him that everything would be all right. Hymen was contented, and Hans had Peter transport Hymen to his father's house that day. Hans called his father telling him that he was sending him help for his farm. As Hymen was leaving, he looked behind and said softly, "Thank you, Hans."

COMMUNICATIONS

Days had passed since that first bombing of the camp. Hans had heard nothing from anyone. He tried several times contacting headquarters, but the phone was dead. Hans even tried sending a telegram again, nothing. Hans was now wondering where the General was and anything happened. Hans already knew that Berlin had been heavily bombed but knew nothing about headquarters. Hans realized that he was on his own for this short time. Hans then called Otto in to help him gather all information, hoping that someone would contact the camp, or at least try to. Hans told Otto that the camp had a problem with communications and that we needed supplies. Otto said he would go to Berlin to get them for us and try to learn about the problem with communications. Otto left and did not return for hours. Hans was hoping that all was well with him. When Otto finally came back home, he had plenty of food, bread and medical supplies. Hans asked him about communications. "Sit down, Hans," he said. "Hans, communications are down and we are on our own until the lines are restored. We can get supplies but we cannot speak to anyone directly." Hans thanked Otto and asked him to deliver the supplies to the kitchen and hospital. Hans said, "If communications are down, then we are on our own until we are discovered again; and the question is, when?"

INSPECTION AGAIN

Hans got on his horse that a local had given to him. Hans named the horse Zurich. Riding to the blocks where the prisoners were was something he had to do. Most of the prisoners were out in the fields and at the roads. The heat was less, and more could be accomplished by putting down the tar. Hans was hoping that he job would be done soon for the sake of others. Hans could not get down from his horse, and he went to block 1-10 for inspections, taking Private Heisenberg to these blocks so he could help with inspection. At the first block, Hans rode in with Zurich. Private Heisenberg opened the door and called everyone who was there at attention. This block housed the women. Some were Polish; others were German and Jews. They stood there very quietly; then Hans noticed younger women at the end of the block. Hans used these young women to help clean up and do chores around the camp. Hans didn't want the officers to use the whip on the women, as he kept a close eye on the officers. He knew when someone was whipped. Hans also checked for any sign of sickness or for an unhealthy women. As Hans stood in the middle of Block 1, he gazed at them and saw that so many of them were pretty. His heart wanted to free every one of them. He knew if he done that, others would capture them and kill them. As Hans and Heisenberg passed by these young women, most of them had their eyes on Hans. He had his black uniform on with his shiny boots, short haircut, and his glasses. Hans was only twenty-two years old. Hans seldom wore his hat, but he wore it when he had to meet someone important. What made Hans stand out even more was his horse which caused attention. Zurich was very attractive. He was white with brown spots. Hans always rode with his rifle by his side, just in case. Hans told the women that he was inspecting for any sickness and told them that if any were ill, they were to be treated right away. Hans was pleased to find that none were sick. Hans told the prisoners to carry on with their work and that the inspection was over. Hans then moved to the next blocks. Blocks 2-6 were all in order, clean and without problems, but he found two women who were sick and he told the Jewish leader to take them over to the hospital for medicine. He also told the leaders to tell the doctor that Commander Hans had sent them for evaluation. Block 7-10 was passable, but not to the point of being clean. Hans saw hay from the beds was on the floor and rodents running around. As Hans looked around the block, he determined that it needed changes. Although conditions were passable, they were barely livable. Captain Hilda came in as she heard me speaking. Her job was not to bother Hans, but to assist him. He told her that the conditions were filthy and reminded her that she is solely responsible for the women to clean it up. "As far as the mice are concerned, kill the mice with a rock," Hans said. Any of the prisoners become sick, she is to send them immediately to the hospital. Captain Hilda stood there until Hans left on his horse. He then went over to the officer's club where he saw Peter.

THE OFFICER'S CLUB

Several of the officers were at the club where they met each day before and after their duty. They went for a cooked breakfast each morning and to exchange gossip. A few of the officers were hard core meaning that they followed rules right to the point. Even though they did not agree with Hans on a lot of things, still they said nothing to him. Whatever they did when Hans was not around, Hans did not want to hear about it unless it was necessary. When they enforced the rules upon any prisoner, they made sure that Hans was not around. Small talk was always a favorite topic at the club, and so was romance. Several of the women officers were also there because as they helped with controlling the prisoners. Loneliness was their only friend, and the environment made it even worse for them. They had to look at the barbed wire, gates, and weapons; and they had nothing else for their lives. Hans walked in on his crutches. Everyone saluted him and decided to exchange some of the small talk. Hans had breakfast there, just some tea with eggs because he just did not have an appetite. Captain Luther Geiger came over to Hans and wanted to discuss possible reinforcement and new prisoners. No one was sure what was going to happen especially without communications from headquarters. Hans told Luther that what they had heard so far was all rumor, nothing else. Captain Geiger looked at Hans with astonishment and changed the subject. Geiger asked Hans several times how his leg was feeling, and small talk began again. Smoke filled the room from old German cigarettes and pipes. Hans would smoke occasionally but not often. He felt that he should keep his life somewhat pure away from this habit. Anyway, that was something positive that he was taught in school, a year of brainwashing and hatred. Captain Hilda came up to Hans. She was nothing more than a flirt who happened to need a quick fix for her loneliness. She looked at Hans and admired his looks. He ignored her and asked "how the women were doing and whether any problems were occurring." She told him that everything was doing well and quickly changed the subject. She then asked Hans whether he was going to the officer's party next Friday. "Maybe," he said neutrally. He knew what she was hinting at and decided to pull out of the conversation. Hans looked at his watch and told Hilda politely that he had to return to his office. She then looked at him and said, "You know where to find me." He nodded and smiled to her and said goodbye to everyone

GOREN STRAVINSKY

I am a prisoner of this camp and my name is Goren Stravinsky. I am 62 years old and I am Polish. I have never owned a thing in my life, and yet I had to come to this camp. I had lived in Warsaw all my life before they captured me as a prisoner. My family was weak and died from diseases. I have been here for three months, and before that, I was in Warsaw Ghetto. The Nazi put me on a train, and took all my belongings. I have not been beaten, but I have suffered from not enough food. I came here to have a better chance to live, and the commander here has given me a small chance. Our meals are better, although sometimes we have watery soup with vegetables and bread, and I drink water. My stomach gets sick from the food but it has improved. I work every day except Sunday when we are given a day off. I have been fixing and building the road. The heat burns my face and my hands as I help to lay down the mortal. As I pick up the bucket, the heat from the mix burns my face entirely. I really want to go and forget this place. I heard that the war may be over soon and that our allies may be helping us. I am grateful to Commander Hans. He is not violent as most of the other officers. He has done what he could, but less because of what they want from him. We will see how I am released. I must go now because I am called to work, and I must work.

RETSINA

I have been a prisoner at this camp for more than four months now. My name is Retsina and I have seen many die of diseases and hunger. I know the Germans are all around us, and sometimes they threaten us when Hans is not around. They do not want him to find out. Sometimes they hit us, and we stay silent. Hans is fair to us and tried to make changes. This is a work camp; we work until we drop. As the heat intensifies, we are out as laborers in the fields. There is heat on our faces, heads, and hands. We are burning hot in the summer and freezing in the winter. It makes no sense to this kind of work except we can speak against this treatment in which the officers punch us for no reason. I like the commander because he tries but cannot show many feelings. So he helps us indirectly. I know one thing: the women want to be the commander's worker because he is good looking and young. But many still look at him as a German. So when will this end? I have spoken truthfully. Now let the freedom come. Freedom and truth will set us all free.

SASHA'S WISH

It is a warm day today, and Sasha was baking at least ten loaves of sweet bread. Hans enjoys putting so much butter on the bread and a scoop of jam. Sasha sometimes kept two loaves for them and give the rest to the prisoners. Unfortunately, they are not blessed to have the butter and jam like us, but blessed to have the bread. Tonight she will fry up some potatoes with sauerkraut and serve some red cabbage, too. Hans is usually home by evening, unless he has to do some orders. She usually made some hay mixed with honey for Zurich too. Sasha like to take care of his horse. She was glad that Hans's leg was getting better. The nice farmer gave Hans Zurich. Hans likes to ride his horse around, and he says his boots stay shiny that way. Sasha thought that today, since no one was really around, she would keep a picture of Hans in her pocket. Sasha love looking at him, his blue eyes and his black uniform. His smile tells her he is a sincere person. She really didn't like the Ghetto, the train, and this camp; but she does love Hans who saved her from all the pain. If only she could take his picture and send it to America for her aunt! Today Sasha sat and thought of how she would be if they were married. Sasha often wonder whether Hans would look handsome in regular clothes as he did in his uniform. Sasha wish they were out of there and started their lives together. She wish they were married and she could feel Hans in her arms and she in his. Sasha wish this day and every day that they could get closer to their wish. Sasha hopes that tonight she will tell Hans how much she loves him, and she will also tell him her wish. Maybe he will wish with her or make his own wish known. Tonight will be the night that they will wish together.

"SWEET BREAD AND ME"

Hans came home late in the evening. As always, he first gave Sasha a kiss on her cheek. He always asked Sasha how she was before he took off his uniform and boots. Hans said his foot needs air to cool down. He took a cold shower because of the heat and then he put on a short sleeve undershirt and shorts. He looked so funny in them. He sometimes walked around without any shoes on, sometimes his slip-on shoes. Sasha could see that his leg was still hurting him. It was getting better slowly. He still limped. When he mounted Zurich he usually needed Fritz to help him up. Sasha had dinner on the table. Hans said that this dinner was his favorite, which he remembered eating it when he was a young boy. He took a huge chunk out of the bread and loaded it with butter and strawberry jam. He had a glass of white French wine then just sat back and ate. He usually didn't speak much while eating, only if he found it necessary. Sasha had put a lot of food on his plate, more than he could handle. He usually had Fritz for dinner with them, but tonight was going to be somewhat different. When dinner finishes Sasha intended to discuss her wishes with Hans. She hoped that he would have a special wish too, just like her. Tonight Sasha wanted to feel somewhat romantic and she wanted to use the love that God gave to her to express it. She went over to Hans and decided to give him a neck rub to relieve his stress. Sasha began massaging his neck, and he was pleased that he felt better. She told him that she wanted to be married and live with him for the rest of her life. For once, Hans agreed and said that he first wanted the war to be over with. Sasha told Hans how much she really loved him, and she thanked him for everything he did for her. He rose slowly, reached for her wrist, and pulled her closer to him. There he gave Sasha a kiss, a kiss that opened every door to her soul. Sasha smiled to herself: another wish was granted.

TEARS FOREVER

The prisoners had now been fairly well established for ten months. Some lived, although some had died, not because of Hans but because of diseases and old age. A lot of them lost weight; Hans had a hard time looking at these prisoners. He felt he was to blame, but Sasha always told him that it wasn't his fault. Still Hans secretly held pity in his heart for these people. He went over to all of the blocks to see the prisoners. Hans started with the men and found many in their beds, sick. "Where did I go wrong," Hans asked himself? He knew that he had given orders to the hospital to deal with the sick, yet they still had not achieved his goal. Hans did not know whether these prisoners were new or the same ones who were sick. He took the number of the block and submitted it to the doctor and said that he wanted medical attention to them. Then Hans went over to the woman's block and found some ill also not many but a few. Again, he took the number of the block to present to the doctor. Hans went through the blocks and found a lot of very young women. He just looked at them and smiled and many of them were crying. He felt that tears were their only friend, yet hope was at a distance for them. One prisoner named Olga went up to Hans. She stood only 5'4 tall. She made quite a contrast to Hans, who was way over 5'11 tall. He had to lean downward to hear her speak to him. She smiled at him and put her head on his stomach because her head did not reach his chest. Many of the women who did not hate Hans were well satisfied with his rulings. Many hated the Germans and didn't care how Hans treated them. Olga asked Hans if whether would be safe and not put to death. He nodded to her and said as long as he was commander he would do his best. She asked Hans to bend down; and when he did, she gave him a kiss on his cheek. Hans then filled up with tears, tears that would last forever. He knew it would be a slight promise to save all of them. Yet he promised to do his best. He left the blocks and went to the hospital to give his orders. “Help those people who are ill,” Hans said. The doctor asked who the sick prisoners were, and Hans gave him the number of the blocks where they could be found. The doctor knew better not to reject Hans’s orders even though they sounded unrealistic. So the hospital carried out the orders, and Hans was satisfied with the doctor.

ORDERS

The day August 31,1943: was very hot, and fall was around the corner. Time seemed to be moving faster. Many of the prisoners had been sitting in this camp for months and even years. Hans kept an eye on them and made sure they were doing their work. Roads had to be repaired and doing the grounds in the summer was far better than in the winter when the ground would be too hard to break. Some of these workers were out early in the morning to late at night working. Unfortunately, many died on the ground while working. That day, a letter came specifying that 250 of the prisoners had to be transferred to another labor camp because new prisoners would be coming in by train. Hans's heart began to pound for he knew that he had to follow these orders. The train was to arrive in two days at 6:00 AM to transport them. Then the following day 300 more would be transported to Hans' camp. The rest of the prisoners in Kassel were to stay until further notice, according to headquarters. Hans had to obey their wishes. He then called for Captain Hilda to prepare 125 women and children for the train to leave in two days, and get things ready for new prisoners that would be coming into the camp. She looked at Hans because she liked him, she told him she would do it for him. She also mentioned the officer's party scheduled for Friday. Hans said that he would be there. Hans then called Otto to have the male prisoners ready in the morning. Hans went back to his office and poured himself a glass of sherry. He felt distorted, angry, and bitter towards his own people. He had to figure something to break away or hope that the camp would be invaded by their enemies again. He heard that the Allies were planning more attacks on Germany very soon, but he didn't know how soon.

THE PARTY

On Friday the day was steady with paperwork, business with headquarters, and phone calls. Hans put up the roster for weekends off for the officers and even went one month ahead of schedule. Hans was on duty this weekend ready for the prisoners to be transported unless told differently. Hans tended to go to this party with Otto just to see what it was all about. He really wanted to bring Sasha, but he knew that he could not. Hans was already dressed. Because he had ridden Zurich all day, his boots would still have a shine to them.

Hans had to wait for Otto so they could go over to the club because three of Hans's men were gone for the weekend, leaving only four soldiers, including Hans, plus Hans's guards.

Hans met Otto at his office around 7:00 PM and then walked over to the club. They sat down and had a beer and some brandy. Music was playing. Some officers were dancing, and the women were acting wild. Hilda, on the other hand, sat beside Hans and asked him to dance with her. She was quite bold and pretty but not his type of woman. Unfortunately, she told Hans that her heart was captured by his looks. Hans reminded her that he was her commander and that he could not dance with her alone. Then he changed his mind and danced with her for awhile. Then he sat down with her and Otto to have a beer and something to eat. Hans couldn't tell Hilda that he did not feel the way she felt for him, so he tried to avoid her. Hans just wanted to get this camp going and then find his life somewhere else.

The party continued, but Hans asked Otto whether he wanted to leave. Otto agreed because it was getting late. Hans had to get up early because he had duty this weekend. Hans went inside, took a shower, and went to sleep only to be up early again.

FAREWELL, MY FRIENDS

Monday morning arrived, and everyone gathered the prisoners who were to leave. Hans was on Zurich and stood at the head of the roll call. The call sounded at 5:00 AM, and there he stood looking at every prisoner wondering what was going through their minds. His officers were there, and he saw that Sasha was looking through the window. Hans sat on his horse telling everyone that 250 prisoners had to gather their belongings and be ready to leave. Hans told them that he was sorry but he could not control this decision. Hans wanted to pull away but noticed that every prisoner had come to attention and saluted him. Hans's eyes filled with tears. He saluted them back, then rode away. The prisoners were dismissed and went to get their breakfast, then to wait for the train. Hans was not sure what was beyond this camp but suspected what might be waiting. As he was riding away, he heard the whistle of the train blow and saw the prisoners were standing by the tracks. Hans called it the "disaster train" because he heard what it was and would be. As the train came to a halt, the guards jumped off and opened the doors so they could pile in the prisoners. As Hans was standing there, an officer approached him and asked him to sign the release forms.

As soon as Hans had signed them, he signaled the conductor to leave. Watching the train leave, Hans felt a huge hurt in his heart.

ARRIVAL

The day was a rainy and Hans was devastated that he had to go through this kind of exercise again with 300 prisoners arriving shortly. He sat on his horse waiting for the arrival knowing that the revolving door was not finished. Hans knew by the time the war would be over, he would receive more orders demanding the transfer of more prisoners. Hans knew the process and just didn't want any more to do with it. He waited for that moment when he could wake up in the morning and not hear a train whistle in his brain. It was past 7:00 AM and Hans looked at his watch, "Late again," he said. Suddenly, he heard the whistle blowing and the clack of the wheels on the tracks. Hans wept silently. Every breath he took he created a silent tear, and every breath he let out relieved him. The train was coming in slowly, and he could see the guards on top with their "Maschinengewehr34." Hans wondered whether they were stupid because no prisoner was going to escape through locked gates. The camp's remaining prisoners were still standing in the center waiting for the arrival of more. Hans's guards were guarding the prisoners while Otto helped him to unload. Hans told the soldiers to meet the new prisoners at the doors of the train and let them out. Hans wanted them off fast so he could finish this process fast. When the doors were opened, the soldiers yelled for the prisoners to come out quickly. Women, men, children, young, old, babies in their mother's arms came running out. In the background, Hans could hear these distorted voices mixed with screams and pleads. Hans rode over to the ones who were screaming to assure them that the process would move faster now. Hans directed all of them through his fog horn. Hans estimated that 300 were here along with his remaining 250 prisoners. "Damn them, they gave me 550 prisoners," Hans cursed to himself. He knew that Sasha was watching and crying as she always did with every arrival. Hans knew her pain, and that pain was mixed with his own. Hans knew finally that the arrival of these prisoners meant that more were to come.

PROCESSING

As Hans yelled out to the prisoners and told them they needed to be quiet, all of the noise came to a halt. The newcomers looked at this young man dressed in his dark uniform and shiny boots. With his smooth haircut, Hans looked sharp, especially with his medals on his chest. But there was one problem: he did not agree with the Nazis or Hitler. The uniform became him, but he did not represent the uniform. In reality Hans was a good-looking German soldier serving his country, and behind that uniform stood kindness. He knew that these new prisoners would find out, or the remaining ones will tell them. Hans spoke to the prisoners, introduced himself as the Commander of Camp Kassel; and welcomed them. He also told them that he was turning this process over to his fellow officer, Lt. Wilhelm Frankenberg. Lt. Frankenberg would lead them through the processing to process in, and issue their uniforms. As Hans approached his remaining prisoners, he commanded them to return to their blocks and wait for any further instruction. Hans told his officers to complete the processing with dispatch and report to his meeting room at 5:00 PM. He left on his horse to return to his bunker. The process took four hours, much longer than the officers had expected. Lt. Wilhelm directed all the women and children to report to Captain Hilda, who would process all of the women and children by giving them numbers tattooed on their arms. Then she had to obtain information, see to hair-cutting, then taking all their belongings, and finally taking them to the showers. After the showers, the new prisoners would come out and be sprayed down then issued uniforms. Captain Hilda also gave them her harsh rules. Lt. Wilhelm gathered all of the men and boys and had them follow him. Soon the ground was empty, except the soldiers who were guarding the gates. They were roaming with their security dogs looking or hoping they would find someone trying to escape. Captain Hilda began tattooing their arms, and her assistants took information after they received the tattoos. Some of this tattooing hurt and burned most of the women. The women did not say anything because they were afraid of getting slapped or beaten. Captain Hilda had at least 190 women to process; she finished this part of the job around 2:30 PM. The prisoners finally received their uniforms. One woman soldier then gave the prisoners their gear for eating and told them that if they lost it they would then eat from their hands. All jewelry, glasses, wooden legs, false teeth, gold teeth and more were given to the Nazis who were to collect all of this gear. No one kept anything. As the officers were finishing, they could hear the prisoners' sobs. Some of the officers felt tears as the new prisoners walked into their nightmare. Lt. Wilhelm did the same process for the men. Any man who refused the process were punched. Lt. Wilhelm was a heartless man, ruthless but under the control of Hans. Wilhelm would always hit and smack the prisoners and sometimes shout and yell at them. But he did know that if Hans found out, he would be punished. So he did it when Hans would not see. Wilhelm was a true follower of the Nazis and did exactly what he was taught. The entire process for both men and women was finished at 2:30 PM. After this, the prisoners stood in the court ready to receive their duties. At that time Hans rode over to inspect if everything was all right. He rode around the prisoners looking at them as he stood on his horse in the back of the line, watching. He did not ask, but pulled four men and two women to be guards over their blocks. He had just lost 250 of his prisoners, and most of whom had taken care of many duties. He now had to replace them. For a start, Hans needed a tailor, shoemaker, seamstress, gardeners, guards, and leather-makers. Hans asked those who had these talents to step forward out of line. A number of prisoners stepped forward. Hans dismounted and walked with the horse speaking to the prisoners and telling them to stand on the side. He then assigned Captain Helmholtz to take charge of them and to assign them their duties. All remaining prisoners were to report back to their processing instructor for further orders. Captain Hilda and Captain Wilhelm were to finish the process. Before Hans dismissed the prisoners, Hans went over the procedures about roll call and meals, and warned of the consequences for those who try to escape. After that, he let them all leave. "I pray that God will be with them and also me," said Hans to himself. Hans stood there with Zurich watching as the prisoners disappeared into the distance.

MEETING 5:00 PM

Hans was in great despair and went back to his barracks. Sasha saw that Hans was in great distress, and yet he would not speak much about what had disturbed him so much. In her heart she knew it had to do with losing 250 more prisoners and not knowing where they went. Now, he had new prisoners to deal with and know that the prisoners who had been there longer would face removal next. Hans asked Sasha to make some sandwiches and drinks by 5:00 PM. Sasha agreed and started to work on the sandwiches for Hans. At 4:25 PM, Sasha arrived with the food. Hans thanked her sincerely for helping him. He knew that Sasha was part of the group to be dispatched next. Hans had a plan, but waited. By the time he received the food on the table and a bottle of sherry, the officers had already started to arrive. Because everyone had come there early, Hans had no qualms about starting early. No one knew what this meeting was about, but within five minutes they would get their first hint. Hans cleared his throat, opened his jacket, and poured himself a glass of sherry. "Gentlemen, I have somewhat bad news." The air became thick and heavy as Hans spoke. "I received word from the underground in Berlin that the British and Russians are planning to move inward to Germany within weeks. German officials have said that they expect disaster to hit Germany, and they expect us to be well prepared. If we need equipment, we must put in our request very soon. So I ask everyone here to take inventory and let me know A.S.A.P. with requests." Everyone was looking as though they were distressed and worried. Hans said, "I feel that if we proceed to ask for weapons, we will then be safe," Hans said. Hans also told them that during these days the camp would have drills with the alarms going off so that everyone would be prepared to fight. Hans also told Otto to muster the men and drill them in marching with their gear on every day, no matter what the weather might be. Hans promised his officers that he would be keeping them posted on all incoming messages about this possible attack on Kassel. "We must be prepared or die," Hans told them. He then brought food to their attention. Some ate and some left. Everyone was stunned, and shocked. They knew the destiny of Germany even though the Fuhrer promised that they were going to win this war. Yet Hans thought that finally the dictatorship of Germany would end. He knew that there would be memories of this war, and most of them would be nightmares. "The ghosts of this war will haunt each one of us until we die," Hans sad to himself. "I know my heart hates the Nazis who led Germany to war, and all of the good men will suffer the consequences. We will be hated and disliked by many and will carry on to future generations. God help us," Hans prayed silently.

TEARS UNITED

Hans went into his barracks to have a short rest and dinner. He knew that Sasha was always on time for dinner. Tonight was the night that harmony would be found and their hearts would be healed. Sasha was holding back her tears as they piled up in her heart. She would remember every detail of this war, every friend, relative and prisoner dying. Sasha knew about death, not personally, but at a distance. She felt that through this war her only relief was meeting Hans. Just to think how she met Hans and how her heart danced the day she met him in the Ghetto! How young, innocent and how handsome. She believed that she fell in love with him that day when his blue eyes met hers. At that time she wasn't sure it was love but she had felt a special tingling in her heart, a tingling that no one could ever understand, except her. Her life had found hope, and she knew that God would not let her down. It was her faith. Hans sat on the porch after a cool shower and dinner. His uniform and boots were extremely hot, especially when the temperature reached near 100 degrees. His eyes looked into the future and he kept them focused staring in the air. Hans remembered when he was a little boy and his parents would tell him to believe in what is right and to do good for others. His parents also said that God would bless him if he does follow what he is told. Hans remembered. Only his beliefs and faith could keep him this far. His eyes saw the horror, the murders, the anger, and hate. Yet his eyes have seen hope through faith in God. His eyes filled with tears. He knew that he was alone to find out the truth. He felt distorted over the departure of his prisoners because he did not know where they went, nor did he know the new ones who came. He did not know whether the prisoners just transferred would be killed or sent somewhere to die. Hans pleaded with his thoughts, yet he still remembered his silent prayer that God will forgive him. God had responded to him that all of his sins were forgiven, When he thought this, he had to wipe his eyes frequently. Hans still had some time left at the camp. He prayed for the safety of his friends and Sasha. He thought that God had heard. Sasha came outside and saw Hans with tears still in his eyes, and he had fear and love over his face. She knew that Hans had been speaking to God. When Hans asked Sasha to forgive him, she was puzzled why he would say such a thing. Yet she comforted him with the thought that he was forgiven. As she told him that she forgave him, she felt tears sting her eyes. Hans could not neglect these tears and saw that she was so deeply hurt. He drew her to him and held her close to his heart. There both of them cried and felt all of their tears pour out. They both stood there for at least five minutes before they wiped their eyes. They felt that God had comforted their doubts. Their tears were united as one. Both of them knew that God did not look at their appearances but their hearts. They did the same to each other, and for this reason, their tears united together. The pain and hurt and great bouts of joy had united their tears.

PRISONERS

My name is Rachel and I am a prisoner at this camp. I am 24 years old, and I lost my family in this war. It was not through this camp but in the Ghetto. Two German soldiers attacked and shot my parents because they did not move fast enough. I could not bear the pain of remembering that painful day. I couldn't say or do anything because the soldiers would have shot me. Before my parents died, they looked at me and told me to keep quiet. Sometimes I wish I hadn't. My life now is so empty, and I am a prisoner here without anyone. I came here praying I would be released and I have not seen much abuse, but prisoners are beaten. The head commander never beats us. I see him always on his horse. Sometimes he nods to us, sometimes he smiles. I also wear the star around my arm so everyone knows what I am. I am a German-Jew and I am not sure how to take that. I am quite shy about what I am because I lost a lot of my German friends, who were told not to talk to me anymore. I now pray for death and maybe it will find me soon.

PRISONER 2

I am Mark, captured by the German army who killed my entire family due to resistance. I am only 18, and I never knew how lonely life could become until this war. I was near death after I was hit by a German soldier. I had a headache for so long. When the soldier hit me, a girl named Lena, who is also eighteen, helped me up. I was grateful to meet her, and we both helped one another. My suitcase had all of my parent's pictures; but when I arrived here, I was ordered to surrender everything. My memories are there where I will always remember my family. I am not happy about this prison life. I sit in these hot clothes, plastered with a yellow star on my arm. My shoes hurt, and I am laboring very hard. I eat very little although the soup is much better than it's been. Sometimes we have fresh baked bread, and that makes me happy. I know that food is limited since the first bombing on us and that the water is scarce. I heard that the chief officer, Commander Hans, will be going to get more food. I must wait.

VISITATION

Today Hans wanted to go around the camp and speak with all of his guards. They were his army, his protectors; and he needed the list immediately to order weapons. He rode his horse around the entire camp, speaking in German and his broken English. Most of the prisoners spoke German; and to those who didn't, he spoke his broken English. The soldiers had gathered at the main gate and there he rode over to speak to them. The two soldiers guarding the gate clicked their boots as soon as they saw Hans and properly acknowledged who Hans was. Hans saluted and asked them their names. The one soldier said that his name was Gunther and that he was from Hamburg. The other soldier was Franz from Munich. Hans told them he appreciated their good work, and they were very polite to him. From their speech, he knew they were from the youth school. "Respect yourself, friends and your fellow soldiers, especially to the officers," they had learned. Hans knew all about that. He said, "Carry on," and went to his next post to inspect. Hans rode around the camp picking up the papers from the officers for the weapons that he needed to order. When he rode around the camp everyone knew who he was from his beautiful white horse with brown spots. Hans dressed in his black uniform with his medals on his chest, in a crisp white shirt, and in boots that shined. He wore his hat that dipped below his forehead and his sunglasses. He always rode with his rifle next to him just in case something happens or he was attacked. Everyone knew Hans. When he rode around the camp, the prisoners were deeply happy and relieved. They knew that the officers would stop hitting them when Hans rode by. It was a relief. Hans had never struck anyone, nor would he ever do so without sufficient cause. He wanted to visit the workers and soldiers in the field house where they did the tailoring. Hans alighted from Zurich and tied him to the pole. He opened the door. Work came to a halt from everyone, who stood at attention. Hans nodded, and they continued with their work. Hans spoke to the soldier guarding the prisoners and asked how everything was. The soldier responded with a nod, signifying that everything was under control. Hans moved on to the tailors and watched them clean the uniforms. The prisoners were stunned because Hans watched them but never touched them with a whip or anything else. Hans didn't have to treat them badly, because they were doing their work perfectly. Hans walked to the door. "Good job," he said and walked out to Zurich. As he was untying his horse, he noticed a woman at block six leaning over with a broom. For some reason, he thought that he had seen this woman somewhere and knew her. He walked with his horse towards her. When she saw Hans approaching her, she quietly stood up. There she was looking at Hans for the first time since he was around seventeen. He looked at her and asked her name. She wiped the sweat from her face and wanted to make an impression, but not enough to make it obvious to Hans. She told Hans that her name was Elda Fritz-Berger. "I knew you in Cologne from years ago." Hans exclaimed. She agreed without any hesitation. "Yes," she said, "you're Hans. I am so happy to see you again." Elda was so happy to see Hans again. She was a full blooded German, so why was she here? She didn't agree with the Nazis and this was her punishment. Hans took his hat off and hung his head over his chest so that his hair fell down into his face. His hair, like Elda was soaked with sweat. He pushed his hair back with his hand and was looking at his friend. Elda had known Hans for years. Never had there been anything bad about him. She had always thought that Hans was a handsome blond boy, quiet and always to himself. She was wondering whether he was still the same. Certainly he was still handsome: that is what she knew. Hans looked at her and asked her, "What can I do for you?" He didn't expect to see someone he knew as a young boy in this camp. Thoughts rolled around in his mind, and his only hope was Sasha. She could help him. He said goodbye to Elda and told her he would take care of her. She looked at him with peaceful eyes and told Hans, "I trust you." He mounted his horse and rode again over to his officers to ask for the list. They all gave them a list of weapons needed. He took the list and went back to his office.

They needed "Granatwerfer36," "7.62cm Pak36," "Panzerschreck, 8cm" "Granatwerfer34," and plenty of "STG44." Hans's next job was to call headquarters to order the weapons. He needed plenty of them.

ADVICE

Hans had finished with everything and the next day he will be calling headquarters to order more weapons for his camp. Now he had something more important to do: thinking about how is he to help Elda. When he came home, he took his horse into the back and tied him in the shade until nightfall. Sasha always gave Zurich oats and water before bedtime. Sasha greeted Hans at the door. She always knew when he was coming in; maybe it was his loud boots hitting the floor. Fritz, on the other hand, would click his boots when an officer approached the barracks, so she knew also when someone was coming. This time it was Hans. As he came in, he threw his hat on the table and fell into his chair. He then took off his jacket and hot boots and just sat there in another world. He had a hard day. It was hot outside again, and he was thinking harder than usual. The fans were running, and he felt the coolness hitting his face. He opened his shirt to feel the coolness even more. He enjoyed it. Sasha, on the other hand, had to wear her prison outfit with her gold star on her chest. Hans hated it. But Hans always allowed Sasha to work around the house without any shoes on her feet. Sasha had dinner cooking, and she always made extra food for Fritz or anyone else who might turn up. As Hans sat on the chair, a knock came at the door. It was Peter. Hans was happy to see him. In fact, Hans needed to see him sooner or later. They had a lot of talking to catch up on. Sasha asked Peter whether he would like to stay for dinner. Hans explained to Peter about his childhood friend who happened to have come to this camp. She had been in the camp for weeks. He even explained to Peter that Elda was a pure German, who had disagreed with political issues.

Peter suggested releasing her quietly and taking her somewhere safe. Hans then thought of his father's house. Hans looked at Peter and thanked him for such a wonderful suggestion. He was starting to feel better already. As Hans sat there he was rubbed his forehead from a headache that had come up with from the heat and the excitement knowing his friend was in the camp. As he was rubbing his head, Peter suggested that releasing Elda had to be done at night. "Weekends we do have off, and most officers go home for the weekend," he reminded Hans. Sasha suggested that Peter should take Elda out of the camp at night; it would be the best way. Everyone agreed. She also suggested that it should be done when Goetz and the other officers are away for the weekend. Again, everyone agreed. Hans felt much better about this issue. All he needed now was to figure out when. Sasha suggested when she leaves at night, that Hans should tell the guards at the gate about her leaving with Peter. Hans should also tell them that when Goetz is away, Peter could see Elda to safety immediately. They all knew that is task would not be so easy. They hoped and prayed for guidance.

FAVOR

Finally, Friday morning had come. Again, the day was hot and sticky. At last, Hans had some time off. He put on a sleeveless shirt and his dark trousers, pushed his hair back, and splashed his French cologne onto his face. He didn't have to wear his uniform today; but of course, if there were an emergency in the camp; he would be there to help. The weather was definitely too hot for anyone, and he felt bad that he had to let the prisoners work so hard. He had to make sure they had sufficient water to drink today. Hans went over to his office for a while and called headquarters about the weapons he needed. He asked to speak to someone in the weapons unit and identified himself as the Commander of Camp Kassel. When he said that he would like to order weapons for an emergency, he was transferred immediately. He spoke to Captain Alehaus directly and told him who he was and that he needed to order weapons. Hans also told him that he needed them immediately for possible attack. Captain Alehaus asked what weapons he needed. Hans gave him the list and told him he needed the following: "Granatwerfer36," "6-7.62 cm Pak36," "15-Panzerschreck," "4-8cm Granatwerfer34," "50-STG44." He needed them delivered to the camp A.S.A.P. Because of the recent attack by the Allies, he could not risk another attack without being prepared. Captain Alehaus told Hans that he would have his men gather these weapons and have them delivered by Wednesday. Hans thanked him and hung up the phone. He had one mission finished. Now he had to work on Elda's release papers so Peter could carry them with him. Hans worked for an hour and then put the papers into his drawer. Being released would make Elda feel good, Hans also. Looking over the roster, he saw that Goetz had requested off on the next weekend because of a birthday at home. Hans quickly approved the request and planned on letting Elda leave that weekend with Peter. "Perfect," he said, feeling quite pleased in how this plan was turning out. "It couldn't be better," Hans thought. Now finished in his office, Hans took the request form for Goetz and mounted Zurich to find him. As he was riding, he noticed Elda again working in the hot fields and stopped at her workstation. He stood tall on his horse and looked at her, motioning for her to come over to him. He treated her just like anyone else so there would be no questions asked. She came over to Hans trying to catch her breath. He was looking at her with great hope. He told her to report to his office at 12:00 PM and not to be late. She shook her head "yes" and left. Hans proceeded to the guard and while he came to attention Hans was already speaking to him. "What is your name?" His replied, "Sigmoid Freitenhaus."

"Make sure they have plenty of water today." Hans repeated it twice so that Sigmoid would know what he had to do. He then saluted Hans and went back to guarding the prisoners while they worked hard. Hans rode over to Goetz, who stood there with his whip, watching and waiting. Goetz looked at Hans, saluted him, and asked what he needed. Goetz was always critical to anyone and Hans was not his victim. Therefore, Hans wanted to get Goetz out of the camp next weekend. That was his plan. Hans handed Goetz his request form with his approval and told Goetz that he had next weekend off. Hans had finished this part of the plan, and he needed only to wait now. Hans then rode around the camp before going back to his office. He observed what was being done and what was not. He stood out because he did not have his uniform on, yet he still accomplished his work of today. Hans then rode back to his office and called for Peter. He needed Peter present when Elda came at 12:00 PM. Peter was there when Elda arrived at 12:00pm, they needed to go over their plans. Hans offered everyone a cup of tea. Elda was thrilled to have a cup, she had forgotten about tea weeks ago. Hans, on the other hand, was stirring his tea and was staring into the cup.

For a minute, he closed his eyes, traveling back in time to his boyhood. Peaceful as he was, Hans remained that way for some time. He had to waken himself from the past and take care of the business now at hand.

ARRANGEMENTS

Peter and Elda sat down with their tea as Hans explained his plan. He knew he had to do move quickly before Goetz would returned to the camp on the Sunday. He explained to Peter that on the following Friday he was to take Elda to his Father's house where she would be safe until the war was over. Hans told Peter that he would give Peter travel expenses and food. Hans also said he would notify the guards about letting Peter and Elda leave the camp. This challenge would increase our faith in God, knowing that it would work out for all of us. Hans believed that this mountain would be moved. Elda, on the other hand, was happy to hear all of her planned release, and she stood there crying. She knew she could never repay Hans for this favor, never. Deep in her heart she had always loved Hans but he never knew about her feelings. They were young together and being in the same school meant that she saw him every day. She was flabbergasted at this turn of fortune. Hans saw that Elda was tired and asked her whether she had eaten anything. She said, "Only a piece of bread and some water." Hans told Elda to come to his quarters after this meeting to get something to eat and to clean up. Quickly, he had to get back to his plans, and at 7:00 PM Friday, Peter would be leaving for Cologne and arriving at 11:00 PM. He told Peter to stay at his Father's house and rest until the following day. It would be better this way because of the fighting in town and the weapons could be a danger for him. Peter agreed. Hans took Elda to Sasha to help her get cleaned up and to relax for a while. Hans stood there looking at Elda and knew in my heart that she would be fine. Hans left Elda with Sasha to take care of her and he rode over to the gate. It was still hot outside while Hans rode Zurich over to the main gate, and the horse's steps marched to the beat of Hans's heart. He hurried along to the main gate where he met Gunther and Franz and spoke to them about Friday night. Hans told them that his officer would be taking a prisoner out of the camp with signed papers and that they both had his permission to leave. They assured Hans that they would keep this departure in their memory and they would take care of it for him. Hans thanked both of them and invited them to come over to his quarters anytime for food and drink. Now that Hans's plans were finally unfolding, he would be most relieved when it is all over. Hans went back to his quarters and gave Zurich a cool drink from there, Hans stood with his binoculars, looking at the camp from a distance.

10:00 AM

Hans had just finished observing the camp when he heard a whistle blowing and signaling the gathering of his men. Hans had almost forgotten that the noise he was hearing was that of the soldiers drilling and marching. Hans went over to where Otto was drilling and marching with the men and told Otto to make sure that they were prepared. Hans wanted them to be prepared for another surprise attack and told Otto that he must go over the weapons and their positions. He knew his position as 2nd Commander of this camp, meaning that he had to follow Hans's orders. Otto agreed and continued to march with the soldiers to the outer banks of the camp. Hans walked back to his quarters to see Elda again and to relieve himself from the miserable heat. Hans made sure Zurich was tied to the post in the shade and then went inside to take off his jacket. It was much too hot for anything but not hot enough to tell Elda that she would be leaving on Friday as a free woman. Hans told her that he had confirmed everything with his guards and that they would be letting both her and Peter out of the camp. We sat there listening as the soldiers beat their boots to the ground and heard Otto shouting to them as they marched. Hans was well pleased and knew that all of his plans were unfolding before his eyes. Hans felt now that God was on his side and that although more challenges lay ahead of him, he knew he would get through all of these trials with the help of God.

DISCHARGED

Hans hosed down Zurich, took off his saddle and put his rifle into his quarters where he washed the horse down with mild soap. Hans knew that the temperature was over 100 degrees, so he took the hose and let the water cascade over his head. At last, Hans felt cool. Both he and Zurich were wet, and Hans did not care who saw him. He remembered when he was young and his Father would hose down their pigs; and when Hans was helping, his Father would spray him down with the water. Anyway, Hans didn't have his uniform on, just a tee-shirt and shorts: no shoes because his feet were burning. Hans pushed back his hair, found a towel, and dried Zurich off then himself. Hans put some horse cream on Zurich's hair and then brushed him until he shine like Hans's boots. Hans gave Zurich a carrot and a hug and went inside. Because he was pretty wet, Hans changed his clothes and got a cold drink. There he saw Sasha and Elda sitting at the table talking. Hans overheard Sasha telling Elda that Hans had saved her from death and how they fell in love. She also said something about seeing him in the Ghetto, but Hans wasn't sure what else Sasha had said. He heard Elda saying something about the fact that she was happy for Sasha and that they both had a lot for which to be thankful from God and Hans. Hans then came in without letting them know that he had heard their conversation. He told Elda that he was going over to his office to get the discharged papers. She looked at Hans and said that he was so sweet. She also said that he wasn't going to marry Sasha, she would marry him. Hans smiled and left, knowing that Elda appreciated what he had done for her as his friend. Hans looked over the papers before signing them. He mentioned that Elda had a pure German background and he could not understand why she had been brought to this camp, but that she would leave. After Hans had signed her papers, he called Peter to his office and told him about Elda's discharge papers. Hans gave Peter the papers to take with him and asked him to come over to his quarters so that Elda could see the papers that Hans had signed. Hans and Peter went over to Hans's quarters, and there Hans showed Elda his signature which certified the fact that today she would be a free woman as of that day. Hans told Elda that she had been convicted for no reason and that he was releasing her from this misery that every prisoner faced in this camp. Hans told Elda he could occasionally release prisoners. This time Hans felt that this release was overdue.

WEAPONS DELIVERED

Hans had Otto come to his office and wait with him. The two men walked around the camp, as they waited. Hans let the main gate guards know that a delivery truck would be coming through and directed them to let the truck into the camp. Hans went over to the area where Goetz had charge of the work and found that the road was coming along fairly well. Hans stopped Goetz to tell him that the prisoners were doing a good job but that he needed it done faster. I told Goetz that he needed to speed up the process because the roads had to be finished before winter. He assured me that the work would be done much faster. Hans then walked over to the kitchen to inspect the food supply and also to see how the cooks were doing with the soup. Hans ran into Peter and asked him about the food supply as well as the process of the new soup recipe. He told me the supply was all right and assured Hans that the new soup would be finished today for lunch and dinner. Hans was well pleased about that news and told Peter that if and when the supply went down to let him know so that he could put in the order to headquarters. As soon as Hans walked out of the kitchen, he heard the truck coming past the gate into the camp with our weapon supplies. I walked up to two soldiers who were delivering the weapons. They saluted Hans and asked where he wanted them to be stored, so Hans directed them to the weapon shed. He asked Otto and a few guards to unload the weapons and put into the weapon shed. Hans looked at the paper and he noticed that headquarters had sent more weapons then Hans could handle but that he certainly could use. Hans signed the paper and went over the inventory to make sure that he had everything he had ordered. He found the following: "10-Granatwerfer36," "8-7.62cm Pak36," "15-Panzerschreck," "15-8cm Granatwerfer34," "20-STG44," and plenty of ammunition. The weapons went into the weapon shed, and I handed the paper back to the driver. After they left, Hans told Otto that he must train the men to use these weapons and to see how many already knew how to use them. Hans felt certain that the camp was ready for any attack since it was now well stocked with weapons. Hans felt good about this delivery and began to plan ahead again. Otto was in the weapon cage looking over the weapons when Hans told him that he must start training by Monday. He agreed and told Hans that he would even begin on Saturday. Pleased with Otto and his decision, Hans proceeded to his next job.

PREPARING

Goetz left camp with a few officers who also happened to request this particular weekend off. Hans was in charge for the weekend, and the entire camp was under my command. Hans held roll call with the rest of his remaining officers, letting them know what was ahead for all of them. Hans told them that because the weather was hot again, that he would make sure that everyone had plenty of drinking water. Hans assigned Captain Hohenstaufen over the job that Goetz usually handled. Hans also told Hohenstaufen that he wanted everything done according to his plans. Captain Hohenstaufen assured Hans that he would take care of the roads and the prisoners. Hans reminded him that there would be water available for the prisoners to drink. Hans was exploring the camp during the day and could hardly wait until it was dark so that Elda could leave with Peter. Hans had lunch with Peter that afternoon and reminded Peter to be at his quarters by 7:00 PM. Peter nodded and left for his remaining day's work. Hans went over to his office to do some paperwork, wanting to make sure that everything was in order for this weekend. Everything seemed right on target. Hans went back to his quarters to see Sasha and Elda. They were having lunch together. He went into the kitchen to get something to drink and then sat down on the balcony with his drink. He pulled a cigarette out of his pocket. Hans usually did not smoke, he found that the war helped one continue do this bad habit and others as well. Hans could see the prisoners working in the heat as the guards patrolled the grounds. Hans gave a quick smile to what he was seeing. When he had finished his last puff, he went inside to see the women. There he encountered Peter. Peter asked Hans about Elda's release papers. Hans told Peter that he had signed papers days ago; Peter was amazed at how fast Hans had worked.

FAREWELL, MY FRIEND

With only a few hours left, Hans rode down to roll call. He was exhausted from the day's stress and needed to get through this detail fast. Hans told Peter that he would meet him down by the kitchen to see how everything was going. Peter left, and Hans followed. Hans went into the back, got Zurich, and rode over to the center while the horn and whistle blew. Everyone ran back to the center, and the remaining officers followed. Guards that were in the towers had their STG44's pointed at the prisoners just in case they tried to escape. Hans called everyone to attention while he told everyone about the new soup and more bread. He saw some smiles on the prisoners and Hans knew eventually that they would all agree to this change. Hans told them that their meal was ready, and directed them to eat and shower and go to sleep early because he would be waking them early in the morning. Hans dismissed them, and they went over to the line to receive their food. Hans went back to my quarters and fell on the chair waiting for Peter to arrive. Elda was there with Sasha. She had some things packed. We waited and finally darkness was falling outside. Peter already had Hans's car parked outside ready to leave. At 6:54 PM, Elda was saying goodbye to Sasha, and both were crying. Elda came up to me and kissed me on my cheek and thanked me. "Until we see each other again, goodbye," she said. Elda hugged Hans and Sasha and they bid one another goodbye. Hans's eyes filled with tears because he made someone free and happy. Hans walked outside, closed the car door, and wished them a safe journey. Hans told Peter that he would be seeing him on Sunday. As Peter and Elda started to disappear in the distance, Elda lifted her hand

and blew Hans a soft kiss, just as she did when they were young. "Farewell, my friend," Elda said to herself. Hans, watching as they reached the gate. The gate came up, and the car disappeared into the warm night. "Goodbye my friend, goodbye. You are now safe and free," said Hans half aloud.

WEEKEND

On Saturday morning, at 8:30AM, July 16, 1944 rumors were already spreading through the camp that there would be a raid soon. Some even said that this camp would end in a few months and to expect the worst to hit it. Hans felt relief and knew that he would get through this war, even if Germany did not come out as a winner. Pro-Nazism was fully pledge by a lot of his officers and Hans had to watch what he said and did. Goetz, who is at him with the Nazis movement, would kill Hans if he had the chance. This is why Hans was cautious in what he said. In all honesty, Hans was quite pleased that Goetz had gone for this weekend because he wanted to attend a birthday at home. Now Hans could swing around this camp talking to the guards and anyone else he wished to speak with. He even felt like going into his small pool. Previously, Hans did not have any time to even go into the pool and he couldn't let Sasha go alone. Instead of sitting in this heat, he had found a way to cool off. Hans also thought of inviting Fritz and Otto over for dinner and having them also come to the pool for some fun. "We are having fun here because everything is not just work," said Hans. "If I had to work all of the time, I would be very frustrated with my position." He thought of all of the people who had become his good friends, and who had given him comfort when he needed it. Blessed he and his friends as life gives hardships. Hans's life seemed fine, except for being in this camp. Hans found himself receiving hundreds of prisoners. He worked them hard and those who survived the labor would be transferred perhaps to death camps. Hans never asked because he did not want to know. Hans could not kill anyone, yet he seemed to be remaining in this situation for a purpose. He asked himself: "Can anyone see that I am a person, though in the future I may be looked upon as a Nazi, a full blooded swine who enjoyed murdering?" But those who will survive this camp and including those whom he could set free could later tell his story to the world. Hans saddled his horse, Zurich, and rode around the entire camp. He had taken off his jacket and hat because of hot weather. He did his rounds, observing the guards, soldiers, officers and the prisoners. He rode slowly through the dirt and dust and then he started at the main gate again. Hans thanked Franz and Gunther for taking care of Peter and Elda. They were amazed, smile and went back to their smoking and chatting. Hans proceeded to the left wing of the camp where the guards of blocks 16-20 were and saw that the two towers had guards with their STG 44's pointing at the prisoners while they worked. Dogs were roaming with their masters, who took care of them, and he realized that no one had the chance to escape, no one. Hans had the electric fences tapped with barbed wire and electricity. If anyone had touched the fence they would be electrocuted instantly. Occasionally, Hans found someone who had deliberately gone up to the wire and touched it so he could die. Hans just moved on where he saw numerous of his guards smoking, chatting and watching. As Hans approached, they yelled out, "Attention!", and all came to a full halt to await his orders. Hans told them to proceed with what they were doing, and he continued his journey. Hans decided at this point to go into the men's block and visit some of the new prisoners whom he had not met. He opened the door, took Zurich by his reins, and walked into the block. As Hans approached, he recognized familiar sounds of pain. He witnessed the horrible sites he knew that he would see. At least twenty men were lying in their bunks almost half dead. This situation was never reported to Hans. The guards don't understand that Hans cannot afford to lose any more prisoners unless they die on their own, or the camp will not finish the roads. Hans determined a purpose and the officers would know about it eventually. Hans knew that sick people bring diseases, not only to other prisoners, but to the officers, and soldiers in the camp. Hans looked at these men; He just couldn't catch his breath in what he was looking at. The sight was horrifying and some of the men were standing up to me. Hans had to devise a solution to counter this problem and he had to do it with haste. Hans quickly told them to sit down and asked how long these two people had been sick. The prisoner looked at Hans with a remorse look, yet he answered me. "Sir, they have been sick at least two weeks." He said no more at that, and Hans stood perplexed, wondering why his officers had not reported this situation. The smell was making Hans sick: he had to get Zurich out and leave, but he still stood there holding onto his horse hoping that the animal could give him comfort. Hans worked to summon his courage to open the door. As he did, he held his breath and spoke fast as he told the guard happened in charge to clear out any dead bodies and to have some of the prisoners disinfect the area as soon as possible. The guard nodded, saluted Hans, and left. Hans did not quite finish his investigation because he was overwhelmed in what he saw and wondered whether he would see any more of this kind of scene. Hans rode over to the one supply room and just sat there for a while. He looked at the prisoners and saw so many with despair in their lives mixed with bitterness, hate, and pain. "They only know that I have tried to change some of the rules, and the majority I had to follow," said Hans to himself. He had witnessed first hand one person that created from the hate and anger in his heart and found many followers who had the same. Hitler used this hate to others creating millions of Hitlers. Hans asked God forgiveness for everyone and continued with his investigation. This time he tied Zurich to the pole and just went into any block not knowing what he would find. He thought a short visit with the women in Block 8 would help him. Hans opened the door and found some of the women in their bunks and the rest on the benches with their hands clenched together. He assumed that they were praying. Some of them were coughing: others were crying, and still others remained silent. Hans looked at everyone as though he knew them; his eyes saw young, old, and middle-aged. Some were walking, but some could not. Hans became aware of their eyes, their eyes frozen in pain. Hans couldn't believe how many were so young, around his own age, and they were beautiful. Some had blue eyes and brown eyes, and their hair was dark, light and medium. Most of them spoke German. Hans asked them whether they were all right with the food and drink. Some nodded; others didn't. Although many looked scared, yet some seemed eased by what Hans was saying. He told one woman to bring some fresh water for everyone. She and another prisoner went to fetch some water with their large jug. Hans then rode back to see Sasha and Fritz to release Fritz from his guard duty. Hans invited Fritz if he wished to take a swim in his pool. Fritz took the offer seriously, leaving immediately, for his swim. Hans had to sit down because he was horrified at what he just seen. No one could know how he felt. Hans had expected some horrifying sights but not so terrible as what he had experienced in this tour. I sometimes ask God how I am going to live with myself after this war. "Maybe Sasha would be able to remind Hans of his goodness that he has done leaving the wrong out," Hans said to himself. The weekend was just beginning, and already he had his share.

THE RETURN OF PETER

Hans woke up around 5:10 AM on Sunday and could not go to sleep again. He just wanted to get up and get that day over with. The thoughts of what he had seen the day before haunted his life and his dreams, and today he had to face it again. Hans realized that he had no pleasure in his life, and certainly not in being commander of a slave camp. This was no camp; it was the beginning leading to the end of life for those prisoners who lie sick. Hans hoped that the war was winding down. Being at this camp for so many years have taken a toll on everyone. Hans realized that he didn't need to kill anyone to feel what he felt. Just the sight of something had made his life change. Hans knew that soon-because this war was going nowhere-soon he would be receiving new orders once headquarters close this camp. My question is will they? "The hell with them I say," said Hans. "They took every ounce of blood out of me and theirs. We will see." Peter returned to the camp around 1:00PM on Sunday. It was another hot day but with less humidity, although Peter came to Hans's door, his face flush from the heat. Peter informed Hans that he had a very uncomfortable ride because of the heat. He said that Hans's father had made lunch for him and gave him some cool water to take on his journey back to the camp. Hans told Peter to sit down and asked Sasha to get him a cool drink. Sasha brought out a pitcher of lemonade with lots of ice and she poured two glasses of lemonade. "What a trip!" Peter said. Hans asked whether Elda and Hymen were all right. Peter's answer satisfied Hans. Hymen had been helping Hans's father with the farm, and now Elda could also help him. "If I have to send Sasha to my father that would be more help," thought Hans. Peter wanted to rest a little so Hans gave him that request immediately. Peter left for his quarters, his precious job finished. Now Peter could rest upon his pillow knowing they are safe; and so could Hans, who wished that he could free all of these prisoners. Then he really could rest.

INFORMATION

That Sunday night, Peter came to see Hans about information which Hans's father had directed Peter to deliver Hans. Peter sat down with Hans and he told him about the deportation of the Jews to the death camps. He also said that most of the camps were releasing prisoners to Auschwitz where they would be put to death soon after their arrival, meaning that Hans's prisoners probably went to Auschwitz to be put to death. This news made Hans feel even worse inside, so much as that he wanted to tear his uniform off and run. But that wasn't all; Peter said that new prisoners would arrive here at Kassel three times a week, meaning that more would be forced to leave. Hans's father told Peter to be very careful that no one else knew the news. "It is a secret to the outside world and only those who work within knows," Hans's father had said. These things made Hans even more determined to find a plan to free Sasha, Peter, Otto, and Fritz from this hell of Kassel Labor Camp. Hans had the information; he would wait and at the same time make his plans.

PLANS

Time seemed to be passing by much faster than Hans had expected. As Hans could understand from the underground, the British and Russians had began to attack Germany. He was happy to receive this news because headquarters never gave him news of this sort. He decided to make plans each day for the camp. He knew that the camp expected to receive more prisoners, and turn them out faster—and all because the German command knew that their time was coming down on them. Hans could feel it, too. By the end of the week, Hans vowed to have plans and blueprints for Sasha and the rest of us.

DEPORTATION

"Comrades of the SS: You know what the Fuhrer has ordered us to do. We haven't come here to treat these swine's insides like human beings. In our eyes, they are not like us. Any man who is in our ranks and can't stand the sight of blood doesn't belong here. He should get out. The more of these ba . . . . we shoot, the fewer we have to feed," so says Commander Theodore Eicke. The letter also directed the camp commanders to round up all children over the ages of 12-16 and deport them out of the camp as soon as possible. Headquarters wanted to have them exterminated right away, including babies to the age of 11 set for September 1,1944 at 7:00AM.

Hans looked at the letter and his heart ached. His hands shook, and his tongue froze with no words to say. He became a victim of his own shame, and he pleaded to God to show him mercy. Hans had been in charge for all these years as commander, now the time had come for bloodshed. Political prisoners, opponents of the regime of the Reich, Jews: they were all in the labor camps. Whoever Hitler hated he commanded to be killed. "If they only knew my thoughts; I would be killed on the spot with no questions asked," thought Hans. "I am convinced that if I am found out, I will be murdered by my own people or by Russians, or Americans or the British. Someone will surely get me." Hans called Peter, Otto, and the guards to inform them about this urgently message although he wanted to tear it up and throw it away. Hans couldn't, of course, because the soldiers would soon come on that train gathering whom they say they would take. So Hans had a meeting with Peter and Otto to make the announcement to gather all the camp's children by

5:00 AM the next morning. Peter and Otto said nothing, and Hans dismissed them immediately. Tonight after dinner Hans planned to have roll call and make this horrible announcement to everyone. There would be more hearts to break, more tears, and more deaths. Hans knew that the prisoners would blame him, but he would tell these prisoners that these orders came from headquarters, not from him. The hate of one person had spread like wildfire and had now poisoned too many men and women of Germany. Hans refused to allow himself to feel any of this hate for anyone. He offered a silent prayer that God would give him strength to act wisely in this next horror to come. He did. Hans took the letter from his office and went to his quarters. He walked so fast that he did not even remember seeing Fritz. When Hans saw Sasha, he broke down with tears and handed the letter to Sasha so she could read awful news and understand the misery that he was feeling. Sasha read the letter word by word; and as she did, she broke down in tears. Hans sat there so dismayed, feeling so worthless and unable to fight headquarters. Hans just knew this move was coming; now here it was. He made that horrible announcement after dinner. He sat on his horse Zurich with half of his uniform on, unable to look at the prisoners. Hans kept his sunglasses on so they wouldn't see a grown man crying as he told them the bad news for the next day. As he made the announcement, Hans saw that no one dared to show emotions or say anything. Goetz looked at them, too. So did Lt. Stein, but neither of them said anything to anyone. Hans continued to look at the prisoners with tears in his eyes telling them that the children from the ages of twelve to sixteen were to be ready for the train the next day by 7:00AM. Hans felt that these prisoners were either too scared to respond or that they were just tired. Perhaps even some were happy to face death. Hans then released them to return to their blocks. Hans just couldn't face them anymore. Then he rode Zurich slowly back to his quarters, and put his horse into the shed with his food and water. Hans went to his bunker and took a hot shower, ate a little, and sat in his chair. He could not speak to anyone nor could he do anything. He waited for an answer to this horror, an answer that was not human. Hans could not even speak to Sasha; he was so overwhelmed by this situation. He bowed his head and asked God again forgiveness.

MORNING RESENTMENT

Hans couldn't sleep again, he sat in his chair and found Sasha on the other chair sleeping. Hans knew that he couldn't save everyone, understood, but children? He had to think of a way to save them by morning: he had to. He got up, took a shower, and look positive. He even asked Sasha to be his medicine so that he could feel better. He put on his French cologne, his black uniform, his shiny boots, and ate breakfast. Hans also made some tea and had a slice of Sasha's sweet bread. Hans wakened Sasha up at 5:45AM. They looked at each other as though they were meeting in the Ghetto in Berlin. Hans gave her a soft kiss on her cheek and told her how special she was to him. She was surprised by Hans's actions but knew the reason behind them. Hans left and decided to leave the horse home. He walked around, again with his sunglasses on in order to cover up his tears. He did not want the prisoners to see that he had emotions. As Hans was walking, Peter was coming out of the officers' hall in which he had eaten an early breakfast. Hans asked him whether he was here to see the dysfunctional SS men coming off the trains. Peter smiled, knowing what Hans meant. Hans couldn't help feeling despair and so much hate in his heart, not for the Jews or any of the other prisoners, but for his own Germans who had become like vultures. Everyone waited outside. Everyone was so quiet that Hans could hear his heart beating. Everyone knew what was coming, every one in the camp. Hans let his mind wander to the future. As he did so, he heard the whistle blowing from the "death train." It came rushing in as though it was in a hurry to come in and leave. The officers from the train got off and came to me and said, "Hans, how are you doing, surviving this war and heat?" I replied, "Well." As Hans excused himself, the officers were gathering all the children as headquarters had ordered. They loaded the children, all 210 of them who left their families behind. Their families would never see them again. The SS soldiers locked the doors of the train that would take the children to the slaughter. "This was my own people who done this, who allowed others to influence them in a world of hate," Hans said to himself. Hans signed the papers, as soon as he had, the SS men re-boarded the train and left. Hans now realized that humans all have evil in them and that if we do not control that evil, it will overtake us. Those innocent children had done nothing wrong; and Hans knew the SS, the children would be dead by nightfall. As the train departed, Hans heard so many cries, screams, and sighs. He could do nothing but wipe his tears away from behind his sunglasses. Hans walked back to his quarters and sat there thinking again: "If I were found assisting the prisoners, my life would be over with, especially saving Jews and Germans." Yet Hans had to continue to save the prisoners and obeying some of the rules. "Knowledge is power," he said, "and that power I do have." He resolved to continue to save Sasha and others.

TELEGRAM

When Hans went over to his office at mid-day, he found a telegram waiting him. It had come from Colonel Helm telling him that another train would be arriving the next day to deport another 300 prisoners to another camp close by and that following their departure of the prisoners, Hans would receive more prisoners the following day. Hans was upset and feeling guilty. "I would be better off being shot," he said. But then if he were shot, then Sasha would be shot also. Saving her meant a lot and Hans knew that he must continue to save although this time he couldn't save anyone. Again, Hans had to have the prisoners ready to be transported by the train. Colonel Helm did say, "no camp is a holiday resort for anyone; it is a labor camp." He also said that after the war Hans's benefits would continue, and in fact increase more because he was a commander. Hans spit on the letter and threw it into the trash. "Swine," Hans called him, "fascist liar!" Hans had to see Peter and Otto so they could tell the others about what would happen the next day. To Hans, the letter had meant another shot, another lie, and another death.

DECEPTION, AGAIN

Hans rode to the officer's stations in the warm weather. He delivered this nasty message from Colonel Helm to every officer. Hans described the details of what was going to happen. Goetz was walking around. This time Hans caught him hitting everyone he could find. Hans glared at Goetz from his horse with hate in his eyes. As soon as Goetz saw Hans, he refused to take another strike upon the prisoner. He knew it was better for him not to take that whip out and strike anyone. He knew my punishment. Hans thought nothing at this time to take his "Walther P38" and shoot him and eliminate his hate. Hans prayed as he thought this about shooting Goetz. Hans rode to every corner of the camp to deliver the message to all. Hans saw Goetz as nasty as he was in his black uniform telling the prisoners to move the boulders on the road. Hans needed that road finished for his plans. Then he told the prisoners that tomorrow more of them were to be transported to a nicer camp. "Liar!" "Deceiver!" thought Hans to himself, hoping that none of them would believe his filthy lies. He rode Zurich across the bridge and sat there alone thinking and wondering what would happen next. These camps as crowded as they were would take days and days to exterminate. Hans had never witnessed any of these exterminations, nor did he want to. He just closed his eyes, then opened them to the blueness of the sky. He felt as though a hand had touched his head, and peace came over him. Hans just sat there on his horse and closed his eyes again, his hat off and his hair blowing down into his eyes. Hans remembered for a minute when he was young and his hair had always blown into his face. Mama would tell Father that he needed his haircut, and Father always say, "Hans is a boy let him alone." I felt peace but still a pain in my heart. Hans left his hat off and just rode with his hair in his eyes as he rode back to the camp. Hans went to his quarters looking like a mess with his hair and Sasha was preparing lunch for them. Hans told her that he wanted little to eat and food was really not on his mind. Sasha agreed with Hans and saw that his hair was a mess over his face. The funny thing was, she never asked Hans why?

SASHA'S IDEA

It was a very warm day, again. Hans came home, sat down, undid his hot jacket, and took off his boots. He was exhausted from the heat, and mostly from the telegram he had just received. He knew headquarters were hiding the truth that the war was ending sooner than we thought. The SS were asking all men and even women to fight for Germany because headquarters needed more people to fight for their country. Hitler was desperate to win and tried every corner to do just that. Hans was too tired because of the heat, the train, and now the telegram. He was exhausted from all the events and didn't know what to expect today or even tomorrow. He hoped that Otto, as his second commander had the men trained to use the weapons. Hans knew that he had to see Otto that day about these lessons with the weapons. Hans knew that the time had come to make a solid plan so that they can follow the escape when it hits this camp. Sasha came over with a drink for Hans and sat beside him. Sasha said that she was concerned, the only comfort for Hans was her. Sasha was right; Hans felt that he had to tell her about the telegram from Colonel Helm. I made it known to Sasha about the telegram, and exterminations. I also told Sasha that they needed 300 more prisoners from my camp the next day. Hans told her about his concerns for her safety. He suggested that she should go to his father's house for protection. She looked at me with those dark eyes framed by her dark hair and spoke to me in a soft tone. Her English, like Hans's English, was broken but understandable. "Hans, you must do what is safe for all of us. Let us look at everything first, then decide," she said. "I do suggest that I should be deported to your father's house where I will wait for your return. We can then be married and perhaps live our lives again. Hans promise me if I go, that I will be safe." Hans promised what she had asked for, no matter what. Now Hans had to come up with a day for her to leave. Sasha took his hand, kissed it, and told Hans that she could hardly wait to leave the camp and especially the clothes that she had to wear. Hans agreed. The next morning, Hans asked to see Peter for his assistance.

ANOTHER FAVOR

I spoke to Peter about the possibility of transporting Sasha to my father's house. They both felt that Sasha would be much safer away from this tension. Peter agreed because he knew that the tension was coming to an end soon. He felt the tension and the hate. He knew about the bloodshed cruelty and he didn't want Sasha to be exposed to this either. Peter agree that the time had come to set Sasha free. Peter was Hans's best friend, and Hans trusted Peter's opinion although he had also been in Hitler's Youth, and then in officer's school before coming with Hans. Hans had helped Peter to be removed from the harsh fighting that he had been sent to do. Peter was at this camp to help Hans. Hans knew that Peter would help him in return. Hans told Peter that he would give Peter a date and time for taking Sasha away from the camp. Hans knew that he would speak to Gunther and Franz for another favor in letting the car out. Going over the plans was necessary, for Hans saw how circumstances were changing drastically. Hans told Peter to join him at 6:00PM for dinner and a short meeting. Hans also intended to invite Otto and Fritz, who must be told that the plan had to go forward immediately.

TRAIN ARRIVAL

Sickness was in the air again. This time 300 of Hans's prisoners were to be deported to a nearby camp, as they say. Hans had heard that many prisoners were being or shot and beaten. He was so concerned that these 300 prisoners were to face such cruelty when they left his camp today. Hans had heard that over 500 prisoners had already been murdered and burned each day and sometimes the count went into the thousands. The details sickened Hans and sometimes they were too awful to believe. Yet they were true. Hans had a friend who was an officer in one of the other camps who told Hans that the process was making him so sick that he could not watch it anymore. He had witnessed so much death and so many murders that he had no desire to help Nazis anymore. Yet the Nazis kept the trains coming and anyone who was a Jew was murdered in cold blood. Anyone who resists politically or not was also murdered. That day the "death train" came again. Hans sometimes wished that he could do something, yet he knew that he was helpless. The world does not realize how we were bribed when we joined the party and told the opposite. They had to pledge themselves to Hitler and if they refused, death was immediately at their door. Fighting a war was one thing, but murdering and taking people against their will was uncalled for. With the arrival of the trains, death hung over all of the prisoners. They would all be gone by nightfall, just like the children. I gathered the prisoners again, and told them that headquarters had ordered this camp to release 300 more prisoners so that they could be transported to a nearby camp. Hans couldn't speak anymore. As he turned away he heard a yell, a yell that told everyone to salute him. Hans turned around and saw all of the men, and women, standing at attention in honor to him. Hans took a deep breath and raised his right hand to salute all of them in return. Hans then left in tears and waited for the train. The train came fast on this day. The guards packed the prisoners into the cars like cows, had me sign the papers again, and left in a hurry. The only words the guards said to Hans was that on the next day again, Hans would be receiving 400 more prisoners for hard labor. Hans held his breath and left for his quarters. He had 200 prisoners left today but the next day that number would grow to 600. Hans retired for the day and had Peter take charge if anything went wrong. Hans was happy about one thing: he was Commander and he could do almost anything he liked. Hans went inside and took a long shower, and lay on his my bed. He arose briefly to take his uniform off and put on a shirt and trousers. Mentally he was exhausted, although physically he felt all right. Hans fell asleep in mid-day but had nightmares about things to come. These nightmares all came from his day's work: trains, prisoners, paperwork, and calls had all become a nightmare. "May God have mercy on us all," Hans said half awake.

MORE LABORERS

Hans awoke, had something to eat, and he asked not to be disturbed by anyone. He fell asleep again and this time stayed asleep until the next morning. He awoke early because he had to wait for another train delivering 400 more prisoners. He now had to go through his same situation every day. Headquarters told me to get used to this action. Everyone of us are involved in this, his officers especially. They did the same thing each day, take the prisoners' belongings, giving them numbers and uniforms, cutting their hair, ushering them to the showers and then giving them a cheap meal. Because of this growth of people, Hans had to go over to the kitchen and ask them about supplies and whether they could make a better soup. Hans pretended that he ate the soup once in a while and told the cook that he needed to upgrade the recipe. Hans spoke to the cook in charge and asked about the soup. The cook said that he could put more vegetables in the soup and make it more tasty for Hans. Hans told him to put less salt in the soup to let him taste the soup before the cook hands it out to anyone. Supplies were fine; Peter was taking care of that detail for Hans. Little that cook knew that soup was not for Hans, but for the prisoners. "Fool!" Hans said to himself. The head cook also had plenty of wheat flour for making bread. Hans ordered him to get his stuff ready for a lot of bread each day. Hans told the cook that he had purchased huge amount of wheat flour, but nobody had been using it for baking. "It must be used," said Hans. He assigned four other soldiers to help in the kitchen each day, rolling out the dough and making over 50 loaves of bread every day. Hans told the head cook that if his orders are not obeyed, the cook will be put out with the prisoners to do some hard work. Hans was not fooling around anymore, not with the tense feeling that he had been having. "Obey me or pay the price," Hans said. The head cook never said a word except for promising that he would implement the command. At 2:30PM, Hans decided to call roll call so that he could meet the new prisoners. Once again, the weather was warm. Hans tried not to wear any of his hats because of the heat. He had his sunglasses on, and his hair was pushed back this time. Hans made himself known as Goetz gave him the number of prisoners. There were 555 prisoners, including children. Hans needed new laborers for tailoring uniforms and shoemakers to make shoes. Hans asked those who had experience in this kind of work, to please step forward. More than 25 prisoners stepped forward, and Hans chose whom he needed. Hans tried to use as many of those 25 because he could spare them. Hans told those 25 to stay, and released the rest back to their leaders. Hans gave them all the rules of the camp and warned them against trying to escape. Hans outlined the penalty. The prisoners seemed to understand. Hans had the remaining 25 prisoners before him and began to assign them their duties. Hans called Otto over and told him that he needed to assign these prisoners to the sheds and to put them to work immediately. Otto saluted Hans and left with these prisoners. The sun was beaming down its rays upon Hans, who was sweating profusely. He continued to push his hair back. He always kept it long on the sides, making it easier to slick it back. Hans took out his handkerchief and continued to wipe his face off while he decided to walk around. Hans followed Otto to the sheds so that he could make sure that the prisoners knew what to expect from him. Hans told Otto that the prisoners were to be doing tailoring, and making shoes and boots. Hans divided those prisoners into teams to have 14 tailors and 11 shoemakers. Their work would be divided into half a day in the sheds then the rest in the fields. "Keep me posted on how this works, Otto," Hans said. Otto smiled and began to do immediately what Hans had directed him to do. Hans left to return to his office.

FIXING THE DAMAGED BRIDGE

The bridge that connects to the main gate had been heavily damaged from past bombings. Although it was still usable, it needed extensive repairs. Hans told Goetz to deploy more men out there to fix the bridge without any hassle from him. Hans commanded, "Do it now or else!" Hans knew that these men already struggled over 15 hours a day at work by moving boulders and concrete. He even saw a lot of them dying from this work. For that reason, Hans told Goetz to make sure that the men ate and had plenty of water. Hans came very hard on Goetz knowing that if he did not, Goetz would just stand there whipping them making the work even slower. Hans told Goetz that he would not tolerate any maltreatment of the prisoners. He also told Goetz that if any prisoners died, they must be properly removed and buried. "If I find any bodies lying around," Hans told Goetz, "you will be burying them personally." Hans stayed there observing since this bridge was the biggest and important project, not just for Hans, but for all. The prisoners, however, had no idea the bridge's importance to the camp. Huge rocks needed to be moved, and sometimes it would take twenty men to push one of those huge boulders. The prisoners worked on this bridge as the heat pounded on their bodies. At least 200 men working, and Hans realized that sometimes 50 of them might die from the heat. Hans left the bridge site. He planned on having that bridge finished by next week. Pleased with the progress so far, Hans returned to his office to attend to the papers on his desk: some requiring signatures, some memos to answer and mostly papers to read on the prisoners. Hans looked through the papers of his prisoners and saw their ages and where they were from. So many of the prisoners were young and a lot were older. Hans looked through what he could tidied up his desk and left for the day.

DINNER PARTY

Sasha and Hans had decided to have a dinner party that night and to go over their plans for the future days. They planned a menu of roasted chicken with mashed potatoes, string beans with plenty of Sasha's sweet bread, lemonade and plenty of brandy. Hans told everyone to come hungry because they would have plenty to eat. The weekend arrived, and it came Hans's turn to be on duty along with Otto and Peter. All the others, including Goetz, went home for the weekend. So Sasha and Hans had some time to discuss their plans. Once everyone had arrived, we sat down for dinner as Sasha served us the roasted chicken and mashed potatoes. In our grace, they asked for God's blessing and to keep them safe, also the prisoners. Everyone ate and ate until no one could eat anymore. Sasha always cooked well and told us that she used her mother's recipes. At the end of dinner, Sasha collected the plates, the men went and to the den to discuss their plans. Sasha came in briefly to announce that she would serve cake and tea. Like Hans, the officers felt that soon this war would be over and they discussed that theory. They also agreed that the reason that the camp was taking prisoners was facilitate the murder as many as possible. Time was growing short. Hans also had to figure out the time we to get Sasha out of the camp to take her to his father's house. Hans wished that he could have saved Sasha's parents and brother. "If only I had been there at the time, I would have found a way to free them," Hans told himself. Hans felt that they were watching from heaven and smiling that their daughter has been saved by God and him. As Sasha was washing the dishes, the men went into the living room to discuss future plans. Sasha announced that the cake and tea was ready and the cake that she made. It was absolutely delicious. Actually all of the officers had a second piece, making Sasha happy because she did not need to save any cake. As we were going over our plans, we all felt that the war would end very soon. We concluded that the killing that has been going on, was part of the Nazis plan to get rid of as many prisoners as possible before the war ends.

Time was growing short for these murderers. Hans also had to figure out exactly when to send Sasha to his father's house. Everyone suggested, including Sasha, that it had to be by the end of this month before winter could set in. Again, we agreed on something. When the war would end, Hans and Sasha would stay at Hans's father's house until things settled down. Hans knew that life would not be the same for anyone. Hans was relieved that his father's house was in good shape and had not been damaged by any bombings. The farm was still intact, and the house had plenty of room for everyone to live temporarily. Once the officers had left, Sasha and Hans continued talking about their plans. Sasha always suggested that they we could go to America to stay with her aunt and uncle if they wished. Her relatives live in New York, and they owned a huge house that was connected to another house. Sasha would explain to her aunt that she and Hans would be coming there because of the war, but she would not say anything about Hans's position. Although if she had to, she would tell them that Hans had saved her from death and not be ashamed at how he did it. Sasha even had Hans's portrait put away in the den so it wouldn't be destroyed. She adored that portrait of Hans when he was younger, but just as handsome as he was just then. The picture reminded Sasha of the day that she first met Hans in in Berlin. Hans told Sasha that eventually he wanted to destroy that picture because his uniform represented hate. Sasha said "No, it will remain with me, just as it is."

KIEV, A PRISONER

I am Kiev, and I am not a good writer. Excuse me, please. I can explain my purpose. I am a Polish Jew. My father was Jewish and my mother was Polish. I had four sisters and two brothers, all of them are dead. We were all in our apartment eating when someone knocked at our door. The Nazis came in and shot my parents, and threw us in a wagon. They brought us here and I believe there is no hope. I pray every day for help. Many here are sad and hungry. "Please help us God," I say. Today, I think it is September 8, 1944 in Kassel, Germany.

GORSHEV, PRISONER

I am a Gypsy, born in Hungary and deported here by the Nazi's. My family is dead, and I am the only one alive. I have no one but myself. The Nazis have persecuted because me because I am a gypsy. I have no political issues; I am not a Jew or anything else they may say I am. I cannot agree with them so I keep my mouth quiet. They still beat me, though, I do hard labor every day. My back hurts so much, my skin itches, and I am always hungry. I do not like the Nazis anywhere, not just here. They are so nasty looking, but I do feel that the officer in charged of the camp is different. I don't know why I say this. I do not see much of him, but I have heard others talking about him. They say that he helps others without the Nazis knowing. So many are nasty and heartless.

I must go now, or they will find me writing this on September 12, 1944, Kassel, Germany.

PRAYERS

Sasha prayed that night and cried through her entire praying. Her heart was very heavy, afraid of the future. She asked God for help, "Dear Lord, please help us and thank you for your help and all the blessings. Thank you for Hans and please keep him safe for me and everyone else here. Help us to get out of here soon. Please help all of us here; please give us a miracle." Her prayers were simple. As she prayed, memories of her parents and her brother Melvin flooded her mind. Sasha missed them so much. Sometimes she could not believe they were all dead. But she did know that in this moment, she was safe and out of danger.

Sasha ended her prayer, in an unusual way by saying it very compassionate, "Please Lord; bless all the officers. I pray for all of those men who do not believe in you, and those who do."

REBELLION

The prisoners were very restless. As Hans rode around the camp, he saw many who were yelling, and great hate in their eyes. Hans had not paid much attention to such things before he had warned the guards and officers that there might have trouble coming from the prisoners. Hans had received a notice recently that riots had broken out in a number of the labor camps in Germany. General Heisenberg told Hans that shooting the prisoners was the guards' best defense. His officers were now on high alert about possible rioting. Hans could not risk a riot, because his men and Sasha could be hurt. Hans had to protect his men and everyone else who would not be involved. Hans carried on inspecting his camp as usual, praying that nothing would come out of the prisoners' restlessness.

FREE TIME

Because Hans was so concerned that the war would end soon, he decided to give the prisoners some free time to do something other than lying in their bunks. Most of them were outside playing ball anyway, so he finalized the action. The men had found an old ball and a flat wooden stick and just played. Hans couldn't take this only joy from them. The prisoners who were too weak stayed in their beds, but many were still in good shape played happily. Hans had watched them play every day, sometimes hitting the ball across the camp. At one point, they almost hit one the guards standing in the tower. Hans laughed, for as long as the prisoners were playing on good terms, Hans had nothing to say. Hans went inside his quarters and changed my clothes because the weather was still very warm. He put on a short sleeved shirt and shorts. He had on his trademark sunglasses and enjoyed letting his hair blow in the cool breeze that blew occasionally. Hans had his free time, and he had decided to go over to the prisoners and hit at least one of the balls. He held his hands signaling to a prisoner to give him the bat. Around 25 men had been playing. Now they all had their eyes on Hans. Some looked afraid of Hans while others were cheering him on. As soon as Hans picked up that wooden bat, they were amazed. The older man who was pitching to me didn't know what to do when he saw me at the base. I told the prisoner, "I do like to still have fun, so pitch the ball." When he threw it, Hans hit a home run across the camp. They were amazed; and so was Hans. Hans thanked them, noticing that the prisoners all smiled at him. Then they continued with their game. Goetz and some of the officers told Hans that he gave the prisoners too much freedom in which Hans disagreed. Hans told them bluntly that even though they are having a good time, still someday soon they would be walking to their death. Goetz and his colleagues said nothing. Hans thought that the situation was fine. “If I am caught, then I will worry about what will happen to me,” he told himself. “For now, I am contented and so are the prisoners.”

THOUGHTS

The week went by fast, and Friday had come once again. Hans remembered looking forward to Friday when he was a teen. Elda, Peter and I and a few others would go down to the candy shop every Friday to have milkshakes and pastries. They had loved the fun. They would laugh but never talk about anyone or thought that they were better than anyone. They certainly never thought of a war together. Hans had also looked to Sunday because his mother always baked fresh bread and pies on Sunday. He had loved these times as a boy.

Looking forward to Friday in this labor camp was something else because it really did not seem to matter anymore. If Hans had the weekend free, that was one thing. If he did not, he did little more than sit in the camp looking at misery. The officers who had every other weekend off, they could go home. Hans, however, usually stayed around. Sometimes he took a long ride on his horse but soon turned back, just in case anyone needed him. This particular weekend, Hans couldn't wait to sleep late, read, and take another ride on Zurich, perhaps to discover something new.

URGENCY

Hans received a disturbing memo from Karl Schoenberg, one of the commanders at headquarters in Berlin. It read: "Hans, we will be closing down in maybe three weeks, I am not sure. Burn all your files in the camp today, and I will be in touch with you soon. We are losing the war. Karl." Hans looked at the memo again and sat down quickly in great shock. He had to call everyone who worked in the office including all of his officers who had files. Hans read them the message and told them to burn all the files immediately for what reason he did not know. He assumed that the camp might be attacked again, soon. He made sure with Peter and Otto that all of the camp's new weapons were tested and ready to go. Hans told them to begin this job immediately. They both left; then Hans faced Goetz and the rest. Hans told them that Germany was losing the war. Rudely, Goetz stood up and excused himself, saying "Last time I checked, we were winning the war." Hans looked at him and told him the truth: "Not this time." Goetz sat down quickly and quietly. Hans released the officers to burn the files so that he could begin to burn his files also. Hans assigned a few extra guards to help the officers with this big task. They were to burn memos, files, and messages and to empty all of their drawers. "Leave nothing behind," Hans commanded. "Burn everything in the middle of the camp and put them ablaze. From the names of the commanders to the guards and staff, everything must burn. No evidence of this camp must be saved. Nothing." The prisoners had papers, which had to be burned also. All evidence beyond the office was also burned. Pictures were burned; nothing was to be left. After making a huge pile, the guards threw gasoline all over it. After they torched the files, everything was gone. Everything was finished. Hans felt at ease but concerned because he knew nothing about why headquarters had issued this order. He had his suspicions. Hans called headquarters but was told that they were closing down for a while. All of the top officials had their offices there. For this reason, everything was destroyed and moved. Hans's camp was left to him now; everything was all in his hands: his decisions, his commanding, and finally, his peace.

THE BIG DECISION

Hans was in his office at 12:30 when his phone rang. He picked it up and heard the voice of Colonel Ludwig Heisenberg. "Hans, good day. I want you to destroy any papers, any evidence of the camp, today," he said. Hans excused himself and told him that he had received a call from Karl, who had already asked whether Hans had done that job already. Hans told him that the camp had carried out the burning and it was all finished. The Colonel congratulated Hans and told him that the command would reward him for his performance for which Hans had earned the highest medal. Heisenberg also told Hans that he would visit the Kassel Camp the next day. Hans invited Heisenberg for lunch. The Colonel accepted. Hans realized that he had two medals already and this would be his third. Hans did not know what to do next. In his excitement, he even thought of creating the next riot and releasing the prisoners. Then he thought again, "Maybe I should let God handle it for me. He knows best," Hans reminded himself.

ANNOUNCEMENT

Hans announced at the evening roll call that Colonel Heisenberg would visit the camp the next day 9:00AM. He told everyone to make sure that they had all papers burned and if they found any left, to torch them that evening. Hans asked Sasha to do all of the food planning for him. She said that sweet bread was at her top list and suggested making red cabbage, brats, green beans, and fresh baked apple pie for the Colonel's lunch. Hans told her that he could not ask for more.

"COLONEL HEISENBERG"

The morning came quickly, and Hans was fully dressed in his uniform, hat and all. I even had my "Walther pistol" strapped to my hips and my medals shined. Elegant as Hans looked, he also put grease into his hair, because he still had his Hitler youth haircut, and combed it back. Hans was all ready for the Colonel. He put everyone on alert about Colonel Heisenberg visit, even though he had said he was just coming to see Hans. "I know how he works; he says he is just seeing me," Hans reminded himself, "but at the same time, he observes everything around him."

It was 7:05AM. Hans had a short breakfast so that Sasha could finish preparing lunch. By 11:00, Sasha would have everything prepared and ready to eat. She laid out sweet bread, plenty of meat, fresh lettuce and tomatoes, potatoes, homemade pickles, and strudel with cream topping. It was 9:00AM, the car arrived with Colonel Heisenberg and a few of his top officials. Hans had his guards and Peter meet him as he got out of his car. Hans greeted Colonel Heisenberg and escorted him over to his quarters. As they passed Fritz, his boots clicked so loudly that the Colonel jumped. Hans took the Colonel inside to the den, and there they talked and had their lunch for hours. The Colonel informed Hans that headquarters had moved for security reasons and assured Hans that they would be in touch with him. "The Allies are starting to destroy Germany and that we have to be on high alert.," said the Colonel. The Colonel said that he could not guarantee Hans security or safety. "Because all of your records and papers have been destroyed, plan on being out of this camp by December 16th," said

Colonel Van Hoyden. "We will be closing this camp permanently and removing all prisoners to a nearby camp. All of your staff will be released and taken to Berlin. There the 268th Headquarters will be meeting them and taking them to an area where they will be needed and safe." As for you Hans, he said, your job here would be finished, and you will be released from your post. I will keep you in touch about your next commanding position; but for now, I am giving you a check that is worth 50,000 marks, which will be your pay for the next two years. After that, you will be paid every month and it is because of your high commanding position. Hans then asked the Colonel what would happen to his pay if he left Germany for a while. The Colonel assured Hans that nothing would happen. Hans had only to supply a change of address. Because the Colonel knew Hans's father, he would have the checks sent to his address. Colonel Heisenberg asked Hans to send his regard to his father and tell him that he hopes to see him again, soon. "The best to you, Lt. Colonel Commander Hans Schweitzer. Good Lunch!" the Colonel said. He also thanked Sasha. Hans walked Colonel Heisenberg to his car. Before the car pulled away the Colonel looked out of his window and said, "Wait for my instructions and the best to you Commander; may God be with you." The car pulled away, leaving a pile of dust behind. For some reason Hans felt as though he was in a dream; but yet he felt that he was waking up from it, finally.

PREPARATION

Time seemed to accelerate very fast. Getting out of the camp had seemed beyond his dreams because Hans had so much on his mind: Sasha, the prisoners, what to do after this duty of commander, and so much more. Hans sat in his office for hours alone except for four interruptions, two phone calls, three bathroom excuses, four cups of tea, and two short meetings. The phone call Hans received came from the Colonel telling him about the possible extermination of all his prisoners within a few weeks. Hans held his breath while the Colonel explained to him all of the details of this process. Hans choked on his words, and so did Colonel Heisenberg. Hans had prepared his staff, Sasha, his friends and over 450 prisoners telling them what was coming. Hans already had all the paperwork destroyed and now what to do after this event. Hans now wondered whether he could save all of these prisoners or not. He planned to ask Sasha for her advice and his staff tonight.

PLANS AND A TOAST

Hans called Otto, Peter, and Fritz and, of course, Sasha to the meeting. He had her prepare a light dinner and brandy to drink. The plans finally were coming to a head and ready for discussion with his two top officers, Peter and Otto. Everyone arrived at 7:00PM. Hans had just taken a shower and made himself comfortable, ready to make that speech. Everyone gathered at the table eating and drinking and there made history. Hans told everyone by December 16 Camp Kassel would close for good. The prisoners would be going to nearby camps and exterminated. Hans also told his officers that by the month of January, they could be released from their duties. Where we will be going, I did not know. Peter suggested everyone could go to the house of Hans's father's and wait. Otto suggested that they should all leave Germany and find a new life. My faithful guard, Fritz, said that we should release everyone. Sasha said, "My beloved Hans, let us get married." Hans complimented everyone on the wonderful ideas, but they needed to have the main event happen first. Hans asked Sasha to get some glasses and the brandy. Peter looked at Hans with a gleam in his eyes as though he was waiting for the final approach, the final curtain put an end to these horrific years of anguish. Sasha gave everyone a glass of brandy. and Hans said, "Gentlemen and Sasha, let me make a toast to our final days at this camp: To us and to you my friends." They drank the brandy in one sip. "Hans, can you tell us the plans that we need to follow?" Otto asked. Hans answered, "I am going to set up our own riot where all of the prisoners will be rioting and rebelling. This chaos will lead them to being released from the camp. I am going to gather a few of my prison guards, talk to them, and tell them about our weapons and their locations. I have to figure out in details the rest, but in due time I shall tell all of you everything," Everyone looked at Hans with great astonishment and drank another brandy. Hans asked whether anyone had any questions or suggestions. Some did, and some didn't. Peter and Otto wanted to know their role and how they could help. Hans told them to be patient, and that he would keep them posted about the preparation of the riot to come.

Sasha poured them a third brandy. Everyone sighed a sigh of contentment.

SPEAKING TO ISAAC

Days have been passing by so fast, and each day Hans waits for the call from the Colonel. Still the plans had to be finalized and ready to go. Evil must be stopped. So that day as roll call approached, Hans set out to find Isaac, the Jewish helper who takes care of the prisoners. He intended to keep them in order and to enforce strict rules. Issac knew that the rules had to be obeyed, no matter what. He also had to keep the prisoners busy with much labor. Hans called Issac to see him in his office as soon as the roll call was finished. The weather was cooling down, but still Hans did not need a coat. The prisoners wore their light old jackets over their uniforms in which some were still cold. In between roll call, Hans managed to get some breakfast at the officers' club but decided to take it to his office. Isaac came over shortly, and we spoke in private. He saluted me and stood there as though he was stiff. Hans told him to sit down and listen to what he had to say. Hans ordered him to keep his mouth quiet and not say anything. "If you tell what I have to say to anyone, I shall have you whipped and put out of this camp," promised Hans. He couldn't afford anyone outside of our team to know what we were planning. Hans explained to Isaac that Germany was losing the war and soon the Allies would find them and try to murder them all. Hans also told him that he needed to gather enough prisoners to lead the fight. "I intend to release all of the prisoners as soon as I get word from the Colonel about transporting everyone out," Hans promised. "Further, I shall cause a riot to occur, and then you will be shown to the compound where our weapons are stored. You will be directed by Otto and Peter, they will leave the door open where you and your men will smuggle weapons to the other prisoners. As soon as they get their weapons, you will proceed to the rioting. You will not harm me or anyone else, unless they shoot at you. Understand, Isaac?" Isaac stood there amazed while Hans continued with his orders. "I will command the guards at the main gate to open them so everyone could leave," said Hans. "I cannot promise that everyone will live, but at least you will be free to go your way. Only shoot those in the towers and you will make the run. Now as time moves on I will keep you in touch. Understand, Isaac?" Issac saluted Hans and said in German, "Es ist eine Ehre lhnen zu die nen Kommandant." or "It is an honor to serve you, Commander." Hans told Issac to go back and continue his work. He reminded Issac again not say one word to anyone or else he would pay a heavy price. When Isaac left, Hans sat back in his chair and sighed a huge sigh of satisfaction.

CONFIRMATION

Hans received a short call from the Colonel on October 13, 1944. He gave me the exact date when the train would arrive to pick up the entire camp. He confirmed the date as December 16, 1944, just before Christmas. He said it was his gift to the camp for Christmas. Hans laughed to himself and said, "You stupid bas . . . . It is your gift for yourself." Hans had the plans now confirmed and reinforced ready for his own battle as Commander.

BRATS AND SWEET BREAD

Hans finished his day very tired and drained. Hans went back to his quarters where he found a familiar smell lingering in the air. I knew the smell belong to brats and the aroma of sweet bread. When I walked in, I saw the table filled with plenty of brats and loaves of sweet bread. Hans was extremely hungry and asked Fritz to join him for dinner. Fritz agreed enthusiastically, and they both ate until they couldn't eat any more. Hans felt very full and too lazy to do anything else. To make this meal more interesting, they had made the leftovers from the previous day into a feast. Fritz ate so much that Hans released him from his guard duty until morning. Hans told Fritz that he did not expect anything to happen overnight and that he would see Fritz in the morning. Fritz, Hans's personal bodyguard, had orders to shoot anyone who tried to harm Hans and Sasha. Fritz was also a wonderful friend, young at heart. Fritz had been schedule at the beginning of the war to leave for the front, but he was transferred at the last minute to Camp Kassel. Hans had been very happy that Fritz was with him.

SURPRISE VISIT

Another weekend, and a few of Hans's officers including Goetz, went home to visit family. They left late on Friday and ordered to be back here on Sunday. Hans himself always stayed on the camp grounds no matter if he had the time off. On his free days, Hans would either ride Zurich or just exercise by running. He was putting on his regular clothing when he heard a knock at the front door. He couldn't imagine who this might have been. Hans opened the door, and there stood an old friend, Heinz Von Bruin. Hans was totally shocked to see him because he was completely dressed in his full uniform. He looked at Hans and said, "Hans, how are you doing?" Hans replied, "What are you doing here?" Hans could not believe his eyes. Hans ordered him to come in and led him to the den. Hans asked Sasha for some tea and offered Heinz breakfast. As they ate, the two friends caught up on their news. Heinz told Hans that he had become a Lieutenant of the 1st Division in Berlin. "I see you made it to Commander, Sir," said Heinz. Hans looked at Heinz and turned down the "Sir thing" and asked him if he heard any news of the war. Hans put his tea cup down and got up from his chair, pacing up and down as though something was wrong. Heinz looked as though he should have been down in Berlin running headquarters. His left arm was draped with a swastika, and his pants were neatly pressed. "Just to think I knew him from officer's school, and he still had his hair hanging down his right side and he seemed deeply disturbed," Hans observed. Gently, Heinz came over to Hans explaining to him about the horrible scenes that he had witnessed. Heinz looked at Hans and asked, "What was this war supposed to be about?" Hans answered him with honesty and told him, "self-righteousness." It is about one person who enticed a country into evil and promised us that we were the best country. We were promised the world, power and freedom. Heinz agreed that he and Hans had been fooled to believe in our leaders. "Hans, I have nothing left in Germany, my home was destroyed, my family is missing, and I have nothing." Heinz took another sip of his tea and continued his conversation. "I am promised nothing, nothing at all. Will the leaders take care of me when the war is over?" he asked. Heinz told Hans that they didn't have a choice in this matter and they have to serve high command or else die. Hans and Heinz continued their conversation, neither slowing his thoughts. Sasha served them some finger sandwiches with ham, cheese and tomatoes on her sweet bread. She even gave them some potato salad. Heinz looked well convinced that Sasha could cook and told Hans that. Heinz downed five of the sandwiches, and breakfast was no longer breakfast. Hans thought that because Sasha had left-over sandwiches from the day before, Heinz wouldn't care having them so early. He actually thanked her for the sandwiches and told her how sorry he was about her captivity. However, Heinz put his jacket on and told Hans to call him if he needed anything. As he started to the door, Heinz turned around and said, "I hope to see you after this war, best to you my friend, and thank you for the food." Heinz got into his special car and speedily left the camp.

INVITE

The weekend was quite cool. Hans enjoyed riding his horse around the camp. Sometimes he rode bareback and forget the saddle. But he always rode with his rifle at his side. Hans had never shot anyone, but he still kept the rifle for any emergency. He wore his casual on-the-side hat, his white shirt, and his black trousers. Everyone knew who Hans was when the horse passed by. Hans sometimes rode outside the camp into the woods. He usually rode as fast as he could to avoid anyone spying on him. The guards never had a problem at the front gate in letting Hans into the camp. In fact, they were always polite to him and proved that they were good soldiers fighting for their country. Hans always spoke to them in German, because they spoke no English. Hans invited them to a holiday dinner. Hans told them that the date for this dinner would be on October 28 at 6:00PM. They gladly accepted the invitation and thanked him and let Hans pass. I left the camp with thoughts of which he had and many. Now he needed time to prepare his thoughts with complete satisfaction.

DINNER PREPARATION

Hans invited many people to the holiday party including guards and officers. He wanted this occasion to be a party and fun, not a lecture about the war. Hans was surprised that everyone accepted the invitation. Hans had Sasha prepare the entire dinner including desserts and appetizers. At one point when some of his untrusted officers had gone, Hans wanted to speak to Gunther and Franz, the main gate guards, about the future riot. Tonight would be their final preparation for the day that would come. Sasha and Hans had planned the party to be very casual, no formal dressing. As before, Sasha prepared the food: appetizers, caviar, lamb roast, potatoes, string beans, red cabbage, sweet bread and desserts. She wanted to make a chocolate cake, pastries, and apple pies and have some coffee and brandy. Sasha was going to prepare the entire meal by herself.

HARD WORK

Monday came, and Hans felt ready for anything. Hans felt even better when he had finished his breakfast. He rode over to Goetz, Schrieffer, and Buchwald. He warned them that the bridge work had to finish by November 30. Finishing it was a must because the bridge was collapsing. Hans told them to finish it or else. He was not fooling around and very serious about the bridge's being finished. These officers took the orders and immediately told the prisoners about the orders. Hans needed the bridge finished so that when the planned riot occurred, the prisoners could escape quickly when the gates were opened. Hans watched every day to make sure the work progressed steadily. Hans saw a lot of the prisoners working on the bridge, and he knew it was hard labor; but he knew that later on the prisoners would thank him for this opportunity. Isaac looked at Hans as he passed, Hans nodded to him in return.

Hans rode over behind the tree where he stood, watching and observing the entire camp. He was planning the escape as though it was happening that moment. Hans rode from one end to the other, knowing that the prisoners had their eyes fixed on him. Hans noticed that most of the men were rolling out the hot mortar and tar by now and mixing it with water. Some were carrying heavy boulders, so Hans knew that the road work could be finished. However, no one knew anything about the escape plan, except Isaac. Most of the women whom Hans saw were working in the storehouses, working in the fields, and cleaning. Hans tried to go past them so he wouldn't disturb them. The guards were coming down on them yelling to hurry on and work faster. Some guards whipped the women, and Hans stopped that practice fast. Hans asked the guard, "How can you get work out of someone if you whip her?" Hans stayed around feeling sorry for every woman he saw. They knew nothing of his plans. He looked at them with pity and sorrow. Hans passed by, he saw another guard was beating a woman with the end of his rifle. Hans rode up to the guard stopping him immediately. The guard was malicious. Hans intimidated him about his barbaric actions. Hans went to the woman and gave her his hand. Hans helped her up, he offered her water from his canteen, and told her that she would be all right. This woman was young, no more than 24, and very pretty. Hans told her that it would be all right to drink some water. Hans asked her name and she replied, "Mela." Hans told her to carry on her work and yelled in German at the guard, "Don't do it again or else." Hans told him to curb his beatings because he needed every one of those workers to complete his mission. The guard saluted Hans, who told the guard to carry on but without any more beatings. Mela kept her blue eyes on Hans as she was working. He smiled at her and rode away slowly. Then he backed up and watched for any beatings. Hans watched Mela. He shook his head to Mela, and she said quietly to him as he watched her lips, "Thank you." Hans nodded to Mela and rode away.

ROLL CALL AND FOOD

Roll call came at 5:00 PM. The weather had turned breezy and cooler. Hans rode over to Isaac to invite him to the party on October 28 and to tell him that the plans would be finalized by then. Hans also asked him to bring that woman who was standing near the door. I also informed him that her name was Mela and she lived in Block 5. Hans wanted her to come to the dinner with him. He accepted with delight and promised to invite her. In the chilly air, Hans waited for the order that all the prisoners were present and none missing. As he waited, he noticed Mela. Her beautiful eyes met his several times. Hans wondered whether she was being treated properly and not beaten. In his mind he thought, "Mela, it will be over soon, I promise you." Hans heart ached for her. He knew he was single and committed to Sasha. Mela, on the other hand was beautiful, young and innocent. He wanted to be her savior, to help her, and yet his heart was in despair. Mela was touching his heart in a different way that Sasha had not touched. She kept her eyes on Hans during the roll call and once in awhile he would be doing the same. Mela knew that Hans was looking at her. Hans received the orders that everyone was here. He told Otto to get the prisoners to eat. Hans went over to the pot of soup the cooks were serving. Hans tasted the soup, "Much better" I said, "much better." Many of the prisoners were very hungry. Hans told the cooks to give those prisoners more if they were still hungry. Hans did not want any leftovers in the garbage. The cooks agreed. As Hans watched Mela eating, he knew that he was just standing there because he was falling in love with her. Hans knew that he had to leave before his heart would feel obligated to her. Mela's eyes followed Hans as he rode into the distance where he wiped a tear that he shed for Mela

YOU OR ME

Hans went back to his quarters. He quickly had something to eat and drink, and then he went over to his office. As Hans sat there, his thoughts were confused and his heart was pounding to see Mela again. Hans wasn't sure whether she wanted to speak to him or whether she felt anger because of what he was. Hans was going to put the matter to a test just one more time by going over to where she worked. Hans intended to make it an excuse to see the men working, but in reality he wanted to see Mela. Avoiding much of the cold air, Hans went over to the area in which she was working. He rode slowly looking at every detail of the camp, and finally he arrived at her location where he saw the same guard. Hans asked the guard whether he was doing what Hans told him to do. He said yes, saluted Hans and went back to his job. There he saw Mela working. She picked up her head up and looked directly at Hans. When she did, she melted Hans's heart. He asked the guard to have Mela come to his office immediately. Hans had just returned to his office when Mela knocked. Hans asked her to come in and sit down. As soon as she did, Hans stood up and looked at her and she looked directly at him. Hans felt a special rush to his heart, and he had to control his feelings. She never moved and allowed me to touch her face and wipe the dirt off her cheeks. I reached down to her and kissed her lips; she pulled herself closer to me. She then laid her head on my chest, and her arms held me as I held her closer to my heart. Hans looked at Mela and told her that he was falling in love with her. He also told her that he wanted her to work in his office. I wanted to help her and not to see her hurt by anyone. Hans knew that he had cheated on Sasha, but he tried to justify himself on the grounds that he was single. He wanted Mela because she was beautiful and offered her love to him so freely. She told Hans that she was grateful in what he had done for her. She confessed that she had fallen in love with him a while ago. Hans told her that he had a plan to save her. Hans told her that he wanted her to be his and to love her. Hans was only 24, and thought that finding love could make this war go by faster. Mela held onto him. Hans released her and knew that they were both now in love. Hans asked her about her family. Mela told him when she was twenty one, her family were all killed by the Nazis. She told Hans that she was now alone. She told Hans that she had never married and that she lived by herself. Hans knew that he loved her and that this feeling was more than Sasha. Mela was grateful to Hans. She knew that Hans was German but that fact did not bother her. She felt that death was upon her and that her hour to die would come. Hans reassured her that she would be safe with him.

Mela and Hans met each day. Each day they would kiss and embrace and made plans for their future. She told Hans that she was so much in love with him and said that if Hans asked her to marry her, she would accept. Mela continued to tell Hans how she would take care of him and never let him go. Like a fool, Hans asked Mela to marry him someday. Hans told her that he would be arranging something special for her and that they could be married, start a family, and forget this war. Hans wanted to arrange for her to go to his father's house to be protected and safe. Hans wanted God to assist him and to let Sasha understand that he had fallen in love with another woman. Hans asked God to forgive him as his flesh became weaker. On our third meeting Mela asked Hans to love her and to take care of her. Hans agreed, and loved her every day without anyone knowing about their affair. He needed her as much as she needed him. Hans was more determined than ever to have her put into safety and away from this misery. Hans wanted to Mela to be protected and to be away from this camp. Hans wanted Mela and thought that even if he did marry Sasha, Mela would always be a part of him. Hans loved

Mela like a little boy who fell in love and felt so much joy for the first time. Hans wasn't sure whether he had this feeling because of not kissing Sasha as much or what it was. Mela was just special, and Hans told her she would always be special to him.

OCTOBER 28TH

Sasha had everything cooked and baked for the party. Hans took a chilling ride on Zurich and didn't return for hours. He really didn't want to be at his quarters until the guests would be arriving. He really wanted to see Mela again. Hans had her transferred to do work around his huge office building. Each day he had his guard bring Mela to his office. Mela would clean, wash and do so much more. Then Hans would have her in the fields just around three hours a day. The guards knew to send Mela back to Hans for duties at his office building. Hans rode by the fields where he stopped to look at Mela. When he did, he saw so much love in her eyes. Hans nodded to Mela and rode on to his next destination. He covered the entire camp and watched a lot of the workers. He knew that recently he had lost over 25 prisoners due to exhaustion. Hans told Goetz to give them more breaks and water to drink or else he would be taking their place building the roads. Goetz moved fast on this order.

Hans then visited the kitchen and asked the cook in charge whether they were working on a new recipe soup that gave more nutrients than the soup that they had been given. They told me that they working on the soup and they should have it much better than the previous. Hans told the head cook he should work for improvement each day. The cook suggested that the cooks could add more potatoes and carrots to the recipe. Hans agreed and told him to proceed with that idea. Hans also told the cooks that he would be back and to check on the soup. Hans then left and found himself again riding past Mela, who made sure to look at him. Hans had to see her again, alone. So he had Mela come over to his office earlier pretending to do her chores. As she came into his office, Hans dropped what he was doing and walked up to her. Again he wiped her face off with his handkerchief because of the dirt on her face. She looked at Hans and grabbed his hand and kissed it. Mela told him how grateful she was to him. Mela even told Hans that if they never were married, she would always be obligated to him for what he had done for her. Hans looked at her and drew her warm body to his. They locked themselves together for hours and where time seemed to stand still. It was a moment of love and special wishes. Right there, Hans made that wish. He wished that Mela would always be his no matter what happened. Mela agreed. She knew that Hans had to see her each day just to draw her love to him, and Hans took the chance for her to be with him. Hans loved Mela in his own way. He told her that he had to save her and that he would be making arrangements for her to leave so that she could be safe. Hans couldn't risk her being hurt if the camp fell under another attack. Mela wanted to know when because she wanted to be with Hans as much as she could. Hans told her that he would let her know. Hans made sure she knew about the party and to come with Isaac. Mela said that she would not miss the party for the life of her. Hans told her he had to go back to his quarters to get the party ready. They kissed for a while. Finally he let her go out of his arms. Shortly after 5:00PM, Otto and Peter arrived, and minutes later came Fritz and Heinz. They heard another knock on the door, and Isaac was there with Mela. Hans's heart beat so fast when Mela's eyes caught his. They smiled at one another. They knew their secret, and Hans was not about to spill it out or give it up, so he continued welcoming his guests. Soon Gunther and Franz came to the door as well as a few of the soldiers Hans invited. The ones I could not trust did not come, and Hans felt blessed that they didn't. Hans invited everyone to go to the table for the buffet. They started with their appetizers then proceeded with their main course dinner, and then their course dessert. They had plenty of brandy, lemonade and coffee. The guest had no time to really say anything because they were busy eating and eating. Hans was pleased with the party and how everyone was getting along. As they all sat down in the living room drinking their coffee and pushing down the cake and pie, Hans told everyone about our plans and the possible outcome. I mentioned by December 16, this camp would be finished and that the prisoners would be gone. Hans didn't tell them right away how the prisoners would be gone. As they kept drinking and eating, Hans made sure that the plans were unfolding, and he made them known to the guards at the gate. They told Hans that they would take care of the gate for anyone whom Hans would tell them to let go. Hans directed them to open the gates as the prisoners would run towards them, but don't shoot at them. Hans told Isaac not to kill his guards at the main gate but to proceed outward. Isaac assured Hans that he would take care of that detail for him and that no one would be hurt. Hans had given the instructions clearly, and everyone knew what he had planned. They were now ready for the day to come.

URGENT CALL

Hans woke up early the next day. He took his usual shower and dressed. Because he found it to be quite cooler outside, Hans put on his leather black coat. Hans had a little breakfast and spoke very little to Sasha because he told her that he had much business to take care of that day. Sasha never asked Hans for any details because she knew his position. Hans went over to the shed to get Zurich and rode over to his office. As Hans went inside, he heard his phone ringing. It was Colonel Heisenberg again. He wanted Hans to drive to Berlin right away so that they could go over the plans for December 16. Hans told the Colonel that he could be there by the afternoon. So Hans ordered the roll call, gave the orders and proceeded to give everyone his pay. Hans had over 241 guards and 20 officers, so distributing their pay took time. Hans started at the main gate and ended with Goetz. In between he stopped to see Mela hoping she was doing well. Mela waved to Hans; he returned her wave. Hans rode back to his quarters and had Zurich put into the shed until he could come back from Berlin. Hans asked Sasha to feed Zurich and to make sure he was warm. Hans had to leave quickly for this meeting in Berlin because it would take nearly five hours or so to drive there. Hans left Otto in charge of the camp until his return later that evening. Sigmund, Hans's assigned driver, drove Hans. Hans made sure that they had some drinks and sandwiches as they traveled. Hans was dressed in his full uniform because he wanted to impress the Colonel with appearance. En route to Berlin, most of the roads were dirt. "Actually it feels good to be out of the camp for a while," Hans told himself. On the way there, Hans saw a lot of

German soldiers on the roadside marching to wherever they were going. Hans looked at them and thought, "Just as I was young when I joined, so were many others." Most of the ones he saw were injured and fragile, looking to find a way back home. Hans felt sorry for them because it was cold outside. He was sure that they wanted to meet their destination fast. Hours later, Sigmund and Hans arrived in Berlin. They saw as many horrible sights that Hans hardly recognized Berlin. Buildings had been bombed and destroyed; corpses were piled up on the sides of the streets. Hans was appalled at what this war had created and he knew that this meeting with the Colonel was going to be a joke. Finding no place really to park, Sigmund parked in front of the building. A guard came over to open the door for Hans and stood at attention as he walked towards the steps to the building. The front door of the building was heavily guarded, and the guards came to attention when they saw him approaching. The front desk had a guard posted, and Hans told him that he was Commander Schweitzer there to see Colonel Heisenberg The guard instructed Hans to go upstairs. Hans passed more guards, all of whom saluted him. As Hans approached the door he saw the Colonel sitting at his desk typing. The room was smoky from his cigar and quickly the Colonel greeted Hans and offered him a cigar and coffee. "Hans, how are you doing?" he asked enthusiastically. Hans replied that he that was doing well. When Hans sat down, Colonel Heisenberg introduced me to Lieutenant Frank Rosenberger from Munich. Hans shook his hand as he expressed delight to see Hans. Rosenberger told Hans that he had heard a lot about him, that Hans was considered one of their best commanders. Rosenberger wanted Hans to hear their proposal. These men were pure Nazis who would die for Hitler; little they knew that Hans would not. Hans would only die for his country but not to destroy. The Colonel explained all about December 16 and described the procedure for closing the camp. He also said that the high command would have a private office for Hans and his staff. They would be transferring only the military personnel they could use, any soldiers would be deployed to the front lines to fight. Hans was now sure that the war was coming to an end very soon and that Germany had lost a lot of good men. The Colonel told Hans that Russia was closing in on

Germany but that German troops were putting up a an ferocious fight. "I was glad for that information, and I do hope it continues that way," Hans told Colonel Heisenberg and Rosenberger. Hans accepted the Colonel's offer for his transfer and asked him about food at his camp. The Colonel guaranteed Hans that he could take back plenty of food, and ordered the one guard to load up the truck with plenty of food and follow Hans to Kassel. Hans then asked the Colonel whether he needed anything else. "No, said the Colonel, everything was fine for now." The Colonel told Hans that if any changes should occur, that he would be in touch with Hans on the phone. Hans thanked him and he bid the Colonel and Lieutenant Rosenberger farewell. Hans met the guard at the door with his truck and thanked him and joined Sigmund downstairs. He quickly got into his car and Hans told Sigmund to proceed back to the camp. "The truck with food will be following us," Hans said. Hans felt contented with the meeting, for now he knew that the plans were unfolding and that he could breathe, somewhat.

BAD WEATHER, AGAIN

Hans and Sigmund arrived at Camp Kassel just as a heavy thunderstorm hit. Hans had Sigmund pull the car up to his quarters and directed the truck to the kitchen for delivery. Hans told the driver to have the head cook sign the papers after he unloaded the food and to return so that Hans could sign the papers also. Hans went up to his room to change his wet clothes and just sat there feeling a huge relief. He really thought that this meeting was not necessary and the only thing that had come out for the good was the food. Hans knew that he had a lot to accomplish in a short time because they were already in November. Hans had everyone waiting for the signal to proceed with his orders. His first urgency was to get Mela out of this camp alive, and he decided that it would be this weekend. He wanted to get his feelings aired out and tell Sasha about the news. They were sitting in the den when Hans saw a flash of lightening. He was afraid for a minute and asked Sasha to close the drapes. The rain was pouring outside, and Hans looked out to see that the dirt was turning into mud. Everyone was inside, and Sasha had begun to prepare dinner a little sooner than usual. It was almost 6:00 PM, and Hans had to make his final decision before that day could end.

SAVING TRUTHFULLY, YOURS

Days had gone by since the bad weather. Hans had to get Mela to his father's farm. Hans cared for Mela so much, yet he could not leave Sasha. If he did, he knew that he would have no peace. Hans felt it was out of feeling sorry for Sasha and not true love. Hans met Mela in his office. He had missed her so much that he couldn't stay away from her. He wanted to feel her close to him once more. So they stayed with each other hidden away from the world where they spoke to each other and stayed in one another arms for hours. Hans told Mela that he would not see her for awhile and that he was very worried about getting her out of the camp. It was so hard at this time to fall in love in Germany especially if the person was a Jew. Hans recognized that he had to follow rules but knew that sometimes rules had to be broken. Already he had broken rules-twice-but was not ashamed. Hans told Mela that he would miss her so much and miss their secret days together. Mela told Hans that she loved him also and would pray to see him again. "I want you to know Hans that I am "Truthfully, Yours" forever," Mela said to Hans. He said the same to her. He also told her that he would have Peter take her to his father's house. When Friday came around, Peter loaded the car and Mela reached over to kiss Hans on his cheek. She whispered, "I love you Hans." Hans wished her the best and told her to take care of herself until he would see her again. Mela also told Hans that she was thankful for everything that he had done. Hans felt a horrible pain in his heart. He was so upset that Mela was leaving him. The car started, and slowly they left. Hans stood there with a knot in his throat asking himself questions, "Can I love her?" Time would tell the truth to him and he was willing to wait for that time. Hans watched the car passing the guards and the gate. Hans was so stricken with grief, yet now he had to make his big decision about his life and how it would be after December 16.

BIG WISH

This has been a week and Hans was grateful that he was off this weekend. Basically he stayed by myself in which Hans had time to think. Hans sat in the den sipping a brandy. The aroma of the sweet bread was in the air, and he felt as though he had a wish to make. Hans enjoyed the comfort of being alone, thinking and making plans for myself and the camp. As he sat in silence, his mind focused getting out of the camp, releasing the prisoners, and maybe marrying Sasha. Hans knew that he had an affair with Mela, but he also knew that if he didn't have Sasha, he would have married Mela. Mela will always be special to his heart, and she knew that. So his biggest wish was to get married. Hans knew he couldn't do anything at this moment, but he surely was planning. Hans needed to see Issac. He asked Fritz to get Issac for him. Fritz left and found Issac at the storehouse. Isaac then followed Fritz immediately to Hans's quarters and found him sitting in his den. Hans asked him directly whether he knew anyone in the camp who could marry Sasha and him. He replied with a quick "yes" and asked how soon? Issac told me that a Rabbi named Jacob lived in Block 8. "The Rabbi is healthy and a good man and if you wish I could have you speak with him," Issac offered. Hans asked Isaac to have the Rabbi come to my quarters as soon as possible. Within twenty minutes, the Rabbi stood before me. He was quiet and looked as though he needed to have food and water. Hans offered him both, and sat down with him talking about the marriage to Sasha. He spoke to me with tears in his eyes and Hans felt that he was a very cheerful man, cautious but grateful. Hans told him that he would like him to be there in the morning right after the roll call. He agreed and Hans mentioned to him that he would help him leave this camp and be safe from this bloodshed. Hans bid him goodbye, and he rushed to see Sasha. I sat in my chair and realized that another wish was being answered.

SHOULD I?

The night was cool. Sasha was in the kitchen cleaning and it was past seven. Hans was very tired. He asked Sasha to come to talk with him. Hans told her that he loved her, and she told Hans that she would never forget how she had met me. She then told me that she loved me very much and wanted to marry me someday. Hans asked her whether that was her biggest wish and she said, "Yes!" Hans explained to her that they would married tomorrow after the roll call in the morning. Sasha was totally shocked and didn't know how to respond. Hans told her that Rabbi Jacob, a prisoner, would be performing the ceremony. Because Sasha was Jewish, Hans felt that a Rabbi would make her feel at home and comfortable. Hans believed in her. Sasha's tears rolled down her cheeks as she remembered how Hans had saved her and how she met me in the Ghetto. Hans told her to put on something pretty and all she had to do was look presentable. She said something about a dark skirt and a white blouse and that was fine with him because he would wear his full uniform. Hans couldn't wait for this event to be over with and a thing of the past. Tomorrow Sasha would be Mrs. Sasha Schweitzer, wife of Hans Franz Schweitzer, finally together.

WEDDING DAY

Hans woke up around 5:00 AM. He was somewhat nervous and excited to be married. He had Mela on his mind and was tearful about her. He would see her again; he knew that. He wasn't sure whether he should tell Sasha about his affair with Mela, but he assumed that they were not married and there was no reason to tell her anything. It was his business and only his. Still, he loved Mela. He was hoping once he had married Sasha his desire for Mela would be finished. To get rid of this feeling he went into the shower. When he came out, he shaved. Hans put on an enormous amount of his French cologne and got dressed. His uniform was well pressed and his boots were shinning. He had his hair cut the day before so that his hair would not fall into his eyes. Hans was so handsome that any woman would be proud to marry him. He was the Commander, and he stood for truth. Because of those values, he loved a Jew and was now marrying one although doing so. However, Hans did not care. The love was forbidden but he did not care much about that. He based everything on faith, trust, and the grace of God. Sasha was up even earlier because she had to make the wedding cake and prepare the food for the ceremony. She made a lot of potato salad with plenty of finger sandwiches and put a bottle of red wine in the freezer. She looked beautiful today because her blouse was pressed, and her skirt fit for her body. Her hair has grown and she put it into a bun. She also put on and put a little makeup. When she was ready, she refused to see Hans before the wedding and according to her customs. Hans went over to the officers club to have breakfast, and there he met Peter and Otto. Peter had returned last night from dropping off

Mela to Hans's father's house. Something inside told Hans to be quiet in asking how Mela was doing. Yet he waited for Peter to mention something about her to him, and he did. In matter of fact, Peter handed Hans a note from Mela. Hans's heart stood still in his throat, and he refused to look at the note while sitting with others. He would read it only when he would be alone so that he could feel that joy again. Hans told Otto and Peter about his marriage to Sasha that morning and invited them to be his witnesses. Hans quickly finished his last sip of tea and met everyone at roll call. Everyone had their eyes fixed on him. He was completely dressed in his black uniform with all of his shiny medals on his chest. His boots were polished that the sun actually reflected off them. He even wore his dress hat and left traces of French cologne in the air as he passed. Hans spoke to everyone explaining that the road must be finished before the end of November. He commanded all of his officers to make sure that the work was accomplished. Hans turned around, went back to his bunker, and walked into his dreams. Several minutes passed; then Peter and Otto were at the bunker waiting for the historical moment to occur. Peter thought that Hans was rushing into marriage but Otto said nothing about it to Hans. Peter knew about Hans's affair with Mela and thought that Hans was young and needed to wait, but he couldn't tell Hans that. A few minutes later, Isaac and Rabbi Jacob showed up for the wedding. Fritz was stationed outside but came in occasionally to join the ceremony. Hans told Fritz that if anyone came looking for him to say that he was in conference and that he would return later on. Gracious and faithful as Fritz was, he agreed to Hans's wishes. Sasha joined Hans in the den, all dressed, hair in place, looking as she did when Hans first met her. Then Sasha looked at Hans and saw the man she truly fell in love with that day. Her eyes filled with tears with happiness and with sorrow because her family was deceased. "If only they knew and lived, they would be happy; and Papa could have married us," Sasha said to herself. She wiped her tears and proceeded with Hans to Rabbi Jacob. Hans, pure German, knew very little about the Jewish faith, but was eager to learn. He even agreed that the children would be raised in both religions and would learn to respect those who were different. Rabbi Jacob joined their hands together as he prayed and asked God for blessings over them. He also thanked God for the miracle that had occurred, and everyone knew what that miracle was. He then had Hans kiss Sasha and pronounced them man and wife under the eyes of God. They had two glasses under their feet which represented good luck, which they had to break with their feet according to Jewish custom. Everyone clapped, and Hans and Sasha kissed. They were now married; Sasha was Mrs. Hans Franz Schweitzer and a proud wife of him, indeed.

THE NOTE

As Hans was enjoying his first hours of being married, he left his marriage ring off his finger until he was out of the war. He had given Sasha his mother's beautiful pink pearl ring with diamonds. It looked splendid on Sasha's finger, and she swore never to take it off her finger. She kept her vow and wore it to her death. Hans had to go over to his office to do some work and noticed that he had the note that Peter gave to him from Mela. This was his private moment to read the note, and he didn't want to answer her as yet. He felt that he was married and that he had to live by his vows. However, the note was on white paper. The smell of the ink was upon the paper, and it read: "My Dearest Hans, words could not express my heart in what I feel for you. You have done so much for me and I could never repay you. Thank you for saving my life, again. You will always be my friend and I hope you feel the same way for me. Be safe, my love. Always until we meet again, someday," "Truthfully, Yours," Mela.

Hans quickly folded the note, brushed his tears away, and stuck the note into his wallet. Only someday he would pull it out and read it over and over again. He based the note on what he did to save someone and not feelings. He knew the truth and stuck with it, until that day would come again where he would meet Mela, again.

LOVE

Night came. No one came around to see the Schweitzer's, so they had their dinner and decided to spend their wedding night earlier. Finally Hans could kiss Sasha and be returned in passion from her. They went to Hans's room and forgot about the war, Mela, and the world. There they both found their dreams, love and hope in their lives. Hans held Sasha in his arms and both melted into one another where they soon became one. Soon after midnight, the stars came out and they both fell asleep in each others arms. They were snuggled in a warm blanket, and the fireplace was crackling as they kissed goodnight. They were both satisfied that their dreams had happened in such a beautiful way, the way they had prayed for. They had been married on November 18, 1944, in Kassel Camp, and soon they will be on another journey.

PROMISES FULFILLED

As promised, Hans told the Rabbi that he would take him to his father's house. He had the Rabbi come to his quarters. Peter was to drive the car to his father's house. This journey was Hans's excuse to go and see his mistress, Mela. Peter was shocked to find that Hans wanted to go to his father's house but knew the real reason. He was hoping that this visit would not lead to anything negative. There Hans stood in his full uniform as though he was getting married again because he had so much cologne on his face and uniform. He walked over to Sasha and he kissed her goodbye, promising to return the next day. He told her that he wanted to spend time with his father and speak to him about his plans, and the reason fit perfectly into his excuses. Soon, however, he would find differently. Sasha held him in her arms as though she knew something there was waiting for him. He smiled and left as they disappeared in the morning sun. Hans promised himself and especially for his wife's sake that he would not let himself be tempted.

FORBIDDEN JOY

As Peter and Hans arrived, bringing Rabbi Jacob, Hymen, Mela, and Elda met them at the door. As Hans got out of the car, Mela's heart jumped for so much joy and saw how handsome he looked with his blond hair and his uniform. She hated that uniform but not on Hans, for he had made that uniform stand with a different purpose. Hans ran inside to see his father where tears and joy fell over his father because it has been years since he had seen son. Hans sat down and introduced Rabbi Jacob to everyone and told them to save the Rabbi also. He told his father that he had just married Sasha and that he would be sending Sasha to him very soon. As he was telling his father the good news, Mela came in. Hans stood up as he met Mela's eyes. Her eyes were damped with tears and ran right into his arms. There Hans had his second dream. He was most happy to have her in his arms again and he felt his heart beating with the feeling of wanting Mela to grow inside him. He looked at her and couldn't help but kiss her and he felt his body wanting to have her again, yet he couldn't shake off this feeling. He didn't want to let her go, yet he knew that he was married; and he had to be honest with Mela about that. He told Mela that he had married Sasha and that he loved her. Mela said that she understood. She told Hans that she still loved him and she would always until she died. That night they spent together, loving and lying in each others arms. They had so much passion from the camp and they could finally let it all out. It was hours before they fell asleep. They became one many times that night. Hans told Mela that he loved her so much that he wish he could have married her. He also told Mela that he married Sasha but that he wanted Mela to remain as his mistress whom he secretly loves and wants. Hans didn't know where the passion actually lay, with Sasha or with Mela? He gave Mela money so that she could take care of herself until they would see each other again. His father disagreed with Hans but knew he was older and had to live his life. The visit was bliss, passion and forbidden love, yet Hans wanted every bit of it. He left Mela with love, little hope, and a child of his to bear from this affair. The war was finally showing its true self with loneliness and confusion, leaving many questions never to be answered. That day Hans left Mela only to return to, his new wife.

SASHA'S THOUGHTS

Before Hans returned, Sasha had the chance to do some serious thinking and was wondering why Hans had really left for his father's house. She suspected it was because of Mela. Call it a woman's intuition, but only time would tell and Sasha decided to keep her thoughts to herself, perhaps to keep it a secret until she dies. She was sure that she knew the truth. The question remained: did Hans's passion for Mela change her love for Hans? "Never," vowed Sasha. She determined to keep her faith with prayer and hope.

RETURNING

As Hans left his father and said goodbye to everyone, he waved to Mela and left. In the car, silence fell upon Hans, and Peter knew the truth. Peter could not express his opinion, because he knew that he would suffer the consequences. As they rode, they saw dozens of wounded soldiers being transported to Berlin. At one point Hans got out of his car to visit the soldiers. Many were weak from the war, fighting, and hunger. They couldn't even come to attention both for Hans and Peter. Yet Hans felt so bad for all of them and even for himself. Hans and Peter got back into the car and headed to the camp. Finally Hans broke the silence and said, "I was wrong, yet I am not sure of what I truly want." He admitted to Peter that he loved Mela very much but that he loved Sasha at the same time. He knew that he couldn't have both. Hans told Mela that he could only be her friend for now on, and she agreed. "But what am I supposed to tell Sasha?" asked Hans. Peter suggested to tell the truth and to have her forgive him. Hans agreed but was in a state of depression because he loved Mela. So he dropped the subject. Before they knew it, Hans and Peter were at the main gate ready to go in and face his destruction. Hans walked up to his quarters, and there stood Fritz with a click to his boots which alarmed Sasha that Hans was home. She ran to the door knowing the truth in her heart, but willing to forgive. She grabbed Hans and kissed him, waiting to hear his confession. He looked tired, and worn out; his face spoke a thousand words. She knew that when Hans was upset, he would speak strictly in German; but when he was not upset, he usually mixed both languages of English and German. Sasha knew that something was terribly wrong. Hans sat down and opened his jacket exposing his suspenders hooked on to his white shirt. He then took his jacket off and his boots and waited to catch his breath. Finally, he admitted his affair with Mela. Sasha looked at him and spoke before he did, "Hans, I know the reason that you went to your father's house; it was to see Mela. I know that she is your mistress, but this is a mistake. You must understand that you are hurting not only yourself and me, but also Mela." Hans then burst into tears and confessed that he did have relations with Mela and now felt very sorry. Sasha forgave him, but she asked him not to hurt anyone else again. Hans blurted out, "I told Mela that I cannot see her anymore and that I suggested we could be friends; she agreed." Sasha looked at him,and forgave him, but she told Hans that he must now live up to his mistake. Sasha brought out the most important question that Hans didn't even think of to ask, "What happens if she becomes pregnant?" He told Sasha that he would have to live up to the responsibility. "If she does have my baby, then I must take care of the expenses. It would be my responsibility without a doubt." Sasha agreed, wiped her tears, and moved on, trying to put this situation behind her. Hans could not understand how she could forgive and forget in what he has done. Now he needed to make his peace with God.

ANNOUNCEMENT

Weeks passed by. It was now almost December. Sasha wasn't feeling too well. Her body didn't feel right, and she had no friends to ask anything. So she went by her own intuition that that was she was having her first child. Her body was changing, and she needed to tell Hans about the good news; and yet she wasn't sure. Sasha waited until that night when she was going to sleep in Hans's arms and everything was quiet and forgotten. Still, she didn't say anything because she was not sure, so she fell asleep and didn't say a word. The next morning Hans took his horse out for inspection, and his first stop was Goetz and the bridge. As he approached the bridge, he saw that the boulders were in place and it looked as though it would only be a few days before it was finished. He mention to Goetz that he wanted it to finished by December 3rd, and it was already November 30th. Goetz reassured Hans that it would be finished and invited Hans to come by to see. Hans agreed and left for his office. He passed by where he first met Mela and felt a thorn in his heart. He quickly had to get rid of the feeling he carried for her. He went over to his office and found a bowl of soup on his desk, took a few sips, and left to see his wife. There Sasha had prepared a delicious meal for Hans and invited Fritz to join them both. They sat at the table eating their pork with beans and potatoes. After dinner, Hans went out to the porch and had a glass of brandy and smoked a cigar. He then took a shower and put on his night clothes. He always wore his pajamas with no shirt, showing his muscular chest; Sasha thought he was handsome. Sasha turned off the light as they climbed into bed and had the fireplace working. Hans held Sasha next to him and asked how her day was. She remembered her words and told him that she had something to tell him. He told her that she could tell him anything and he would listen. She stumbled on her words and finally she said, "Hans I just wanted to tell you that we are going to have a baby." Hans sat up quickly and said, "Me a father, you a mother? Sasha, I am happy for us." Now he had to get Sasha to his father's house before anything happened to Sasha and the baby. The biggest problem was not letting anyone see Sasha pregnant, or else there would be questions asked.

ACCIDENT

Hans wanted to send Sasha home so he could prepare everything before December 16. He planned to meet her after that date at his father's house. He then saddled his horse and rode around observing everything around him. Today, he had a very uneasy feeling in his heart and he knew the reason. He knew deep down in his heart that he missed and loved Mela. He carried his feelings for her and always would because he knew that he would not be able to be with her, for now. He was depressed over the war, camp and now Mela. So he just rode around on his horse to get the feeling out of his heart and concentrate upon the fact that he was married and his wife was expecting. Still, the feeling lingered. Hans just let it go-for today. Hans wanted to look at a few things; and as he got off his horse, his boot got caught in the stirrup. The horse began to move. Hans was being dragged upside down with his head and body hitting the ground. Hans was screaming with so much pain because his right knee torn into the ground ripping his trousers. Several of the guards came running to help him. They held on to Zurich and pulled Hans leg out of the stirrup. Hans was hurt. The fall was so bad because the ground was frozen. Unfortunately, the frozen ground cracked his knee injuring his ligaments. He was then carried to the hospital as the staff came running to assist their Commander. Hans was screaming in so much pain that the doctor had to give him a sedative to calm him down. As the doctor was examining Hans's leg, he discovered that Hans cracked his knee and had developed a tear. Not good news for Hans because he had this mission to accomplish soon. He had to put his plans into action and now this accident. The doctor told Hans that he had to be off the leg for a while and not to ride his horse. For at least two weeks Hans had to use crutches or just rest. The doctor gave Hans medicine for the pain, and a nurse completely bandaged his leg. He felt like a fool with a torn knee and his uniform completely covered in dust and torn. Hans had to use the crutches again that Hymen had made for him months ago. To Hans, this accident was a repeat from the first one. Hans was then carried to his quarters where Sasha came running to assist him. She was very upset and asked what had happened. Hans told her everything as she helped him take off his uniform. Hans asked Fritz to get Otto for him. Several minutes later, Otto came to the quarters finding Hans injured and in great pain. Hans explained his accident and needed Otto to act as commander for the day. Hans took the day off to rest his leg and bruises and still deciding on his plan. All he did for the day was eat and drink and think of Mela. He was ashamed of himself because of the accident and needed to lay his head down and just rest. He knew that Otto would take care of everything including inspections of the bridge. Hans thought that no accident was going to keep him down because he had promised his friend Isaac that the prisoners would be set free, and he would keep his word, no matter what.

"AIR RAID ATTACK"

That morning of December 6, 1944, Hans went outside on his crutches to call roll call. His right leg was in extreme pain. He spoke very little to everyone. Today he was making preparations for Sasha to leave. He knew he had to do it today no matter how injured he was, and he knew that he could take care of himself with the help of others. His concern was for her and the baby, and he had to put his leg out of the plan. He was about to go into his quarters when suddenly four bombers appeared in the sky. Hans quickly yelled to sound the alarms and start using the weapons. As he was yelling for everyone to get down, he saw the bombs dropping from the planes hitting the camp ground. One after another the bomb fell, and his men were using all of the weapons that Hans had ordered. At one point, one of the bombers was hit and crashed on the bridge that was being fixed. Hans heard screaming, machine guns, and more bombs. He could not move as he lay behind one of the barrels. His uniform was completely in the dust, and even his hat was blown off when he hit the ground. His blond hair was now full of soot from the bombs, and he had several burn marks on his face and hands. As Hans tried to get up, another bomber kept hitting the camp while his men were fighting back. Finally the attack was finished. Hans just lay there with fresh wounds and heard the cries of others. He didn't know how many bombs were dropped, but he did know that there were many that had fallen. As Hans tried to get up, he scrambled upward and moved closer to the barrel where he grabbed the edge to pull himself upward. His knee was bleeding, and his burns were causing him with great pain. His thoughts were on Sasha and everyone else because this was an unannounced raid that no one knew was coming. As Hans reached for his crutches that were scattered on the ground, he started to walk slowly toward his quarters. He saw with relief that the building was untouched but he looked around at other buildings that had been destroyed. Hans hopped with his crutches to his quarters and found Fritz covered in dirt and dust. He had minor injuries. Hans's great worry was Sasha and he couldn't move fast enough to ease his heart whether she was alive or dead. He saw her running towards him grabbing his neck and kissing him because she thought he was dead. She saw that he was injured again, but he paid no attention to those injuries because his mind was now in the camp. Hans went outside with the strength he had left looking for Peter and Otto for details of injuries and casualties. As Hans moved through the smoke filled air, he saw Otto coming towards him, and was grateful that he was all right. Hans asked for a report, and Otto said he would give him one immediately. Hans saw that Otto was completely in soot and dust and asked if he were really all right. Otto told Hans that he had minor injuries and said that Peter was fine. He then left hoping the report would not be too serious. Hans proceeded to inspect the buildings that were burning and destroyed. The kitchen had been completely destroyed, and bodies were lying all over the ground. Some were Hans's men, and the others were prisoners. Hans was completely devastated because he had no hope at this point, and when he received the report from Otto, Hans knew that his hope would be turned into horror. Hans had to sit down for a while to catch his breath and to wait for Otto's report on the damages. Minutes later, Peter came to find me. His uniform was totally destroyed. He did tell Hans that he was all right except for a minor injury to his leg, but he could still walk without difficulty. Hans told Peter that he sent Otto to bring him the report on damages and deaths. As Hans and Peter were speaking, Otto came running towards them with all the details. Hans held his breath. "Sir, the hospital was completely destroyed, storage room damaged, several blocks were destroyed, four officers dead, several prisoners dead, guards dead, and the bridge completely destroyed. The list goes on Sir." Hans asked him who the four officers were, and when Otto told him, he couldn't bear the pain anymore. "Goetz, Reiner, Braun and

Schlesinger were among the dead," Otto reported. Hans looked at Peter and Otto with so much pain in his face that they started to sob about what has happened. Hans couldn't understand why the enemy had bombed a camp when they knew that prisoners were occupying the blocks. "If they wanted to save the camp, they should have never done this attack," said Hans. Hans went back to his quarters and wept profusely and waited for the smoke to clear so he could see the damages. Meanwhile, Hans asked Peter and Otto to get help and have them put the dead bodies in one pile so he could examine who they were. They left and Hans knew that there were many bodies. Hans also knew that he had to face this challenge as he did in the past. His next decision was to release the prisoners.

Lt. Colonel Commander Hans Franz Schweitzer

Hans Franz Schweitzer, 33rd Division, Munich

Mela (former prisoner of Camp Kassel, Germany)

Sasha Schweitzer (wife of Hans and former prisoner)

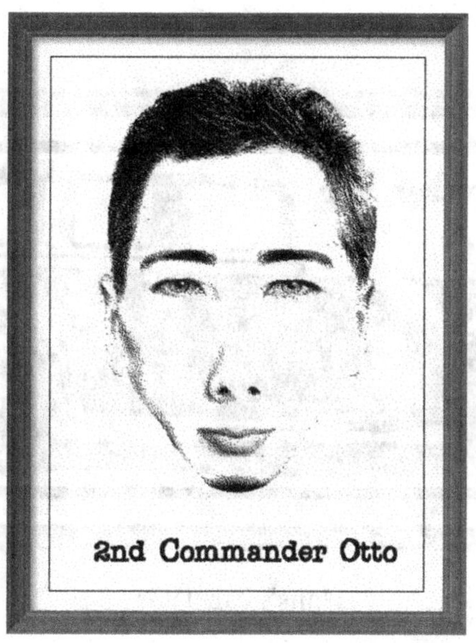

Lt. Major Otto (Second Commander, Camp Kassel)

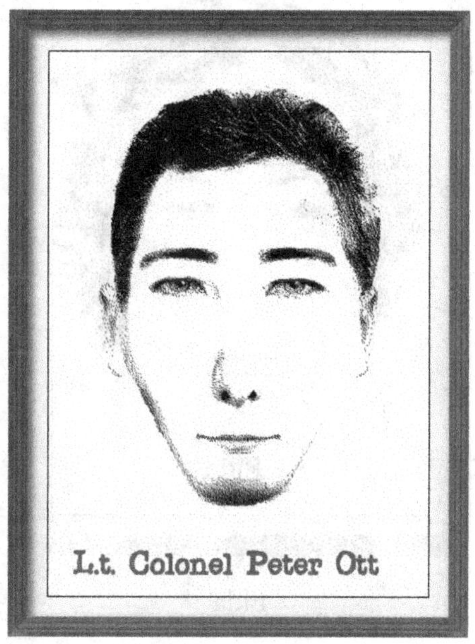

Peter's picture, (Peter Ott, Hans's best friend)

Hans's car, 1935

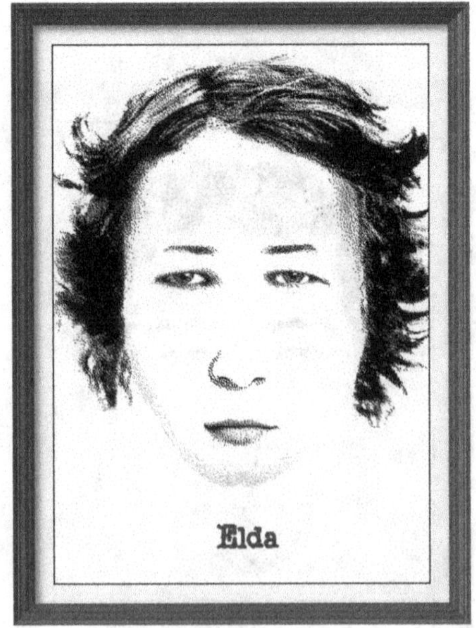

Elda

Rabbi Jacob

Han's horse

Hans Purple Heart
RVERDIERSTE IM LUFTSCHUTZ

Hymen

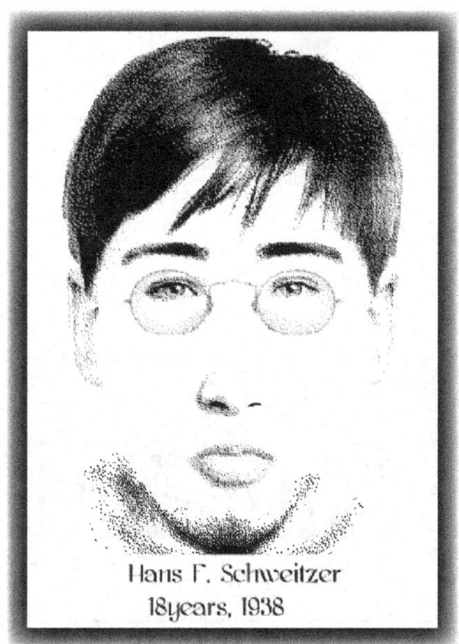

Hans at 18

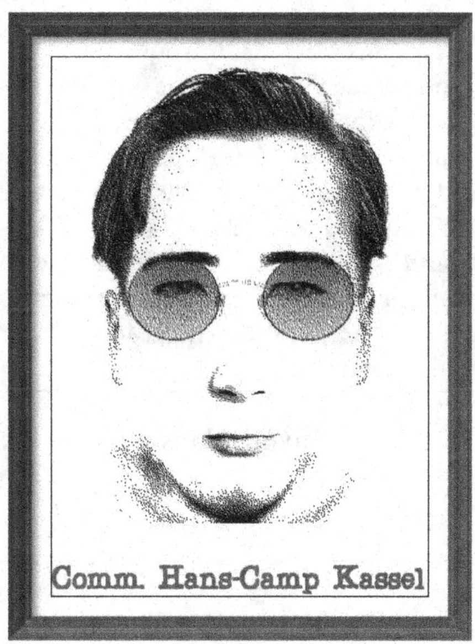

Camp Kassel

The Daily J

Monday, August 25, 1947

"Save Former Commander I

Former Lt.Colonel Commander Hans Franz Schweitzer was arrested last week and kept in custody of officials. Schweitzer who served as high command over 2,000 prisoners at Camp Kassel from 1940-46 and possible deaths. Schweitzer, claims he is innocent and has not killed anyone. His trial will begin on Wednesday, August 26, 1947 at the courtroom in Berlin. Anyone who has any information to this, please meet at the courtroom on Wednesday, August 27, 1947 at 10:00AM. If Schweitzer is found guilty, immediate execution would be enforced.

Ren
foll
imp

The
that
rela
the
beh
of a
exp:
in li

Saving Hans

LIVING ON HURT

Hans had ordered that all the bodies be piled up. As he walked around them, his heart was torn apart by the sight. He saw over 100 bodies dead and many injured. Hans then called roll call the best he could. He had 16 of his officers and men left. The prisoners were gathering in their places. Hans stood there in pain and started to speak to them about his plan. Hans told them that several unexpected bombs had fallen upon the camp and caused great damage to buildings, killing many. Hans told them that the one supply shed was spared and their food was safe and not contaminated. Hans assigned several prisoners to get this food to his quarters where Sasha would be cooking. At the same time, Hans decided that the next day he would allow the prisoners to leave. As Hans left them with duties, he walked over to his office slowly, pleased that it was not damaged. As Hans walked in, his first action was to see if the phone was working. He reached for the phone and tried calling the Colonel. The phone was working, but no one answer. Hans tried all day but still no answer. Hans assumed that they had been attacked and perhaps dead. In the camp, there were around 150 prisoners left. All of Hans's major officers had been killed. Hans had Isaac come to his office for instructions. When Isaac came to Hans's office, Hans told Isaac to gather everyone again for roll call immediately, giving Hans some time to get to the shed and try to mount on his horse. The pain was unbearable, but Hans blocked it out of his mind because he had a major decision to make. In Hans's mind, he had no time for physical pain, only emotional. Hans rode over to the center of the camp which had not sustained damages. The prisoners were there waiting for his orders. They were all quiet and exhausted from their stay at this camp, and so was Hans. Hans gripped the reins of his horse and announced to the prisoners: "Today is a very sad day, not for only me, but for everyone. We all lost someone we cared for, but this does not mean that we will give up. This only means we are to get up from this loss and move on. The camp is totally destroyed. We have little food left. Possibly our water has been contaminated as I am told." Hans continued: "Being the Commander of this camp, I decide to open the main gate tomorrow releasing all of you in this camp who are prisoners. You will have freedom starting tomorrow and will be transported to the nearest refugee camp so you can be taken care of with food and shelter. I am not responsible after you leave here tomorrow. Those who are strong will move on but those who are weak in their bodies will be transported to a nearby hospital. God bless all of you."

As Hans started to ride away everyone stood there. Then Hans heard Isaac shouting to the prisoners to salute him. As Hans turned Zurich around, he saw every prisoner standing at attention saluting him. They were waiting for his command. Hans thanked them and directed them to carry on their duties until the next day. Hans was sobbing from what he had seen. Never had he experience a scene like this one. Hans never knew that prisoners would salute their Commander as his had just done. He then rode to the main gate and spoke to his guards. They have been hurt but not enough to keep them down. Hans was grateful for that. He told them that the next day the trucks would be leaving with the remaining prisoners and that he would have everyone's orders at that time. Hans went back to his quarters and waited for the next day to come. Perhaps God had a different plan in mind. Part of Hans's plan had begun to unfold and good would come out of it because still they could leave.

FAREWELL, MY FRIENDS

Hans arose early because he had to face another day of pain, and release all of his prisoners to the hurting world. He dressed in only his shirt, suspenders, trousers, and long coat and had a light breakfast. Hans kissed Sasha goodbye and prayed that they would all be safe that day. Otto came into Hans's home and asked whether Hans was ready. "Of course I am," Hans replied. They walked over to the area for roll call, and there Hans met the remaining prisoners. He told them that they would have a light breakfast and that the trucks would be ready in one hour to take them to their destination. Hans then called the supply Sergeant over to his area as he released the prisoners for breakfast. I had Sergeant Wolfe meet with me and asked him whether he was ready for his orders. He acknowledges that he was, and Hans told him to gather several men to help him transport the prisoners. Hans told him that he would be going to the refugee camp in Berlin dropping off those who are strong in body and taking the weak to the hospital. Wolfe was to leave as soon as Isaac had gathered all of the prisoners after breakfast. Sergeant Wolfe gathered enough men for the journey to Berlin, and had the trucks wait in the center of the camp. They had a convoy big enough to be noticed as they rode. Hans called back Sergeant Wolfe and told him to be very careful and to have his men ready for anything that might occur. "You are relieved from Camp Kassel, "Hans said sadly. He saluted Hans and continued his work. Breakfast finished, Isaac had those who were able to load the trucks. Those prisoners who were sick and weak were on stretchers. A good hour later, the trucks were ready and proceeded to the main gate. Everyone on the trucks waved goodbye to Hans as he stood, leaning on his crutches. Zurich stood behind him along with his men. Many of the guards had been hurt, and they wanted to leave the camp. After five years of being at the camp, they wanted to leave to search for their homes. Hans told the ones who were hurt to wait until the next day. Hans wanted the medic of the camp to attend the wounded and to make their beds in any of the blocks that were not damaged. The camp's supplies were down, as for bandages, medics used old shirts and whiskey to put on the guards wounds. The medics bandaged and cleaned everyone who was injured, and Sasha even helped. She knew the pain that Hans was facing as a Commander and a husband. Hans never thought a turn of events like this one. "In honesty," said Hans to himself, "I am tired of thinking and making plans. Tomorrow I shall release my men who I know will go home. Let them start a new life and the search for their homes that they left behind." Hans went over to his office to call the Colonel. Still he had no answer. Hans was sure that he was either gone or dead. Now Hans had to be the main one to make the decisions. He had nothing to fall back on because of this bombing. Hans felt that he had made the best possible decision that anyone could make. Hans had proved his bravery in this camp, and commanded it for almost five years. He had gone through the pain, sorrow, hate, good times, and bad ones. He had been there alone facing every challenge. Hans felt proud of himself and vowed never to regret this experience. He was relieved that the prisoners who were alive now had a chance of living and facing healing in their lives. Hans had given them that opportunity. "I am convinced that they will always remember me. Someday I may need them," Hans told himself.

FINAL RESTING PLACE

Hans returned to his quarters and he lay on his sofa; resting his weary body, and fighting every painful move that he made with his leg. As the pain overtook his body, Hans took pills to take that pain away. His leg was still injured, and now he had new wounds on his body. As Hans was resting, Sasha came in to see if he was all right. Hans was a pathetic sight and needed her attention to help him. Sasha helped Hans remove his jacket and boots. She noticed his right leg was swelling from being on it too long, so she took off the old bloody bandage and cleaned Hans's wound. She put on a fresh bandages and told Hans to get some rest because the coming day would be a big one. As Hans was closing his weary eyes, Otto came to his quarters asking for orders. Hans told him to make sure that his men who had died were buried in the nearby field behind the hospital, and to attend the wounded. "Make sure they eat and do what you have to do," Hans told Otto. "Also find Sergeant Heinz and tell him to bring all remaining trucks and transporters to the center of the camp ready to leave tomorrow." Otto left, and Hans didn't see him for the remaining night. Hans fell asleep and kept himself warm. He was now contented because he had Sasha by his side. He had to make sure she was not under stress because of the baby. Another challenging day had ended.

JOURNEY

Hans awoke, feeling refreshed and ready for this challenging at hand. He dressed in his uniform and went outside and saw that the trucks were started and ready to go. His men were waiting for their orders. Hans saw Sergeant Heinz and ordered him to gather the men on the trucks for transport to Berlin. Hans ordered any injured to go to the hospital. Now that everyone was on the trucks, all of Hans's men were anxiously ready to leave. Hans said good-bye to them and thanked them for all their years with him. They all had their papers with them bearing the code justifying their release. As the trucks started to leave, Hans saluted them as they saluted him. The camp was now a ghost town. Everyone was gone except for a few who were getting their cars ready to leave for my father's house. When Hans returned to his quarters, he found Otto and Fritz in the den while Peter was sitting back on the sofa with his head resting. The two cars were outside with a hitch for Zurich. Hans helped Sasha to the car. She was weak from so much work and excitement. Hans hoped that when this journey ended, that perhaps they could all get rest. Hans wasn't sure what to do next, but he went to his office so that he could try one more time calling the Colonel. As Hans dialed his number, he finally received someone whose voice was not familiar. Hans asked for the Colonel, but the voice said that he wasn't there. Hans identified himself and said that he needed to speak to an officer in charge. The speaker quickly put on Colonel Hausmann, who was acting Commander of the Headquarters. Hans explained what had happened at this camp, and said that the camp had no one to direct them with orders. Hans told Colonel Hausmann the complete story in which the Colonel told us to abandon the camp and leave. He told Hans to call as soon as he arrived at his destination. Hans thanked him and returned back to his quarters. He informed everyone that he had at last reached Berlin and that he was instructed to abandon the camp and leave. Hans also told them that he had to call headquarters for new orders once he reached his intended destination.

"ABANDON THE CAMP"

The date was December 13, 1944, three days before the original date that Colonel Heisenberg wanted to transport the prisoners. Just as they were ready to leave, Peter told Hans that he heard that Berlin was being bombed. Hans's heart broke. He thought of the prisoners and his men being transported to Berlin. Now Hans knew that he didn't need the Colonel to give him orders again. They effectively had no orders. They left with whatever they could carry, having to leave many things behind. Just as Hans's car left the front gate, he stared at what was left of the camp as memories lingered in his mind. Hans remembered his first day when he found Sasha to the end of this camp. He said good-bye silently to his memories. Except for a few remaining buildings, the entire camp was buried in rubble, and while everyone that was killed, was buried in the fields. Camp Kassel was no more. Leaving the camp was the easiest, but the hardest was finding life again. They had to look at the road ahead now, a journey of almost three hours before they would reach the house of Hans's father.

THE FARM

Hans and his group finally arrived at the farm. His father knew nothing about what had just happened to them. As the cars pulled up slowly to the door, where Hans's father came out; so did everyone else that they knew. Hans couldn't walk because his leg was badly swollen and he was in extreme pain without his medicine. Hans helped everyone including his wife to the door, and they all went inside. Hans's father asked whether he was all right. Hans told him about his injury that happened days before the bombs were dropped over the camp. Hans couldn't go on with any more stories, so he left the narrative until another day. Hans's father asked to see his leg. Then he had Mela and Elda get some antiseptic and bandages so he could clean out his wound. When Hans saw Mela and Elda, he was happy that they were safe, and didn't have to go through what he just experienced. Hans looked at Mela, and his heart jumped for joy to know that he would be seeing her every day. Mela smiled at Hans, and her eyes looked at him as though she wanted to say something. Hans just sat there while Sasha helped him to take off his jacket so he could rest. His father gave him some pills for the infection and pain. He told Hans to rest and try to stay off his leg. Hans was tired of this leg and needed to get himself going because he had new matters to attend. Hans told Peter and Otto to hide the vehicles in the barn and put Zurich in the shed. He then got the phone and called headquarters about our situation. He and his men were still enlisted men, and he did not want any of them to be called deserters. I had to find someone in charged, and we did, a few days later. Father had Sasha and Hans sleep in his old room. Everyone else was scattered throughout the entire house. That night Sasha helped Mela and Elda make dinner for this big crowd; Hans knew that Sasha would make her sweet bread. Some two hours later, Mela came over to Hans. Hans did notice that she had become much heavier and her stomach was protruding somewhat. He had a gut feeling that Mela was going to have a baby, his baby. Everyone then sat down to eat and had fun laughing and enjoying the food. Many had seconds of the chicken, salad, and corn. Sasha had made two loaves of her famous sweet bread, which everyone ate happily. As they sat around discussing their next adventure, Sasha leaned over to Hans and told him that Mela was pregnant. She also told him that he had the responsibility to speak to her and to help support his child. Sasha never said anything to Hans about it being a mistake, but he did. Hans was in pain that he had to speak to Mela, so he went into the kitchen and told her that he knew about her having his baby. When she started to cry, Hans told her that he was sorry what had happened and he assured her that he would be man enough to support both of them. Hans told her that Sasha knew and agreed for me to do this for the baby. Hans also mentioned to Mela that Sasha was having a baby too. Hans had to pay for his passion and now he must learn his lesson. Hans wasn't sure that it would be a lesson because silently he still loved Mela. Hans had promised to keep Mela as his friend and this obligation put a lot on his mind. Now Hans had to face his demons that stood before him.

BERLIN

Hans made several calls the next day, and this time he reached a Colonel Buchwaler. Hans told him that he was the commander in charge of Camp Kassel and that he had to abandon the camp under the order of Colonel Heinz. Hans explained to Colonel Buchwaler about the air raid. Buchwaler asked whether Hans's staff could come to Berlin. Hans told Buchwaler about his accident and his injury from the raid also. Buchwaler said that today in the afternoon would work with him to see Hans and his staff about their future orders. Han told him that they would leave immediately because they would be coming from Cologne and would need several hours to reach Berlin. Colonel Buchwaler said that he would see them later in the day. Hans gathered his men and asked Peter to get his Mercedes so that they could leave for Berlin. He told everyone to be fully dressed because they would be meeting with the Colonel. Hans had his full uniform on, including his boots, which Sasha had shined them for him. He asked his father whether he had any hair cream. Hans's father directed him to go into the cabinet just as he had done when Hans was younger. There Hans found a plentiful supply and still good to use in his hair. Hans slicked his hair back so that it would not fall in his face. He put on his side hat and long coat and then the groups left for Berlin. The ride always seemed as longest no matter how fast they went. The roads were filled with so much mud and water. Everywhere they saw German soldiers. Hans didn't care for the long ride as long as they arrived there safely. In less than five hours later, they pulled in front of the new headquarters because the original one had sustained severe damages. Peter knew about the building because he had picked up supplies there. Hans had not been in Berlin much and didn't realize how heavily Berlin had been bombed. When they arrived, several soldiers met them. Otto and Fritz were out first. Peter came to get Hans, who had a hard time getting out of the car because of his injury. The guard saluted Hans and the rest, all except Fritz. They walked up a pathway where the guards were protecting the inside, and Hans asked to see Colonel Buchwaler. The guards asked for their identification cards, which they produced faster than the guards thought possible. They then directed Hans and his men to the top floor where the Colonel was waiting. He shook our hands and saw that Hans had trouble walking. Hans told him about his accident and about his injuries from the bombs. Colonel Buchwaler also notice that his visitors all had burn marks on their faces and hands. He said that he felt bad that he did not have enough time to warn them about the raid. The Colonel looked at Hans and told him that he was temporarily released from any outside duty although he would still be enlisted as commander. Colonel Buchwaler wanted Hans's leg to heal, and he felt that an easy job would be good for Hans to do at this time. He told Hans that he had another assignment coming up as commander in Munich but that he would let Hans know later on more about it. He then wanted Hans and his men to report to him tomorrow at 7:00AM for work in the office. He explained that they would have no overnight work for any of us; it was strictly commuting, for now. Colonel Buchwaler also told them that they would be expected to wear full uniform to work and that Hans's temporary position would be Commander of Operations. Otto, Peter, and Fritz would be under his command. Colonel Buchwaler welcomed them aboard and gave them each a glass of brandy for celebration. He said goodbye until the next day and wished them a safe return to Cologne. Hans went down the steps slowly wishing that he could see a doctor for his knee because the pain had grown so intense. He walked as best he could. Hans knew that Berlin would be a great change for us, and he knew that his challenge wasn't finished. It was only beginning.

DISCUSSION

That night, Hans explained to Sasha about his job in Berlin and described his hours. She was pleased in what she was hearing. Hans also told her that he had enough money now and that eventually, if she wish, they could get their own place to live. I also noticed that Sasha was getting larger although she had only six months left. Hans was wondering when Mela became pregnant or at the same time that Sasha did. Hans did tell Sasha that He couldn't wait to see the baby born and hoped it would be a boy. Sasha asked him what happened if it's a girl? "Well, you will have to teach her to sew," she said. Hans laughed. Hans also told Sasha that he would teach his son to farm. Sasha rolled her eyes. That night, Hans and Sasha talked about everything from his pay to how many children they wanted. Hans told her that he would like only three, and she said five. "So we just wait to see how many we would have," said Sasha. Then Sasha told Hans about how Mela was becoming depressed because she had very little money to support her baby. I told Sasha that I would be supporting my child and that it was my responsibility to take care of both of them. Sasha also told me that she has been working with Mela during the day and that she talked with her. "Hans, I honestly think she might commit suicide if we do not help her. I feel you need to talk to her more, encourage her. I am sure you do not want Mela to end her life because you made a mistake." Sasha urged him. Hans thought for a minute and told Sasha that he would speak to Mela in the morning. Hans kept saying to himself, "It wasn't a mistake."

NEW ORDERS

Hans, Peter, Otto, and Fritz all woke up at around 3:30AM because their ride to Berlin. It would take nearly five hours. Hans showered and dressed and had breakfast. Hans kissed Sasha good-bye and the men left in Hans's car. Peter drove the car to Berlin; and when they arrived, they saw German soldiers marching into Berlin. Peter parked the car in front of the headquarters building, and Hans went upstairs with his men. This time, Colonel Buchwalter greeted them and took them to their office. The Colonel gave his orders, and Hans had a briefing to attend at 9:00AM. Hans had a strong feeling that this operation would be hard as he sat in his office reading his duties. Hans had to sign papers, and at 9:00AM, he met the Colonel and Major Heinrich in the briefing room. They served breakfast and told us that the war was losing many good men. They also told Hans that the war was going downhill and Germany was losing. Then they told Hans that his job was to control excess spending and to supply the weapons to all of the German forces. They prepared a paper that showed Hans how much money could be spent and what was needed. Hans's job as commander was back on track and ready to go, this time without a labor camp.

FRIENDSHIP

Meanwhile back in Cologne, Sasha and Mela had developed a close friendship. Sasha made lunch and dinner while Mela made the bread. They laughed together and talked about their Jewish roots and their babies to be born. Sasha helped Mela roll out the dough and cooked the chickens. The day was almost over, and soon Hans would be home from work. Sasha remembered how Hans used to come home for lunch while Mela remembered how Hans had saved her. "Hans was a knight in shiny armor on his horse dressed all in black and he saved me!" exclaimed Mela. Sasha told Mela how Hans and she had met. Then Sasha told Mela to sit down for a while because she found something upstairs. She brought Hans's picture downstairs and showed the picture to Mela. "This was his picture before we met," said Sasha." "Hans was only 19 years old and ever so handsome."

When Mela saw the picture, she told Sasha that Hans was a good looking man and that she should be proud of him. Sasha proudly put his picture away, and they both continued to cook and bake. Soon Sasha and Mela realized, they had become good friends and that forgiveness was their answer.

SPECIAL GIFT

Hans had to get up early to go to Berlin again. He and his men had to be there by 7:00 AM to start work. Hans had called a meeting today for 9:00 AM. He had to decide on the operations; and Peter, Otto, and Fritz had to attend. That day they worked only until 12:00 PM because Christmas would come in one day, and Hans had to stop in town to get something for Sasha. Hans finished up the meeting and work and left to go shopping in the Ghetto near headquarters. Hans also wanted to buy something for Mela and for everyone else. Hans, Otto, and Peter found an interesting store. The lights were beautiful in the windows, and Hans saw a beautiful music box in the window. Hans went in and asked the clerk if he could look at the music box. She took it out of the box for him, and wound it up so that it played a very beautiful German waltz. Hans agreed to buy the music box. The clerk asked whether he wanted it wrapped. Hans nodded, and she offered a beautiful blue and silver paper with a white bow. Hans continued to look around and was amused by a lamp that had an angel holding a small baby. Hans wanted to buy this lamp for Mela. He asked the clerk want to please wrap it up but in a different color. Hans's father was easy to shop for, and he saw a nice card to put money into it. Hans also picked up some cologne for the rest of the men and I was delighted that in a short time that he finished shopping. Everything was even wrapped. She gave Hans a discount because he was in the army and she wished him a "Merry Christmas." Hans then took Otto, Peter, and Fritz to lunch at the local tavern in which they had so much to eat and drink that they couldn't move. The men enjoyed lunch and then headed home for the holidays. Because they were exhausted from traveling and work. Hans couldn't wait to get home to put on regular clothes and rest. His leg was hurting because the healing was very slow, and he worried about a severe infection. Hans resolved to see a doctor as soon as Christmas had finished. The men traveled back home to Cologne, Hans wondered whether his father had the Christmas tree up as he usually did on Christmas Eve. Mother always had him put the tree up earlier in the day so she could sit and watch the lights twinkle for a bit longer. Hans was convinced that he had it up today now that he had everyone to help him. Just as the men reached home, it started to snow lightly. As they got out of the car and opened the door to the house, they saw the tree blinking and smelled warm apple pie. Music was playing, and everyone was sitting around talking and laughing. Sasha was sitting down with Mela and stopped talking as they saw Hans approach them. They asked about his day, Hans told them that they had a half a day and then went shopping and had lunch. The women were amused and continued to smile as Hans took off his wet coat and hung it up. Sasha stood up and said, "Well, my handsome husband, how about a kiss?" Hans took her in his arms and kissed her gently. He went upstairs to wash up for dinner but kept his uniform on for a while because once he changed clothes, he was often ready to go to sleep. Otto, Peter and Fritz had already changed while Hans sat there in his uniform. He had been so used to having it on at the camp that he felt as though the uniform was part of him. After dinner, Hans after excused himself from the table, undressed, and took a warm shower. He then sat on the bed thinking about so many things that he had to act on the next day. First, he had to go to the hospital for a check up on his leg because it has been paining him a lot. Then he needed to speak with Mela about his support for her and the baby. Hans knew that he had to do what he had to do instead of putting it off. Hans was also thinking about Christmas, about his presents, and about his father's house. It looked so quaint when he walked in seeing the tree lit and heard German Christmas music playing. He loved the fireplace on, and the crackling noises it made. He felt at home again for the first time in a long time. Hans lay there in bed for some time before he decided to go downstairs to see what was keeping Sasha from coming upstairs. Downstairs, he discovered everyone sitting and talking and looking very happy. Hans's father was in the kitchen telling Sasha and Mela about Hans when he was a young boy. Hans laughed and went back into the living room. The hour was late, so Hans decided that in the morning he would begin to build two cribs to give to Sasha and Mela for Christmas. Hans knew that his father had so much wood to use, so the material was already at hand.

THE CRIBS

Hans woke up very early so that he could go into the shed where his father had all of his tools and wood. Hans remembered that his father had built him a small boat when he was a little boy so he could put it into the river. Hans had play with it so much because his father built it for him and it was so colorful. Hans still had that boat safely in his room tucked away.

Hans drew a blueprint for the layout of the design and worked out the amount of wood that he needed to cut out for the cribs. Hans had to draw only one blueprint because the cribs would be identical to each other. After he built the cribs, Hans planned to put a shine on them so they would be ready for Christmas which was the next day. Hans knew that time was short and that he needed to work intensively and fast. After Hans drew the blueprint, he set it aside in order to follow it. By mid-morning, Hans had the wood all cut for both cribs and ready to put together. As Hans was putting the first part of the cribs together, he decided to go inside for some coffee and breakfast. He locked the shed because he did not want anyone in there until he had finished. Everyone else was already there having breakfast. Sasha asked Hans where he had been. He told her that he was in the shed doing work and that he had come in for coffee and pastries for breakfast. She told him that she had made some hotcakes and toast and that his breakfast was in the kitchen on the table. Sasha came in to greet Hans with a warm kiss, asked whether he was all right. Hans said, "Fine!" and continued to eat every bite off his plate. Then Sasha asked him what he was doing, he told her that she would know on Christmas Day. Sasha looked puzzled at Hans. Then she asked him whether he would be talking to Mela later that day, and he replied, "Yes, but only after I finish what I am doing." Sasha chuckled and said, "Hans, I really adore you and how you do things." She then kissed Hans on his head and returned to the living room to continue talking with the others. Hans finished his breakfast, took his cigarettes and went back to the shed. He enjoyed so much building those cribs because it reminded him of how he had helped his father build barns around Cologne and parts of Germany. Although he was young, he surely had learned the skill. "Now I am using the skill for my family," he exclaimed. Hans was amazed at what he had learned from his father. Hans continued with his work, first fastening the wood together with the screws and then finishing the entire frame on both of them. Next, he put the shine on them. He noticed that they were so cute and small. "The best thing is that Sasha and Mela would be able to rock the crib back and forth," Hans exclaimed out loud. He felt pleased with his work. Hans wanted to go into town today knowing it is Christmas Eve as soon as he finished with the shiner to buy some blankets for the cribs. This painting would not take long even though Hans painted each grain of wood to perfection. Finally, he had finished both cribs. The job had taken him five hours to complete. Hans put the cribs on the side to dry, and locked the shed, and went inside to get his jacket. Hans grabbed his long coat because he had no other coat. He kissed Sasha and told her that he had some shopping to do for Christmas and went to get the car. Hans had to warm up the car because the weather had turned cold outside. As he was leaving, it started to snow lightly, so he drove very slowly until he reached town. Hans parked the car in an area where no one was and he got out slowly because of his leg. He walked around to look for a shop that sold baby blankets and surely he found a youth store. Hans went in as quickly as he could and he asked the clerk for four baby blankets. She asked whether he wanted a bigger one or a small size. Hans told her to give him two sets of both sizes in yellow because he was not sure whether the babies would be a boy or girl. Hans looked around and saw a lot of baby clothes displayed. He asked the clerk whether she had anything for newborn babies, a neutral color. She pointed to sleepers and said that babies mostly wore this garment when they were born. Hans asked for five of each in the same color as the blankets. The clerk asked me whether these items were gifts or whether they would be used immediately. Hans told her that he wanted them for his wife and a friend for Christmas. The clerk smiled and wrapped every gift for him. Hans paid the clerk for the blankets and clothes and gave her some extra money for being so nice to him. As he was paying her, the clerk asked Hans whether he was in the army. He told her that he was Commander in the Army. She was quite impressed and said that she knew that fact because of his coat. Hans had forgotten that he had it on and thanked her for everything. The clerk smiled and said, "Merry Christmas." Hans replied, "Merry Christmas to you also." Hans then went over to several other stores just buying what he could from cards to socks. He was so overloaded with bags that he decided to go home and get ready for Christmas Eve. Hans felt so happy and excited for his life that he started to sing, "Alle Jahre Weier Kommt das Christusking," {Every Year the Christ Child Comes Again.} and smiled all the way home. He felt so blessed for his life that God had given him, although he had made so many mistakes. Hans believed that the little baby who was born on Christmas Day saved him from destruction. Hans silently thanked Him.

CHRISTMAS EVE

Hans came home with so many packages that he needed help getting into the house. Sasha met him at the door. Her face was glowing from the reflection of the Christmas lights, and she asked Hans whether he needed help. Hans said that he could use an extra hand to help him out, so Sasha carried some of the bags and put them on the sofa. Hans asked her to stay away from them because they were gifts that he needed to put under the tree. She laughed as she sat down next to Mela and Elda. The women were all looking at Hans and laughing, who just shook his head at them. Hans took the gifts out of the bags. He left the blankets inside so that he could go into the shed and put them into the cribs. As Hans got down on his knee, he was fighting the intense pain in his leg. His hair was falling into his eyes, he heard Sasha saying, "Isn't he handsome girls?" Hans quickly grabbed the bag and said that he was going out to the shed again to finish his work. Hans looked at them still laughing, pushed back his hair and left. Hans opened the shed again and examined the cribs. Because of the coolness of the air, they had completely dried. This was his chance to put the blankets into the crib. He put a small blanket down in each crib and then hung the larger one down slightly. The cribs looked beautiful. Hans stood back and admired his work as a carpenter. God only knew how he wanted to give the cribs to Sasha and Mela right now, but it wasn't Christmas. So he had to wait for the next day. Actually Hans was thrilled to wait because he knew that they would be so happy with their gifts. Hans sat in the chair that his father had sat in when he became tired while building. He took a cigarette out and just sat there thinking about everything.

He knew that he had to speak with Mela, and he had to decide when that would be. Knowing his feelings for her, Hans kept it a secret from Sasha although he felt that Sasha knew his feelings for Mela. Hans knew that these feelings were wrong, but he also knew that sometimes life could be strange and that fighting those feelings was hard. Hans wanted to be her good friend and always be there for her. Yet he was deeply devoted to Mela because of what happened, and he couldn't walk away leaving her in this situation that he had put her through. Hans felt that Christmas Eve was the beginning for him, that everything would become new and old things would pass away. According to Christianity, forgiveness would be offered to all who accept its terms, and Hans wanted to be part of that plan. Hans thanked God for everything: his life, the plans he had made, his understanding to his position as commander. Without my position as commander, Hans would have never met Sasha or Mela, nor would he have had the chance of releasing the prisoners from death. Hans realized again that Christmas is not about food and family or about presents, but about that Baby who was lying in a manger. Hans was thankful that God had given him the wisdom to build those cribs for the babies. "I know He has a plan for me," Hans said aloud. On this holy day he decided to follow God to the very end. "Christmas came early for me today," said Hans. "I am grateful for everything I have, even the mistakes I have made," Hans cried out to God. Without mistakes Hans wouldn't need Him to help him learn. Hans vowed that he would trust God so that he could learn and pass along the wisdom on to others. "I will let them know that it is all right to make a mistake because we are forgiven," Hans prayed. "On this day I thank You." Hans went inside to prepare his gifts and to be with his friends and family. He knew that his heart was already prepared for the unexpected knowing that this Christmas would be special. Indeed Christmas Eve was already special and one of the best that Hans had ever had.

CHRISTMAS DAY

Hans went to bed late after enjoying their Christmas Eve dinner and gathering. When Hans awoke on Christmas morning and saw the falling snow, he had a wonderful feeling inside. He quickly put on his coat to go to the shed to see Zurich and to bring in the two cribs and put them under the tree. He needed to be quiet so no one would see him. When he went into the shed, Hans found Zurich warm but he put an extra blanket on the horse and turned on the small heater for him. Hans grabbed the two cribs and went back into the house to put them under the tree with the rest of the presents. He also turned on the lights and started the fireplace for warmth. He wanted everyone to be surprised when they woke up. Hans was looking at the tree when the telephone rang. It was the Colonel who wanted to wish Hans a "Merry Christmas" and tell him that he and his men were to report to work on January 2. Hans was delighted, but detected that something was wrong with his voice. Hans returned the Christmas greeting and wished the Colonel a joyful New Year. Hans wasn't worried about the call and just took it for granted that it was the holiday that slowed the work down. The week off before he had to report for duties gives Hans enough time to go to a doctor. As Hans went to the kitchen to make some coffee, he heard footsteps coming down the steps. He quickly put the pot of water on the stove for tea and cocoa and went into the living room to see who had come down. There he saw his father, Sasha, and Mela. They were amazed to see the tree and to hear German holiday music playing. The fireplace was crackling, and their faces were surprised. They just didn't know what to say to Hans. He looked at them happily and told them to find their gifts with their names on the packages. He went over to the tree and gave both Sasha and Mela their cribs. They both broke down in tears, unable speak a word to Hans at that moment. Sasha and Mela asked him whether he had made these cribs. "Yes," laughed Hans, "that's the reason that I was in the shed." Sasha and Mela told him over and over how beautiful the cribs were and marveled that the blankets were so soft and cuddly. Hans made a joke and told them, "All we need now is the babies." They both laughed, and wiped their tears, and sat down. Hans wanted everyone as they came down to take their gifts and cards from under the tree. Everyone looked so amazed and surprised. Hans told them it was better to give then to receive. Hans also told them that he had received his gift from God and nothing else is needed. They quickly went to the tree and helped one another find their gifts and cards. They opened their envelopes to find money in them, and Hans's heart was delighted to see them so happy, so they tore open the wrappings. Surrounded by traces of paper and bows they all looked at Hans and thanked him profusely. Sasha, grabbed Hans gave him a big kiss. "Thank you for the best Christmas I have ever had," she said. Mela gently kissed him on his cheek and thanked him for everything. She looked at Hans as though she wanted to tell him more but couldn't. Hans felt for her and knew that he needed to speak to her soon. Sasha came back to Hans to thank me him for the music box. She adored it and she was actually crying because she loved the music box and because it played the music that her mother had liked. "German Waltz." Hans was stunned because he felt her pain. He reached for her and tried to hug her sorrow away. Sasha knew that Hans was a good husband although like everyone else, we make mistakes. This was the best Christmas even though she was Jewish and a delightful one. Sasha was grateful to God that Hans had saved her and everyone else from death. She forgave him for the sin he committed with Mela, but asked him to take care of his mistakes with forgiveness. Again, Hans said to himself, "It was not a mistake." In her excitement to open her gifts, Sasha had not opened her card. It was a card that Hans had put money into for her needs. As she opened the card it read, "Merry Christmas, my love, I love you, Hans." She put her arms around Hans and said thank you so many times. Everyone else followed again thanking him for everything. Hans then asked Rabbi Jacob to say a prayer asking Hymen and everyone else to join. It was beautiful just to be grateful that we were all alive together as family and friends. Hans felt that everyone had a lot to look forward to in the New Year, and they were just going to celebrate on that special day. Everyone then sat down to a huge breakfast with eggs, sausage, toast, and bacon and of course, love. They talked, laughed, and spoke about their days at the camp. They were thankful that the camp was gone forever, but they knew that the memories would always be there. Hans often thought of his prisoners and how they are doing at the refugee camp in Berlin. He wished them a "Merry Christmas" too. Hans thanked the Lord for a wonderful Christmas, for forgiveness, and for a Child that was born on this day. As everyone prayed, they were all locked in silence. After the "Amen" Hans saw that nearly everyone had tears in their eyes, and they wished each other a "Merry Christmas and a Happy New Year."

A SURPRISE CHRISTMAS DINNER

Everyone was singing and laughing and feeling the warmth of the fireplace. Sasha and Mela were putting the pies into the oven, making the filling for the chickens, and then stuffing them. They were also preparing fresh mashed potatoes, string beans, dumplings, red cabbage, pies, cakes, cookies, and plenty of brandy. We had so much to eat and share with anyone who was hungry. Both Mela and Sasha were wonderful cooks and the smell of the food filled the entire home. When dinner was ready the table prepared, everyone gathered at the table for grace and to eat. Hans invited Rabbi Jacob to ask God for blessings over their food. The entire house fell into silence. "Dear Lord, thank you for everything that you have given to all of us this day. Thank you for saving us from death and blessings upon my friends. Thank you Lord," he prayed. Everyone sat down and happily passed the plates. Before long, they had very little room in their stomachs to put any more food. They would wait until they had room for desserts. Suddenly, they heard a knock at our door. Hans asked his father whether he was expecting anyone for Christmas and he said not really. Hans went to answer the door and saw three prisoners: two women and one child. Hans knew already that they were from his camp because of the uniform and the patches on the side, and they knew of no other camps nearby. Hans asked them in, and called everyone for assistance because the newcomers were wet from the snow. "But how did they make it this far?" Hans asked himself. He asked them no questions; he just helped them by putting them on the sofa and giving them something to drink and making sure that they were near the fireplace so they could be warm. Hans asked

Mela to get him some more blankets for them, as Sasha and Mela went to retrieve some blankets. The visitors were clearly physically tired, so Hans cleared a place to let them rest. The two women were lying on the sofa, and for the child was lying on a warm bed on the floor near the fireplace. When they were ready to eat, Hans would feed them. Everyone else went back to eating. As Hans sat there, he tried to remember whether he knew any of the visitors. No one seemed to know them, either. Peter reminded Hans that the camp had over 200 prisoners and to remember all of them was impossible. But then Mela looked at the women again. Suddenly, she said that she recognized these two women from her block but had never spoken to them. Hans figured that they had been hiding somewhere; and as they were traveling, they saw Hans's house with the smoke coming out of the chimney. Hans felt bad for them and saw his chance again, to help them. Hans then told everyone that the three visitors represented the Three Kings who came to Bethlehem bearing gifts. What gifts did they bring?

MAY I PLEASE?

Hans, his family, and friends finished their dinner, cleaned the dishes and the table, although they left some food covered in wrap if someone would feel hungry. Everyone was happy and felt blessed for everything that they had. Now they had three former prisoners who had found them by the grace of God. They waited for their visitors to get up so that they could eat. The wait was long because the prisoners in their exhaustion actually slept for hours and being warm by the fireplace. Hans stayed by them hoping they would be all right. At almost 6:00PM in the evening, the visitors started to wake up. The child was waking up with the two women. Hans looked at them carefully trying to see whether he could recognized any of them. However, they knew who Hans was and recognized him as Commander Hans of Camp Kassel. He could not deny that allegation. Hans asked them whether they had been hiding in the woods, and they told him they were. Hans told them that a lot of their fellow prisoners were sent to the refugee camps in Berlin and asked why they had not gone to Berlin, too. Olga told Hans that they had been missed, and they had not boarded the truck to Berlin. Hans was distraught, and he asked Sasha and Mela to escort the visitors upstairs to shower and to put on clean clothes. Hans had a lot of extra food and invited them to eat as much as they wanted. These women looked at Hans with question in their eyes: why was he helping Jews? Hans told them he was different even when he joined Hitler's Youth and that he had remained that way even when he became commander. They nodded their head and went with Sasha and Mela. Hans told them to bring down their prisoner uniforms so that he could bury them. The visitors returned in about an hour, and Hans had them at the table with a huge plate of food. He remembered that the one woman told Sasha her name was Olga, but Hans did not hear the other names. The women told Hans that their names were Natasha, Olga, and Miriam: Hans felt odd because he had not known them. Natasha looked at Hans and asked, "May I please have something to eat?" Hans gave her plenty, and she ate so much food which gave her no room to speak to us. Hans saw the visit of these three prisoners as a gift, and he found their visit was special on the celebration of the birth of Jesus. The women asked whether Sasha had been raped in the prison because she was having a baby. Hans replied, "No, Sasha is my wife." They were quite surprised at the news because they knew that she was a Jew, and Hans was obviously a German officer. Hans tried his best to avoid the conversation and asked them whether they would like some dessert. They ate so much that when they lay down again, they quickly fell asleep. As they slept, he looked at them with grief as he saw their drawn out faces, and their skin so pale,their feet full of blisters, and their hair left in kerchiefs. Hans felt overwhelmed by this event today, and he looked at these visitors with so much compassion in his heart. He only wished that this damned war was over. Hans was still a commander, and he had to wear his full uniform, and he knew that the worst part was having to live through the aftermath of the war. He knew what he had done for his prisoners, and he had set them free so they would have a reason and a purpose for living. Hans could only thank God that he had never been assigned to any of the death camps, because he would surely have been dead for resisting his superiors' orders. Hans felt he knew that God had sent the three visitors his way for a reason. To himself, Hans said, "I pray on this Christmas Day that God is pleased with me. I am grateful that these women and child are now safe, and that I shall have a chance to nurse them back to health. Thank you, Lord, for all you did for us today."

BURY THE PAST

Sasha gave Hans the clothes that the three prisoners had worn and he buried the past that almost had taken nearly everyone who was here. He buried them deep into the ground. Now the visitors could live safety and be even more free when the war ends. "Perhaps I can get them into a refugee camp where they will be safe and have food," thought Hans. Hans felt so sorry for all the ones who died. The German world did not know that someone like me objected to Nazi atrocities and helped the helpless prisoners. Hans felt like a piece of dust floating in the air waiting to land. He guessed that the future would probably tell a horrible story about the Germans in the war, and yet no one had seemed to discover anyone who truly had helped the prisoners. "How about Otto, Peter and Fritz, don't they count?" Hans wondered. He felt that the right motives might never be recognized, but only the ones that caused harm. "Any war in any place has good and bad people in it, and just because someone is in the army does not mean that person agrees with all of the high officials. Hans surely didn't. "Yet I will be despised and hated by many just because I am a German," thought Hans. He wondered whether it mattered if he had been another Dutch, Italian, or even an American? "So many of us risked our lives to help the prisoners; so many of us lost our lives and were executed. Many of us never helped the prisoners in front of anybody, yet we can write a story telling others that we have kept this a secret for so many years." Hans continued to reflect: "Yes, we bury the past vowing never to talk about it again and when we do, we will forgive. What is the use of forgetting if we cannot forgive one another? Forgive first, then forget; and if we have to remember, let us forgive and then remember because it will hurt less. Memories will be there, but they will be looked at in a much different way. I, rather, be free; and someday I shall fly as high as an eagle because I have forgiven all."

NEW YEAR'S EVE

Hans, his family, and friends were planning a small party. Hans wanted to celebrate with a new beginning and to put the past behind him. The party as we planned would be a dinner and celebration and probably a few kisses with Sasha and whatever else comes about. Hans needed to speak to Peter about Mela, for he had noticed that those two have been spending time together and laughing so much. Hans finally saw the chance to speak with Peter alone to ask him about Mela. Hans asked Peter whether if he liked Mela as a friend or someone he wanted to date. Peter looked at Hans and asked whether Hans was somewhat jealous. Hans told Peter that was foolish for implying such an idea. Peter admitted that he did like Mela and that he was thinking of asking her out for a date. However, Mela was getting larger and noticeable, and Hans asked, "Does that really matter?" Peter said, "Yes because the baby was not his." Hans knew what he was referring to and that the answer was pointing to him. Hans told Peter to go ahead and ask her out. Hans also suggested that because they were all friends, that he would still support the baby each month. Hans was not sure whether Peter agreed with this motive of his. Peter said, "No thank you," to the offer." Hans then felt bad about his idea. Hans forgave Peter for his bitterness toward him and told Peter that he was sorry. Hans wished Peter the best with Mela, then walked away knowing how he truly felt in his heart about Mela, a feeling which he would admit to no one. Hans went into his den alone and sat there thinking of the past, even missing those days at his quarters. When he felt upset he would always go to his den, pour out a glass of brandy, and think. Here, his father's den was almost the same except having a door that he could close. Hans closed that door, pushing out the present and allowing his past to stay with him. He found his mind shifting to the memories of the camp where he rode his horse doing inspections, and spent the day at his office with Mela. Hans really didn't know how long he had been sitting in that chair. He remembered later that he had drunk half a liter of brandy and smoked an almost filled pack of cigarettes. Hans felt such a dramatic change in himself as he was feeling for his past, his everyday life. Now, Hans felt that he had very little here, and began to wonder whether happiness is truly his friend? "I can only say that time will tell me," Hans told himself. He wondered whether if Sasha and he would live their own or whether they would suffer a change. Hans asked himself: "Would my memories interfere with us as a couple or strengthen us? I wasn't sure if these memories would die or would I still regret to the things I should have done?" Hans got up and and went outside for a while for a breath of air, then he went to see his horse, Zurich. Hans saddled up and decided to take him out for a ride. As Hans mounted the horse, he noticed that his leg had not healed properly because it ached within the muscle. Still, he rode Zurich, and he felt happy that the snow had stopped. Hans rode down the soft smooth snow and made his own path as we rode slowly. The path was deserted. It was cold outside and I really didn't want to put Zurich through too much of this cold snow. Hans returned Zurich to his shed, covered him up, and made sure the heater was on. Hans took his car out and decided to take a ride to the camp that he had remembered so well. Noticing that he still had the two small Nazi flags in the front of the car, he took them down. Hans wanted to live for something that perhaps he had left there. Soon he hoped to find what he have been looking for. "It may not be now, but later on I will find it," Hans reassured himself.

CONFUSED, MY LOVE

Sasha wondered where Hans was going yet "He never told me that he was leaving," she said as she told Hans's father about his leaving. Hans's father said, "Don't worry; just trust him." Sasha remembered that when she had trusted Hans before, he seemed to fail her, and left her wondering about their future. Meanwhile, Mela and Sasha prepared dinner and made sure that it would be ready in a few hours, perhaps when Hans returns. Sasha had made potato salad, and cheese dip with plenty of ham sandwiches. Sasha didn't have the strength that she wanted to have because the time to deliver was coming closer. Sasha was now into her fourth month, and she began to feel the baby kicking inside. Sasha wanted Hans to feel the first kick, but she was sure that there would be more kicks for him to feel. Sasha noticed that Mela was getting larger herself, so Sasha helped her when she had the chance. Mela did the same for Sasha. Sasha was grateful to Mela no matter what might still be between her and Hans. Sasha sat down for a while. She had an intuition that Hans had gone to the camp. She told Peter and Otto where Hans might have gone. They assured her that he would be fine and urged her not to worry. Sasha wiped her tears away and continued with her work. She knew that Hans did things for a reason, and "I must trust his wisdom, I must," Sasha emphasized to herself.

JOURNEY TO THE PAST

Hans was going fast mainly because the road was deserted and no one was around, except the ghosts of his past. He came to where the main gate had once stood, and there stood the sign "Halt" in front of him. Hans passed the sign and drove to the right of the camp where the snow had covered some of the burned-down buildings. His quarters were still there. Memories attacked his mind as he fell into the past and stayed there without any regrets. His office was there just as before. At that moment, Hans did not care whether they were still standing or burned. Hans located the spot where he had hurt his knee. The barrel was still there where he had hidden when the bombs were going off. Hans drove around noticing that the majority of the blocks where his prisoners had lived were still standing although some had been burned from the bomb attack. Hans got out of the car and walked around, remembering how he had once stood in this one area and how he had saved Mela. He could still see the guard beating her and himself sitting on Zurich scolding at the guard to stop beating her. Hans walked into the first block, and there stood all of the bunk beds still filled with hay as though the prisoners were still sleeping on them. The blankets were pulled back just as the prisoners had left them to gather outside for their final roll call. Hans wiped his tears as they filled his eyes. He took off his glasses. Hans's hair began to blow into his eyes as the wind was howling and picking up a faster speed. Hans returned to the car; but as he rode away, he looked back in the mirror to say good-bye again, however, in his heart he knew that he would return again. Hans believed that he had left some of his ghosts behind on that visit but that his pain, his memories and his feelings for Mela would always be there. It was now past 6:00. Hans knew that everyone would wonder where he had decided to go. “They forget one thing,” Hans told himself. “I may be a husband, a friend, and a son; but I am the Commander of Operations in Berlin now, and I respect my position, no matter what.

RETURN

Hans finally returned to his father's house at around 7:30 PM. It was dark outside and cold because fresh snow had fallen while Hans was at the camp. It made it harder to get the car into the shed and I had to maneuver slowly into the small space. Hans closed the door behind him and went inside the house. Sasha ran up to Hans asking whether he was all right. Hans looked at her more closely and noticed that she has been crying. Hans told Sasha he was fine and that he had gone for a ride to the camp. Sasha looked at Hans with a puzzled look and said nothing to him about his drive. The subject was dropped, and everyone sat down to eat dinner. After the meal, Hans poured some brandy and sat back down in the den. He turned the radio on, and there he heard the most upsetting news: that the Russians were closing in on Germany. Hans knew that the war was almost over after hearing that distressing news. He turned the radio off, went upstairs, took a warm shower, and sat on the bed. Sasha came up with shortness of breath saying the steps were getting harder for her to climb. When Hans told her that he would carry her down, she laughed. Sasha asked again whether he was all right. Hans told Sasha that he was fine but was not used to this kind of life. Hans told Sasha that he just wanted to go out and do things, but here he could do nothing. Sasha suggested moving somewhere else but Hans told her it would be the same for him. Hans felt that he was missing something in his life, but he was not sure at this time what it was. However, Sasha knew but said nothing about what it was. Hans told Sasha that he felt lost and that he felt useless there. Sasha knew exactly now what Hans was talking about. Hans looked at her asking, "What am I going to do with myself?" Sasha embraced Hans and kissed him and said, "Hans it is all right to dream and to want the past back, but it is better that we move forward." Sasha felt as though Hans was disappointed in himself that he had married her. Sasha felt that this fact was causing Hans's unhappiness. Hans told Sasha that he was used to being a commander where he gave orders hour after hour, day after day, and now there was nothing to do for him. Sasha told him that the war would be ending soon and that he should accustom himself to a slower pace. Hans agreed with Sasha and dropped the subject. He didn't want to go over it anymore. Hans kissed Sasha goodnight because they had to be up early for work. Hans hoped that his uniform would be clean and pressed and that his boots were polished, they were.

BAD NEWS AND GOOD NEWS

Hans and his men left at 4:30 AM so that they could get to headquarters on time. When they arrived, Hans, Otto, and Fritz got out of the car while Peter parked the car in the back. Otto, Fritz and I went upstairs to Hans's office and were greeted by Colonel Buchwalter, who he said that he needed to see Hans immediately. Hans told the others that to continue on the papers that they were working on before the holidays. Colonel Buchwalter took Hans into a conference room and told him to sit down and enjoy a cup of tea. The Colonel told Hans that Germany was losing the war and he was upset because Germany were so close to winning. However, now the Russians and British were closing in, and many Germans were being taken as prisoners. He wasn't sure when this would happen but he did say very soon. "We have decided to destroy all of our operation paperwork today leaving nothing behind," said the Colonel. Hans looked at him and said to himself, "This is a repeat in what I have already gone through in the camp." The Colonel reminded Hans that he already knew that everything must be destroyed leaving absolutely nothing behind. Colonel Buchwalter told Hans to gather men and have them destroy the papers that are in boxes and anywhere else. Hans assured the Colonel that everything would be done within that day. The Colonel also told Hans that Hitler was asking for more people to enlist. "We are losing good men through death as well as prisoners and deserters, but we will fight to the very end," Colonel Buchwalter said. He also told Hans that the war would not be ended by Hitler, and that all of our German officers, were now being used at the front-line. "We are useless here because the bombs will fall again and again on us, and we need to close down our operations as soon as possible." The Colonel continued this conversation as Hans took another sip of his tea. The Colonel lit a cigar. "You see, Hans, we could have won the war earlier, but Hitler wanted to conquer the entire world with all of our men. Hitler built up Germany and took us out of poverty, planned war, and destroyed us again. We will need years to rebuild and what do we have left? We have defended Germany for over five years and how can we defend a country that is destroyed?" said the Colonel to Hans. The Colonel paused and then asked, "Are we supposed to defend the bricks that hold up the broken down buildings?" The meeting ended, and Hans understood what the Colonel wanted. The Colonel told Hans that after he and the men had destroyed the papers in both offices, then they would leave. "As of today," said the Colonel, "I release all of you; for as far as the war goes, you have fulfilled your duties." He then handed out their paperwork signed by him and also Hans's. The Colonel told me that my job as Commander was finished for now. Hans looked at him not knowing whether to cry or laugh. Hans asked the Colonel about their pay. The Colonel said that they would receive a severance pay each month at the rank from which they left. He also said that "Reserves" was a hidden building and would continue to operate. Hans saluted the Colonel and wished him the best. The Colonel returned the salute and said that he would be in touch if needed. The Colonel then concluded with a "Godspeed."

DESTROY AND LEAVE

After Hans, Otto, Fritz, and Peter had destroyed all of the paperwork, Hans told everyone that they are released from their duty, effective immediately. They could go home, but Hans wondered how they could and what about the other soldiers? Most of them did not even know whether they still had a home or family left? Hans felt sorry that they had to go, but they needed to leave because the trucks were outside ready to take them away from this location. They saluted Hans for the last time in this war. Everything in the building was shortly abandoned, and everyone left for home. Hans held his head down for a while, because he had never thought that such a situation would actually happen. Hans asked himself, "Where is the pureness of our country now?" Hans asked Peter to drive to the refugee camp to see the prisoners who had been under Hans's command. Hans was looking for one particular prisoner, but never said who. They drove past so many destroyed buildings and smoke and a few soldiers on the street. A huge tent appeared connected to a building. Hans decided to get out of the car. Hans saw very few people and asked a guard about the refugees who were here and where they gone. He told Hans that they were moved to a safer area in the mountains. He wasn't sure where but assured Hans that they were safe. Hans asked the guard who was in charged, and he told Hans that no one for now. Hans thanked the guard and told him to carry on what he was doing. Hans pulled the blood stained flags off his car, and got back into his car, and went home. There we left our memories all behind ready for a new life and my question was "What new life?" "Who could have a new life when we have to get used to the world again?" Hans asked. "Where is that life?"

WAITING FOR THE WORD

Peter, Fritz, Otto, and Hans left Berlin only to be home within two hours because the roads were deserted, and more snow was falling. Hans went inside the house to tell Sasha about the news. Hans wasn't sure whether it was true or not. Hans had a gut feeling that this was not over for him as yet not with a high rank as his. I told Sasha that I was waiting, and she agreed with me. She said that she would miss him in his uniform and she would always remember him the way that he had looked when she first met him in the Ghetto when he was so much younger and innocent. Hans was now 24 years old. He had learned a lot in his life and still learning for the best. Sasha admitted that she had pictures of him when they had first met all the way down to his last day at the camp. She even had a picture of Hans on Zurich. Hans told Sasha how proud he was of himself for what he had accomplished. Hans sat down with his father to tell him that Germany was much closer to an invasion from Russia and that they needed to listen to the radio. Then Hans went upstairs to put on his regular clothes and came down to eat lunch. Peter and Otto did the same; and as they were eating and remembering their days as good friend, Hans told them that half of him wanted the war to end while his other half wanted it to continue. Hans believed that he was afraid of being here wondering what will happen to his country. He could do nothing now but wait for the word to come, if any.

WAITING IS OVER

Hans, Peter, Otto, and Fritz continued with their work at home including painting and cleaning up the basement. After one week had gone by, Hans received a call from Colonel Buchwalter asking him to return to duty in Munich as soon as possible. The Colonel told Hans that his new assignment would be as the Company Commander of the 3rd Division of Infantry. The previous Commander had to transfer to another assignment because the army was now short of officers. Hans would be in the unit that was protecting Munich from any disaster including bomb raids and anything else. Hans asked the Colonel how long he would hold this position, and whether he could come home at all. Colonel Buchwalter said, "Sure, when the war is over." He then directed Hans to meet him at the same small building that Hans had gone to a few weeks before in Berlin to pick up his orders. Hans promised Colonel Buchwalter that he would be there the next day. This new assignment meant that Hans would be the Commanding officer assigning all of the soldiers their duties and leading them to fight. The job could last weeks or even months, whichever came first. Hans went upstairs and told Sasha and everyone else in the house that he had to leave for Berlin to pick up his orders in the morning. He also told them that he is assigned as Company Commander for the 3rd Division of Infantry in Munich. Hans knew everyone had been released from their duty unless they would be called again as he was.

NEW ORDERS

Peter drove Hans to Berlin so that he could pick up his paperwork. Hans went into headquarters and saw Colonel Buchwalter again. The Colonel told Hans that he could not go home for a while and that he would be living in a tent for officers. The Colonel told Hans that he had five remaining officers and that he would be commanding the men. Colonel Buchwalter also instructed Hans to keep his car at home and that he would be sending someone the next day at 5:00 AM to pick him up. The Colonel also told Hans to take all of his uniforms and anything else that he might need, and wished him the best of luck. Colonel Buchwalter shook hands and Hans left for home again.

Finally at home, Hans told everyone that he would be leaving the next morning for active duty as Commanding officer in Munich. He also told them that he would not be home until this war ended. Sasha was upset and crying, and so was everyone else. Mela, on the other hand, was upset but wiped her eyes dry. Hans told Mela that he wanted to speak with her alone before he left. Hans took Mela into one of the rooms where they could not be disturbed. He looked at her, and she begged him with her eyes not to leave her. Hans told her that he needed her to take care of Sasha for him. He reminded her that when his baby was born, he had promised to support her. She looked at me and asked me, "Do you love me Hans?" I looked at her and didn't hesitate to answer. "Yes," he said to Mela. She then told him to kiss her before he left for Munich. Hans held her as his tears silently fell. Mela looked at Hans and said to remember, "I am Truthfully, Yours." Then he told her that he had to pack. Hans left Mela in the room where they had been together that night he had visited. This parting made his new orders difficult. Hans packed and went to sleep as soon as he had finished.

ARRIVAL AT MUNICH

The alarm rang at 3:30 AM. Hans got up and took a shower and got dressed. He put on his clean and pressed uniform and his leather issued coat and went downstairs for a light breakfast. Shortly after 4:00 PM, Sasha came downstairs. Hans told her to go back to bed, but she was upset about his leaving. Hans told her that he would be fine and not to worry. In truth, Hans wasn't sure when he would be home again to see anyone, but he had to serve his country. Sasha looked at him through her tears and as he finished his breakfast. Then came a knock at the door. The driver was at the front door and asked whether Hans was ready. Hans told him that he was. The driver took Hans's suitcase and saluted Hans when he got into the car. Hans waved goodbye to Sasha and told her that he loved her and would write. Hans truly loved Sasha, in his own way. The car sped away in the cold. Hans knew that he had this position and had to follow the orders that was given to him. When they arrived in Munich, four hours later, Hans noticed there were several buildings still standing. One with a tent connected. Three officers met Hans and immediately saluted him, then shook his cold hand, welcoming him to the 3rd Division of Infantry. These officers showed Hans his quarters in a tent but fairly decent with a heater and desk. They asked him whether he wanted some fresh coffee to drink before he began his work, Hans accepted gratefully. Hans sat down while the officers briefed him about what was happening. They told Hans that they were bringing more reinforcements and weapons for support. Another Panzer was ordered and would be arriving sometime that day, making the unit ready for battle. Hans learned that his unit would have several hundred men as back up. Hans knew that they must plan this attack carefully. Hans then suggested a meeting as soon as possible with all of his officers and later a briefing for the soldiers. Everyone agreed. Hans put all his belongings near his bed and called for a meeting with his officers. The soldiers were already busy doing their duties as Hans faced all of his officers. This position was a challenge, and Hans knew that he would get through this one just as he did at Camp Kassel. Hans had faith in God for the safety of everyone. He sat at an enormous table, laid out his plans with everyone and introduced himself as Lt. Colonel Commander Hans Franz Schweitzer, new commander of this unit. First, Hans dealt with weapon and procedures. He wrote down everything that they needed to do first. Sgt. Musser told Hans that the unit did not have enough weapons and that the backup would be a blessing to them. Hans asked Musser for the entire inventory, and he listed all the weapons available: Mauser98K, Semi-Automatics, Sub-Machine guns, Grenades, Flamethrowers, Light Mortars, Bazookas and Panzer Faust. Musser estimated that they had enough for fifteen attacks. Hans was pleased with Musser's answer. Hans asked Sgt. Musser what was coming in today for supplies, and Musser said that the unit was doubling up on supplies. Hans thanked him and observed that they were well equipped with weapons. Hans then asked for the status of the men. Captain Faust would assist him. Faust told Hans that 300 men were already out there and that more reinforcement was on their way. Hans told Captain Faust that they would go to see the troops and to call formation. Hans also assigned Sgt. Musser responsibility for the weapons and told him to make sure that they had enough ammunition for the semi-automatics and sub-machine guns immediately. Hans then went outside with Captain Faust to meet his men. Hans had Captain Faust order formation. As Hans stood there, he saw so many men that he wasn't sure they could hear him speak. Hans greeted them and introduced himself as their Commanding Officer. He told them that he and Captain Faust would be leading them to victory. Hans instructed them to have their rifles cleaned and loaded, ready to go in case they came under attack. I wanted Captain Faust to assign several men to put up more barbed wire around the entrance so that the enemy could not have a good chance to get into the building and tents. Hans reminded his men how crucial it was to be ready. He told them that when he had been Commanding Officer at Camp Kassel, the camp suffered two bombing raids and the second one had left the camp completely damaged and with many causalities. Even though the camps had been ready for the second attack, it still suffered huge damage. "We need to be at our weapon station all day and night ready to fire if we need to," Hans urged. He had Captain Faust take care of the details. Hans instructed the soldiers to carry on their regular routine and to direct any questions to him. Hans released them from formation, and Captain Faust went over to the men to direct them in what Hans had ordered them to do. Pleased with what he had seen so far, Hans returned to the tent and sat at his desk near his bunk bed. He thought of Sasha and whether he had missed her. He began to write Sasha a letter telling her that he had arrived safely and that he loved her so much. Whatever his feelings for Mela were, he would always love Sasha, in his own way.

That night, Hans prayed for all of his friends and family back home and for himself. He also prayed for everyone under his charge in Munich. Hans recognized the honor that he had in this command and was thankful that he could lead a company like this one.

INSPECTION

Hans woke up at his usual time and found breakfast awaiting him at the the cooking unit stationed in one of the tents. He had coffee with mush and some eggs. He didn't shower because the shower had a long waiting line; besides, he didn't smell at all. Hans wore his full uniform and, as usual, had his hat off, because it bothered his hair. It would fall into his eyes, leaving him to keep pushing it back. Hans took Captain Faust with him to inspect stations and to see what needed to be done today. He saw that the barbed wire was in place according to his orders. Hans told Faust to set up three sites with guards at the front and two sets in the back. He then called on the phone to see when these reinforcements would be coming to the unit. Captain Faust told me that 400 men would be dispatched by the end of the day. I was happy to hear about all these men that I would have for battle. Hans asked First Lieutenant Goshen to assume command over the gunman because when the Russians would come, they would have no time to think but only to act. Goshen followed Hans's orders immediately. On this assignment, Hans was learning to fight more and to eat outside, and to sleep in a tent. Everyday Hans wrote to Sasha telling her what was happening in Munich. Sasha wrote back several times since Hans had gone to Munich; she told Hans that everyone, including her and the baby, was fine. She also told him that Peter had asked Mela out and that she had accepted. Hans felt happy for Mela but sad for himself. Days and months passed. War became Hans's friend. Already they were into March. The surrounding areas were now fighting off the Russians although they had not broken through the line as yet. Hans had the soldiers ready for battle and told them in formation that they must be ready. "Remember," he said, "war is about us winning." Hans even had soldiers drill every day with their rifles and gear on because no one knew what could happen. "We must be prepared for war and battle," Hans reminded. The officers and Hans remained convinced that soon the Russians and the British troops would attack them. He reviewed familiar procedure again, not sure whether he was lucky or had bad luck hanging over him. As Hans sat, in the tent talking with a few officers, they told him that the war was almost over. One of them said, "We are one of the key units around." Hans told them that they would make history if they followed their strategy correctly. They agreed; but even more they wanted to end the war and go home to their families. Hans agreed and that his wife was having her first baby and he wanted to be there. They asked when she was to deliver, and Hans said, "In August." Chances were that they would all be home by then. Hans met the chaplain of the unit and asked whether he would have a moment with Hans's troops, and he agreed. Hans went outside and called formation, and asked everyone to give a moment of silence for all of their colleagues in Germany who had died for their country. Chaplain Kessler introduced himself to all of the men, and he said that he wanted to say a prayer for everyone. He explained that they would eventually be attacked and that many of them would be killed. He also said that everyone needed to be ready to meet God. The soldiers and officers all bowed their heads, and the chaplain asked them to speak to God about what was on their mind. Hans told God what was on his mind: his family. Hans prayed for everyone's safety and wiped the tears from his eyes as he watched his men doing the same. Later, Hans and his officers sat in the tent going over their orders when the messages came to them. Hans received a telegram from the Colonel telling him that the Russians were now invading Berlin and that they had broken through the lines. He said that Hans should get the men ready immediately and be on high alert. Hans told all of his officers about this message and ordered Captain Faust to give his men this message. Having given necessary orders, Hans began to write to Sasha again telling her that he would soon be under attack by the Russians. "I am not sure what will happen," he wrote, "but if anything does happen, remember that I love you and the baby."

In the months that he had commanded the unit in Munich, Hans had made sure that everyone was ready. He had turned his company into a fist-fighting unit that would fight for their country and life. Hans knew that his men would meet the challenge. Hans went outside to check on the unit's readiness, walking around talking to the men and having Faust and Musser following him. The other officers were attending to the phone and messages so that the unit could be on alert for any attacks. As Hans was walking with Faust and Musser, he heard Captain Alehousier calling him to come in as soon as possible. Hans rushed in to find a memo from headquarters telling them to be ready, that bombers were sighted near Berlin and headed to Munich. Hans told Faust to get the men ready immediately and to be ready for orders. Faust rushed out while Hans was trying to reach Berlin, but no one answered the phone. As Hans made his way outside, all of a sudden he heard sounds of planes approaching their area. He yelled to everyone to get ready to fire and heard the officers telling everyone to be on standby. Hans stood there with his field binoculars, and saw the planes approaching them. Hans screamed out, "There they are!" he screamed. The planes were now right in front of them. Hans ordered everyone to fire and attack. Their guns went off. Panzer Faust, Bazookas, Mortars: They all were aiming at the bombers. The bombs began to fall. Hans had just enough time to tell everyone to scatter. As he did, the bombers struck and dismantled their tents and equipment. Hans ordered his men to fire at the four planes, and they knocked one out of the air. Hans and his men started to shout with joy as it crashed in flames. Hans urged them to continue shooting at the bombers. Another bomber fell from the sky crashing into the buildings before us, leaving only two more planes. The planes continued the bombardment. Finally, there was only one bomber and Hans's men aimed their final target, a bomb fell from the sky crashing next to Hans, putting his leg on fire. Hans screamed in pain as he looked around, seeing that many of his men had been hit directly.

Hans couldn't speak much, and heard in the background Faust telling everyone to aim at that last bomber. It came down like a burning tree, hitting the ground, setting the entire area in flames. Then the raid was over. The final battle that they had prepared for had ended; they had defeated the enemy. The survivors were screaming, "Victory! We've won the battle!"

Hans had so many wounded soldiers, including himself and he wasn't sure how many were dead. Hans lay on the ground in pain and screamed for help. The medic came over to Hans and looked at his wound and he told him that he had to be transported to the hospital immediately. Hans's leg was hanging as if it had been blasted off by the bomb. Hans bravely told his unit that he was handing them-for the time being-Faust. Hans was put on the stretcher, he told Faust to get a count of casualties, and to be ready for another attack. Faust wished Hans the best, and Hans promised him that he would return. Hans was then transported to a local hospital along with more injured men. He did not remember much after that because the pain put him to sleep. He stayed in the hospital for almost two weeks. Hans leg was taken off because of the damage, and the doctor said that Hans would not be able to walk without a fake leg. Hans wanted to see whether his company were all right when he left. I wanted to find out more about my company hoping they were all right. My prayer was answered because Captain Faust came to visit me.

Faust told Hans that the unit had fought one more foot battle and that their weapons were strong enough, thanks to him. They had killed many Russians. After the fierce battle, Hans's men moved out. They had defeated the air strikes and the land attack, and Faust thanked Hans for the proper plans that he had made before the battle. Hans told him that he was pleased with the results. Captain Faust told Hans that the Colonel would be visiting him and the other wounded soldiers. Hans would be awarded the Purple Heart medal for what he had done. Hans was pleased, but in pain. Captain Faust said good-bye to Hans because he was being transferred to Berlin that day. Hans wished him the best and to be safe. Faust smiled and saluted Hans, then left. Hans lay there wanting to go. He knew Sasha might think that he was dead because he had not written, so he asked the nurse, "when would I be going home?" "In a few days," she said. Hans was happy but drowsy from my medicine; he needed to sleep more.

PURPLE HEART AWARD

Hans had a special visitor: today Colonel Buchwalter. Hans was pleased to see the Colonel who wanted to speak to Hans for awhile. He complimented Hans on his excellent job in Munich, when Hans's unit had won the battle against the Russians. Because Hans was seriously injured with a loss of a limb, Hans was awarded the Purple Heart. "You have shown us bravery and I respect that," said the Colonel. Hans felt very proud. The Colonel also told him that he would be going home with an honorable discharge from the Army as Commander. The Colonel handed Hans the paper with his name on it written in gold letters. It read: On this day of April 3, 1945, Lieutenant Colonel Commander Hans Franz Schweitzer is honorably discharged from the Republic of Germany. Hans was so happy and relieved that his job was finished at last. Colonel Buchwalter wished Hans the best for his life. He then said good-bye and promised to be in touch and told Hans not to worry about any money because he had arranged for it to come each month in the mail to Hans's home. Hans thanked him and watched the Colonel award the other soldiers their medals. Hans also did did find out that he had lost 150 men and had 103 wounded. The doctor had to speak with Hans before he was discharged. He was finally finished with the war and would be going home with respect for his country in full uniform with all his medals including his Purple Heart.

IS THEIR HOPE?

Sasha had been crying every day for three weeks because she had not heard from Hans. She had heard that Munich was attacked by bombers and that there were a lot of casualties; she assumed that Hans was part of this attack. Hans's father couldn't believe nor could anyone else in the house think of Hans being dead. Peter told Sasha that she should not give up until she had a call from headquarters. However, Sasha had lost faith and went downstairs to lie down in grief. Her hope was gone, her love was finished. She now prepared for the worse and waited for that moment to come.

LEAVING MUNICH

Hans said goodbye to everyone as he was helped to the wheelchair because his right leg had been amputated and he had not as yet been fitted with an artificial limb. The doctor told Hans that he was to see the doctor at the hospital within two weeks to be fitted for an artificial leg. Hans thanked the doctor thank and everyone waved good-bye to Hans. He looked so handsome going home. He had decided to grow a light beard, and he had his full uniform on and his medals including his Purple Heart. One nurse told Hans that he had been a wonderful patient and that he looked stunning. Hans thanked her and wished her the best. When he arrived downstairs, a car from headquarters was waiting to take him home. As he was coming downstairs, he noticed the survivors of his entire unit from the 3rd Division of Infantry was standing on the steps clapping for him, all dressed in their uniforms. They were grateful to Hans. He sincerely thanked everyone who had made it alive. Hans bid them farewell and slid into the car. He couldn't wait to go home. Hans was tired, and he had to use crutches until he had his artificial leg fitted. He put his head back, resting until he reached home. He couldn't wait to open the door and surprise everyone, and he had made sure that he looked good for his wife. He had not seen his friends and family for such a long time. Hans was prepared for Sasha's crying and everyone feeling sorry for him. But they had to understand that he had sacrifice his life for Germany and that his reputation and bravery were on the line. "Indeed," Hans reflected, "we were all brave."

HOME AGAIN

The car pulled up to the door. Hans didn't put on his side hat, rather slipped it into his coat and picked up his crutches. The driver helped him to the front door. Hans thanked the driver who saluted him with great dignity. Hans smiled and opened the door leaning on his crutches. Everyone was in the living room including Sasha. Their eyes were pinned on Hans as he walked into the living room; they all looked at him as though he was a ghost. Sasha, Mela, Peter, Otto, Father, Rabbi Jacob, Hymen and the prisoners were all sitting and talking. Sasha looked at me and cried, "Hans is that really you?" She then fell on her knees and wept. She told Hans that she thought he was dead. She looked at Hans again. Mela kept her eyes on Hans noticing his Purple Heart Medal and missing leg. Sasha asked him whether he was all right. "I'm fine," said Hans. Then he told her that he had been hurt in the bombing of his unit, that he had lost his leg, and that he had been in the hospital for weeks. Sasha was still on the ground, but Hans's father and Hymen helped her up from the floor. Sasha grabbed Hans as he tried to sit down and kissed him until he told her to save some for later. Mela went inside the kitchen to get him something to drink. Then Hans opened his jacket and told everyone that the war was over for him and that this day was the last day the he would wear his uniform. Everyone was amazed to hear how he had earned the Purple Heart, and Sasha was especially proud of Hans, who said, "I was proud of myself, someday I shall tell the story what happened to the 3rd Division in that attack when we defeated the Russians." Everyone clapped for Hans which made him even happier than before. Hans felt tired now and wanted to go upstairs to rest. He wanted to to take off his uniform and put on his night clothes. Sasha ran to assist him. She helped him up the stairs. He had to take his time, moving much slower than before, especially going up stairs. Hans was breathing faster; he just wanted to reach the top, and he knew that he had to keep moving. Finally at the top, Hans went into his room. He sat on the edge of the bed. He took off his jacket, and asked Sasha to hang it up for him. He wanted to admire his years of being Commander. Hans took off his shirt and pulled his suspenders and his trousers down. He asked Sasha for his night clothes and for help in putting them on. He got into the bed, pulled the covers up, lay there amazed of his accomplishments as an officer. Sasha asked whether Hans was comfortable. Hans started to talk and told Sasha that he prepared his unit for an attack. "I was hit by a bomb as my men were shooting at the bombers in the the air," Hans said. "I was hit and my leg was torn. I was taken to the hospital. As I lay there, not knowing where I was, and I didn't know what was happening to me until I saw my leg was removed. I was awarded the Purple Heart Medal for my bravery, and you can figure the rest of the story. I must go to sleep now." Sasha lay down next to Hans and held on to him tightly as they both slept in peace at last.

GOOD BYE WAR

It was April 30, 1945. We turned on the radio only to discover that the war was over in Germany and that Germany had lost. What was most disturbing was that Germany had surrendered and that Hitler was dead. The radio said that Hitler and his wife Eva had killed themselves. Every dream was over. So many men had lost their lives, and the ones who survived fought with bravery. Hans didn't believe a word about Hitler killing himself and leaving a country so deeply battered. "Hitler loved Germany, he fought for Germany, and now he kills himself and leaves us all to face the aftermath of this war? No one believes it, neither do I!" Hans exclaimed.

"My life has gone by so fast, and I was only a young man when I joined, and now look at me, almost 26 years old. I have so little to live by, and now I must face my entire ghost in my life, as Commander." Hans tried to understand all of this news. "I couldn't, I just couldn't," he said. "I had to live with this war just like everyone else and that was hard to do. Now living in defeat may be even harder."

CALL

Hans received a call from the hospital in Munich asking him about his appointment in May. The hospital wanted to fit his artificial leg for which Hans was grateful. The hospital assured him since he had been seriously injured in the war that he did not have to pay for any of these services. Hans was happy that he could ride Zurich again and that he could walk. The hospital confirmed his date as May 15 at 10:00 AM and to expect to be there fifteen minutes earlier than the appointment time. Hans knew that he had to ask Peter to take him to the hospital in Munich. Hans was pleased about this call.

"DO NOT ASK, PLEASE"

Hans dressed and shaved today. Every other day he grew a slight beard, and then let it go. It gave him something to do. He put on his beige trousers, and Sasha pinned up the one pant leg so it wouldn't hang. It felt odd that he didn't have to wear his full uniform: to think that he would never have to put it on again. He hung it up exposing his medals. Hans would still wear his military shirts and trousers and especially his boots for riding. Hans couldn't wait to get his fake leg fitted so that he could do more things in the house and go places. He went over to the table and had some tea and oatmeal and he took two of his pills for the infection and pain. He was waiting to see who would be up asking him questions about his leg. Then he sat in the den for some peace and to be alone. The weather was so nice, and Hans wasn't sure what day it was any more. The sun was coming up, and the birds were singing. Hans noticed the flowers that were blooming so nicely outside. Hans had so much happening in his life that he wanted to take each day as it came to him. His mind was still involved in the war, camp, and his 3rd Division and now with his leg. Since the camp, he had hurt his leg so many times; this time would be the last time for it to be hurt.

Hans closed his eyes for awhile. Some time later, he heard a knock and there stood his dearest wife. Sasha asked Hans whether he needed anything. Hans told her that he had already had his breakfast. She looked at Hans and said, "If you need anything, please let me know." Hans thanked her and closed his eyes again. After some time, he got up and opened the windows, and thought it would be such a nice day to ride Zurich. Hans remembered how he used to ride around the camp on his horse. "How I long to do that again in my life!" he exclaimed. He had to push away his thoughts, so he went into the kitchen. Hans's father was there and asked how Hans was doing. Then he changed the subject to one that pleased Hans. Hans said that he was fine, offering no more description of his leg. Otto asked Hans what had happened in Munich? Hans quickly answered them by saying, "Do not ask, please!" Everyone accepted his wishes, and Hans was grateful that they did.

DOCTOR VISIT

As time went by, Hans found his life becoming boring, lonely and depressing. He searched for answers for his life. He couldn't wait to get this new leg so he could do more activities than what he was doing now. Now that the war had ended, Hans wanted to do more and perhaps a job or something. Peter was nice enough to drive Hans's car to Munich so that he could see the doctor at the clinic. He had to be there by 9:00AM, so they were up early and ready to leave. This time, Hans sat in the front. He felt strange because he usually sat in the back when he was Commander, having his driver take him to where he needed to go. They rolled the windows down. The warm breeze felt good on their faces. Hans asked Peter the most difficult question: "How are you and Mela doing?" He felt as if he had a knife in his throat as he waited for Peter's response, because Hans knew that Mela still loved him. Peter told Hans they were coming along well and that he had asked her out. Now, the knife sank into his heart because Hans could not bear the pain knowing that he would or already had kissed her. Hans felt his life disappeared before him as he choked back his tears. Peter said that he and Mela were waiting for the baby to be born. Hans felt like telling his best friend, "Never forget; that baby is mine." Hans was so choked up and had the feeling Peter wanted to eliminate him from Mela's life and the life of his baby. Hans also had the feeling that Peter would stop him seeing the baby and he was even intending the paternity. Hans decided right there to leave the subject and stayed quiet until we reached the hospital. Peter parked the car in the back parking lot of the hospital where a nurse greeted Hans with a wheelchair. She knew Hans from when he had been in the hospital. She said, “Commander Hans, how are you feeling?” Hans looked at her astonished but pleased. “Fine, thank you,” he responded. The nurse wheeled him up to the clinic where all the war veterans sat, and she signed him in. Peter came up shortly as Hans waited for his name to be called. As Hans was sitting there, he noticed someone familiar sitting next to him. This man turned to Hans and asked whether he had been stationed at Munich with the 3rd Division. Hans told him that he had been Commander there and injured from the bombs. Hans then looked at the speaker and recognized him as the private who had brought him his mail each day. Hans thanked the soldier for everything he had done in Munich. Hans asked him what had happened to him, and said that he had also been injured that day when the bombs fell. Although he had trouble walking now, he was doing well. Hans wished him the best and asked his name, “Franz L. Schrieffer.” Hans thanked him again just as the nurse called out, “Commander Hans Schweitzer.” Hans wheeled his chair to the desk to let her know that he was Hans; and as did, the entire waiting room was looking at Hans as though they wanted to do something. Hans went in quickly and followed the nurse to a small room where she had him stay. She asked whether he was feeling all right—any pain, fever or infection. Hans told her “no” to all of her questions. The nurse took his temperature, “Normal, blood pressure, normal,” she said and then left.

Hans was very concerned about his prayers and prayed that he would be able to walk again. He was also determined to get on his horse again and ride. “I know I shall ride again, I just knew I shall!” he said. Hans became warm sitting in that room, so he opened the button on his shirt and waited for the doctor to give him his new leg. Hans sometimes could not face being alone because it gave him more time to think. As he sat in his wheelchair, he began thinking about myself again and how proud he was of his accomplishments and of his country. Hans thanked God for the great opportunity that He had given to him and the lives that Hans had saved. As Hans was having that last thought, the doctor came in and asked how he was feeling. He looked at Hans’s half of leg and asked whether Hans was in any pain. Hans wanted to tell him, "Yes, my love life: can you help me doctor?" Instead, Hans answered, "No pain." The doctor then said, "Fine, now for that leg!" Then he went to get some instrument to measure Hans's height. The nurse came in and helped him with the measurements, which he took about five minutes. The doctor told Hans that they would show him how to use his leg and also perhaps recommend Hans therapy. Hans told the doctor that he wanted to ride his horse again. "That is no problem," the doctor assured Hans. "It will take a few days depending upon how busy we are, but the hospital will call you when the leg comes in," the doctor said. Hans was happy that appointment went fast and wheeled himself to the waiting room to say good-bye to his friend, Franz. "Take care and feel better," Hans told him on the way out.

AFTER THE WAR

When Hans and Peter got into the car, Hans asked Peter to drive around to see how things looked after the war. They noticed a lot of buildings heavily damaged by the bombs and trash all over. It was certainly a war scene. The buildings were on the ground still smoldering from the fires. Belongings of people who once lived there were blown all around. I couldn't take it anymore, Hans just couldn't. He asked Peter to stop in the local store and buy a newspaper. There the headlines were very depressing as they read, "A Struggle to Survive." There were so many heartbreaking pictures of Germany and stories about Hitler's failure as a Commander. Hans turned the page and saw an article "Catching Nazi Criminals." It read that the intelligence was looking for any officers who took part in the murders of 50 million people. Hans knew that he had not been part of this murder plot, and he was thankful that some of his staff were living with him as well as others who could testify to what he didn't do. Hans asked Peter to take him home perhaps he could find something to do because he couldn't bear the news anymore. His eyes were sore in what he had just read. More than ever, Hans felt that now was the time for history to heal itself. Again, as we were leaving, Hans saw many Germans cleaning the debris from bombing and crying over what they lost. There were no more buildings left, and those that were, hung onto what was left. The sight was horrifying and depressing. Dead bodies were in the street decaying, hungry dogs mauling at the bodies. At one point, Hans saw people cutting up dead horses for meat and lines of people being served soup. Tears were flowing from everyone and my people are now blamed for this war.

SASHA

When Peter and Hans returned home, they found Sasha had lunch all ready for them. Hans told her what had happened at the hospital and what they had seen in Munich. Hans then showed her the newspaper, as depressing as it was. Sasha told Hans not to worry about anything that he would be fine. She mentioned how handsome he looked now without his uniform. Then Hans asked her," Why did you comment so many times before about my uniform, and how handsome I looked?" "Which is it?" She had said both. Sasha told Hans that she had only two months left before the baby is born. She was thinking of names and it was just too soon, but she needed to have a name for him or her. Sasha made a joke and said, "How about Hans Jr?" Hans told her that she was kidding him because he did not want his name to be used. Hans said to himself, "I had a secret reason why I couldn't have a son called Hans Jr. This was my secret never to be revealed." Hans left it to her to pick out a name. He noticed one thing about Sasha: her hair was long now. However, Hans still saw the same pretty woman when he had fallen in love with in Berlin. With her hair being tied back in a bun, she looked stunning. Sasha was so soft spoken and a good mother-to-be. As Hans was speaking to Sasha, the telephone rang. The hospital was on the line. They were calling to tell Hans that his leg had just come in. "Could you come in tomorrow?" they asked. "About 10:00AM?" Hans agreed on the time. Hans hung up the receiver happily. "Now I can ride my horse back to camp!" he cheered.

HURRY

Hans asked Peter to hurry the ride to Munich because he was so excited to get his leg put on and walk. He also told Peter that he wanted to ride Zurich again. Peter laughed. Hans saw that Peter was going a bit faster for him, and they arrived sooner than expected. Again, the nurse came out to get Hans with the wheelchair. She took me upstairs to the clinic to sign in. Shortly, Hans heard his name called. He wheeled himself over to the desk, and the nurse directed him into the same room as the last time. The nurse came in and asked whether Hans had any complaints. Hans answered, "No." The nurse said, "The doctor will be in shortly to see you, Hans." Shortly after she left, the doctor came in and asked how Hans was feeling. "Fine," said Hans, "and excited for my new leg." The doctor summoned the nurse and asked her to bring the new leg. Several seconds later the nurse came back with it. Even though it looked plastic, Hans was determined to put it on and walk. The doctor took the leg out of the wrapper and showed Hans how to put it on. Putting it on was simple, but the hardest part was becoming accustomed to walking with the leg. The doctor strapped the leg on for Hans and showed him how to use it. Now the hard part was getting up and walking, but Hans knew that he could do it. Both the nurse and doctor clapped for Hans and that encouraged him to continue his determination. The doctor told Hans that it would be better if he started first walking with a cane and gave Hans one to use. Hans was to begin slowly and then gradually increase his speed, until he could walk faster without the cane. Every step was a struggle, a challenge. Hans said to himself, "I will make it to the top!" The doctor asked Hans to come back in a month unless Hans needed him sooner. The doctor continued to caution, "Hans, slowly please?" Hans had his pants leg down and didn't need the wheelchair anymore, so he walked over to the desk to make his appointment for next month. The nurse gave him June 18 at 11:00AM. Hans thanked her and left with Peter, who looked at Hans very impressed. Hans went downstairs and climbed into the car slowly, but determined. Hans wanted to go home on this beautiful day and sit outside.

"I CAN WALK"

Peter drove Hans around the country on the return trip. Finally at home, Peter parked in front of Hans's house. Hans climbed out of the car slowly and walked over to the shed where he went to see Zurich. Hans showed him his leg and told him that within a few days they would go for a ride again. Hans was very pleased in how he was feeling and said good-bye to Zurich. Hans walked into the house and saw Sasha and Mela talking. He asked them whether they saw Hymen and they said, "In the kitchen." Sasha asked Hans about his leg and he said, "Here it is. I am ready to walk and ride." Sasha's face lit up. She turned to speak to Mela. As she did, Sasha saw that Mela was keeping her eyes on Hans. So Hans went into the kitchen and asked Hymen to take Zurich out of the shed and tie him up. Hymen asked whether Hans needed him saddled today? "No, thank you," Hans replied. Hans was so happy that he could walk again. He had never felt as happy as he did at that moment, and grateful to God that he could still walk. All he needed now was encouragement.

"MY HEART TO YOURS"

Hans asked both Sasha and Mela whether they had their cribs ready for the babies. "Yes!" they chorused and continued to sit. Hans felt that he was intruding, so he went back outside allowing them to have their privacy. Hans was glad to walk around the yard. He went up to Zurich to give him a carrot and to brush him. Zurich had been Hans's horse for so many years. Hans always enjoyed taking care of him. Hans brushed down the horse as he was tied to the pole next to the shed. Then he went back to the shed for the saddle and put it on Zurich. Hans saw his Mauser rifle from camp still strapped on the side, and he asked Hymen to help him mount his horse. Hymen looked at Hans as though he didn't want to, but did it anyway. He went inside for a stool so Hans could stand on it. Hans mounted Zurich very slowly, and there he sat. Hans felt just the way he had felt when he was in the camp riding around. He promised himself that he would stay on Zurich and would not get off until he returned back home. Hans told Hymen that he was going to ride slowly to the camp and that he would return within a few hours. He asked me, "Should I tell Sasha?" "I would appreciate it greatly," Hans said. Hymen nodded, and Hans rode toward the camp.

THOUGHTS REGAINED

On this beautiful day for riding, Hans had a small lunch and a drink in his bag. As he crossed the woods and heard the birds chirping, and he knew that he had to say his final goodbye to his camp. No one could understand the feelings that he had and the memories that haunt him each day. Hans knew that he had to face his ghosts and put them to rest. He had been used to working each day and taking care of something that crossed his path. Now, he had nothing. He began to doubt whether he truly had Sasha anymore because the war had ended, leaving him handicapped. Hans also knew that he had changed. As Hans rode up the dirt roads, he heard the birds singing perhaps a love song. He felt in his heart that he loved Sasha, but it seemed to him that they did nothing as a couple. All they did was eat, sleep, chat and babies. The routine had become very boring to Hans who had been accustomed with other people. He would enjoy a picnic or just strolling along the river. He sometimes wondered whether this war had really changed him and Sasha because he began to feel that they had distant themselves. The months in Munich completely changed Hans, who saw himself now as more cautious and colder. "For this reason, I must go the camp to get rid of those ghosts that still haunt me. No one will ever understand me, no one. I must do this visit; I must," Hans said aloud to Zurich. "I have one memory still there that I could never tell anyone, not even Sasha," Hans said sadly. "My heart is completely broken from my secret, and I can only hope that memory will be united again someday to me," Hans cried. Hans rode along the road slowly and presently saw the stack chimneys in the near distance. He arrived at the broken front gate and went through to where his quarters had been. Some of the furniture was still there but damaged. Hans remembered all of the fun he had with Sasha and Fritz, and he thanked God for the memory. Next he rode over to his office. Hans asked Zurich whether he knew this place still, laughing to himself. Hans began to move quickly because it was getting late in the day. He headed over to the road where he had met Mela. How could he forget riding through the blocks suddenly seeing Sasha. His heart began to beat faster as he looked at the site. A lot had been lost since the bombings. Hans knew that eventually this camp would be destroyed and nothing would remain except dirt. Hans knew that he would always remember it as a place where hate never existed from him, because he had given only love and kindness.

Hans found that his mind was drifting, and he knew that he had to leave because the time was already 3:30PM, and the return journey would take some time especially by horse. It was such a beautiful day, and Hans looked back, remembering nice days that he had spent at this camp with his friends and Sasha as they walked around laughing and watching. Hans then turned the reins of Zurich; and as he did, he felt a bad cramp in his leg. Hans knew he had to get off Zurich to stretch his leg. However, he knew that if he did, he would not be able to get back on Zurich. Hans had to think again and fast. He rode over to the barrel where he had fallen during the bombing raid. He kept saying, "God help me!" He put his foot on the barrel and tried to get down. As he did, his foot got caught on the barrel, and he fell off his horse, snapping his leg. The pain was terrific. Hans couldn't believe a repeat of this mishap again. He couldn't get back on the horse, not by this way. His other leg was fine but it was his real leg that was hurting, and forcing him to wait a little longer to try something else. The time was now past 5:30 PM, and the darkness was falling little by little. Hans tried pulling himself up again and failed. He caught his breath and looked around to see what he could possibly do but found nothing at all. "Maybe I should sit here and be part of the camp, and I did when I stayed there and watched as night creep up." said Hans. He could imagine what Sasha was thinking, and he knew that she had everyone upset about him. Hans was glad that he had told Hymen where he had gone just in case they wanted to find me. Hans looked around and felt a light breeze on his face. His hair was falling into my face and covered with dust. Poor Zurich stood in place and waited for Hans to do something, but Hans just couldn't move. He put his head between his legs and fell asleep.

GUESS WHERE?

As everyone was eating dinner, Sasha looked at the time. It was late and she knew that Hans should have been home already. Sasha was convinced that something happened to him on the way or in the camp. Sometimes she wished that someone would burn the camp down so Hans could not go there anymore. It was now past 8:00 in the evening. They had to do something fast before Hans might become worse. Hymen knew where Hans was, and he told Sasha that he was at the camp looking for his past to end. Sasha remained calm and asked Peter and Otto to ride over to the camp and see whether Hans was around the area. All of them went into Hans's car to find him. They had to drive slowly because of the darkness, riding for almost two hours until they came up to the camp. As the lights hit the camp, they saw Zurich standing and Hans on the ground sleeping. Sasha woke up Hans and saw that he was hurt, again. Hans grabbed Sasha and kissed her. He told her that he had been looking around when he got a cramp in his leg and fell off his horse. "Forgive me Sasha, please, I am sorry but all I wanted was to bring all these memories back so I could love you more. Please understand, please," he cried. This was the first time that Sasha had seen her husband weeping. Again, she forgave him.

KEEP FORGIVING

Finally back home, they helped Hans to the sofa where his father and Hymen examined his injured leg. Thank God it wasn't broken, but it was badly bruised; and that was enough for Hans. His father put some ice on the bruise so it would not swell so much, but it still had an open wound. Sasha took over the nursing and cleaned his wound so no infection would set in. She helped Hans upstairs where he would be resting and she could finish dressing the wounds. Sasha helped Hans into their bed where she helped him to lie down. Hans then took off his artificial leg and set it to the side where Sasha washed it for him. She loved Hans so much that when he committed anything wrong against her with Mela, she would always forgive him. That was love, true love.

Sasha prepared to wash Hans and took a washcloth and washed his leg thoroughly. She then washed his artificial leg getting all the dust and dirt off. He was nice and clean and he sat there observing Sasha's love for him. Hans was completely shocked when Sasha even washed his hair getting all the dirt out and letting his light blond hair shine. She then combed his hair back for him, kissed him on his forehead, and then laid him back down so he could rest. As Hans lay down, he suddenly recognized that Sasha had shown true love, such a contrast from Hitler's Youth Camp that had taught him not to mingle with a Jew. Now Hans was most contented that he had found Sasha and had made her his wife, and he couldn't care less who would know about his love for her. The war was over, and he could continue his love for her. No more could he say that their love was forbidden or wrong. Everyone in his unit except a few had said that this love could never happen, but it did. Sasha was cleaning up around him and she put his artificial leg to the side next to the bed in case he needed to put it on. She looked at Hans and told him that she forgave him for everything, and that she loves him more than he could know. So they put out the light next to them where Sasha climbed into bed next to Hans. She held him tenderly as a loving wife; where she whispered softly to him, "I love you my dearest Hans. Thank you Lord, again."

SURPRISE TODAY

Everyone was sleeping when suddenly Sasha got up with great pain in her stomach. She woke up Hans, and he asked whether she was all right. She looked at him and said, "The baby is ready to see his parents." Hans called for Hymen and anyone else who heard the call. Hymen came running in and asked what was wrong. Hans told him that Sasha was ready to have their baby. Hymen woke up Natasha and Olga and directed them to get hot water and plenty of towels. They gathered around Sasha and told her to lie down with her legs up and start pushing. Sasha pushed and pushed until the head of the baby was showing. Olga told Sasha to give some more big pushes until the little bundle of joy arrived. Natasha and Olga screamed, all were screaming, "It's a girl and a pretty one indeed." Sasha was so delighted and wanted to see her baby, but Olga said, "Not until we clean her up and cut the cord." Hans stood back and said, "I'm a father, I can't believe this." Yet he looked at their child born on August 16, 1945. He wanted to give Sasha a surprise by calling the baby girl by her mother's name, Natalia. Sasha broke down crying and thanked Hans for that name of her mother. The baby's name would be Natalia Lydia Schweitzer. She weighed 7pounds 2 ounces. What a beautiful name! What a beautiful baby! Sasha began to nurse her. Then Natasha and Olga wrapped her in the new blanket that Hans had bought her and laid her in the crib that her father had made for her. She was very special.

ADAPTING

Hans found this year very challenging. Now he had a baby in his life. He vowed to do his best as a father. Hans realize as he looked at Natalia that she looked a lot like Sasha, yet she had his blue eyes and light blond hair. The baby was his bundle of joy, and Hans knew that he would always treasure her so much in his life. "I hope that one day Sasha will tell her the truth about her father and what he had done for their mother and others," said Hans eagerly. Natalia would be taught not to hate anyone because of who they are and to ask God to overcome any negative feelings towards another person. Sasha placed the baby in her crib. She slept near her parents. Hans had to adapt to these changes, which was not an easy task. "Right now my mind had been changing concerning the camp and war," said Hans. He had lost his leg, and now he had his baby daughter. These challenges were now ones that he would need to overcome. The year had been so hard for Hans because of the pain felt by so many who had been in the war and had suffered. Many times Hans had wanted to go out and be alone, yet he had such little strength in his leg to do anything. He felt as though he was down low, yet his faith and encouragement from Sasha helped him to grow with hope. He now recognized that time as his friend, and that time someday would let everyone know who he was: Hans Schweitzer, former Oberstleutnant (Lt. Colonel Commander of Camp Kassel.) He had been a German officer who had not practiced his oath completely because he had adapted to the pain, sorrow, and tears of all the people he had met. Hans felt blessed never to have been Commander of Auschwitz or

Dachau, because he would have never have wanted to witness any of the killings that had gone on these daily. Never.

Hans reminded himself that he needed to adapt to his life as a husband, father, and friend to everyone. He vowed to overcome any fear, anything that might come his way with the help of God. "I admit I am not perfect and that I make mistakes," said Hans. "When I do, I know that God will be there for me."

MELA, MY FRIEND

On August 23, 1945, Mela's baby arrived with Peter at her side assisting Natasha and Olga. The baby was a boy with blue eyes and very light blond hair. Everyone said that he looked just like Hans. Mela named him Danderick. Hans saw him only very shortly, but at least Hans did get to be with him for a little while. He was after all the baby's father. He was cuddly and small. Hans was so proud of him, that he kissed him on his forehead and told him that he loved him. Hans suffered within for his wrong decisions and his broken heart that no one sees. Sasha had forgiven Hans for what he done right after his marriage to her, but he knew that she wasn't happy about what he had done. Sasha would not admit to the fact, but Hans could see in her eyes that open to parts of her that only he could see. Forgiveness was their principle, but so was being the father of Danderick. Hans turned over the responsibility to Peter to be the baby's father with a breaking heart. Hans could not bear the pain. Hans knew that Peter would be a good father to Danderick if he decided to marry Mela. Hans told Mela and Peter that he would give on a monthly support to them. Hans felt it important to live up to his mistake and not run from what he had done. He wanted to save his son from hurt and confusion and hoped that someday he would accept Peter as his father, who would love him and raise him correctly. This was another pain in Hans's heart that many soldiers in the war witness. Love was not to be found when fighting in the war because killing could not be righteously done. Call it loneliness, mistakes, and yet Hans's experience pointed to one answer: war was wrong.

Hans loved his baby son, Danderick, within his heart he promised Mela he would always be there for the baby when Peter was not. Mela said that Peter and she were to be married shortly, and Hans was happy for her. Mela was a very beautiful Jewish woman, and Hans knew that Peter would love her dearly.

"Good-bye my son, your father dearly loves you in silence and yet I remain at a distance," Hans said to himself. "You will not have to carry this hurt, but I always will because I truly love your mother. I am sorry that I will not be the one to throw that ball to you and say, "Danderick, I love you. Good-bye, my son, goodbye."

ANOTHER MARRIAGE

Mela and Peter announced on August 29, 1945 that they planned to be married. Peter asked Rabbi Jacob to marry them with me and Otto at their side. Mela wanted Sasha to be with her and assist her in this wedding. Of course Sasha said yes, and Hans was delighted.

Special food was made from Jewish to German and that was fine with Hans as long as everyone would eat and be happy. Hans had to get dress and managed to find a black jacket with a white shirt and dark trousers. Hans had his Ersatz shoes from the war; and they were brand new. He shaved and put on his French cologne and looked the best he could. Sasha said that Hans looked like her knight in shining armor, and she didn't look bad herself. Sasha was always thin and could fit into anything, because she had a baby not too long ago. Hans sat on the sofa waiting for the ceremony to begin while the women were in the kitchen making the food. He had the chance to think how he had regretted Mela marrying Peter instead of him. Hans was stunned at the prospect of this marriage, yet he had nothing to say about whom Mela could marry. Hans had saved Mela from the horrors of the camp including being beaten and everything that went with camp life, but he could not control her life. Hans went upstairs to see his daughter. She was sleeping in her small crib that he had built for her, and she looked so beautiful like her mother. He wished that Sasha's parents were alive to see their granddaughter and that his own mother were here. Hans was still distraught about his feelings for Mela because he knew that they were both still in love with one another. Hans also knew that Sasha suspected that he still loved Mela because of the way Sasha looked at him sometimes when Mela's name was mentioned. Sasha came up to see whether Hans was all right. He gave the excuse that his leg was aching somewhat and that he wanted to see his baby daughter. He did want to see his daughter, that part was true; but the leg part was not true at all. Hans suspected Sasha had guessed the reason that he had gone upstairs to be alone, but if she knew, she said nothing about it to him. She always seemed to know the truth, the truth that Hans could not hide. Sasha looked at him and never said a word about Mela to him. So Hans went downstairs to wish Peter and Mela both the best. It was almost time for them to be married and Hans felt his heart breaking inside and yet he could do nothing. As everyone was standing there, Hans looked at Mela. As she looked back at him, she could tell how he truly felt. Hans watched Rabbi Jacob as he performed the ceremony. Mela had such an unhappy look on her face. Every other minute she would look at Hans hoping that he would do something to stop this wedding, but he couldn't do anything. He could only hope that her feelings would change for him. Then the ritual ended, and they were both married. Heartbroken, Hans still shook Peter's hand and hugged Mela. Hans wished them both the best in life and at the same wishing the same for himself. The food was prepared: potato soup, sausages, fruit and sandwiches and plenty of French brandy. Hans prepared a dish and went into the den by himself to eat and cry silently. Everyone knew when he sat in the den alone, something was wrong. It meant that he was bothered by something; this time, he was bothered by the wedding.

VISIT

Hans sat in the den eating alone, he heard a soft knock at the door. He opened it and found Mela standing there. She walked in and asked if it was all right to see me alone. Hans told her it was fine and invited her to sit down for a while. She asked Hans how his daughter was doing, and then asked about Danderick. Mela said that the baby was fine and handsome like his father. Mela looked at Hans with watery eyes and told her that he would always be his father and that she would always love Hans. She said, "Thank you for saving my life, thank you so much." She grabbed his hand and kissed it and left, leaving him so confused that Hans had to ask himself what just happened? Hans felt that her marriage nor his own would not last many years because of how they felt for each other. Hans finished eating and went outside for some air and to have a cigarette. He had picked up this habit from being in the war and was intending to give it up sometime soon. It was another beautiful day, and Hans remembered how August was at the camp. Hans sat on the front porch alone thinking and wishing that his legs were feeling better. He sat there and watched the birds flying as he listened to their singing. Hans was almost finished with his cigarette when he knew that he had to go back inside and face his past. He mustered all the strength that he had within his heart. He then went back in to face his life.

SASHA MAKES A SUGGESTION

September had come, and the weather finally became cooler. Every day Hans sat looking for that inner peace and solutions for his life. He was still so much in the war, that he found himself putting on his service dress trousers, a white shirt, and my ersatz shoes. A habit or whatever, but he was comfortable and relaxed. He decided to grow a light beard every second day, and then shave. Sasha said that Hans was just lazy and didn't want to shave. How untrue she was. Hans just wanted to do something different. It was something new and Hans welcome that newness. Sasha came outside where he was sitting and suggested that they take a ride over to Berlin and have lunch. Hans was surprised that she said this because she normally did not want to go anywhere. Sometimes Hans felt that she was a shame of being married to a German although Hans never mentioned the subject to her because she would say he was wrong, as always. Hans and Sasha got dressed, and Hans put Natalia in a warm blanket. Finally, they were going out as a couple. Hans took his Mercedes Benz 290 Cab D 1935 out and rode to Berlin for some shopping and lunch. It rode so smoothly to Berlin which took almost five hours from Cologne. When they arrived in Berlin, the city were cleaning up the bombs, collapse buildings and dead bodies all over the streets. Hans really didn't have much room to park anywhere so he parked the car on the side of the pub where they were going to eat. They found some shops opened and people buying and walking around town. Berlin was a horrible sight to see, and Hans was amazed at how much damage the war had done. Hans held on to Sasha because he had to use his cane. Walking was no fun. They came up to a small café that served sandwiches and went in. The café was small and it wasn't crowded. The waiter handed them a small menu. Hans asked the waiter to bring him a beer and whatever Sasha wanted. Sasha ordered seltzer water, and they both ordered lentil soup with fresh bread and a small salad. Natalia was fussing a little, so Sasha gave her a bottle of milk. I was finishing my beer when the the bell rang. The door opened and a thin man, perhaps twenty-nine years old with light hair walked in. Hans recognized him. The man walked over to Hans, shocked to see him, "Hans, Lt. Colonel Commander how are you doing?" Hans acknowledged that he was that person. Hans knew that he had been in his 3rd Division in Munich. He was one of the gunmen who had operated the MG42 machine gun and also the Panzer Faust. He had helped to knock out the bombers, and Hans remembered his name to be a PFC (Gefreiter) Henry Freisenberger. He had actually helped Hans when he was seriously injured as the bombs hit the ground. Hans introduced Sasha as my wife and our new baby, Natalia. Freisenberger gave his hand to Sasha and said he was glad to meet her while Sasha accepted his hand as a greeting. Henry asked again how Hans was doing and where he was living now. "We live in Cologne," realized Hans. "I am doing well and looking for work." Henry said that the only work that they hiring now in Berlin was cleaning up the mess from the war. "It will take years to clean," he said to Hans. Hans knew that already. Hans told Henry that it was nice to see him again and that he hopes to run into him again. Henry returned the compliment and sat at the bar having a beer. Hans called the waiter over for the check and paid him and left with Sasha and Natalia. They went through the town looking at the shops that had opened. Hans told Sasha that he had enough money so that she could do some shopping. They then went into a shop for women where a woman clerk greeted them. She asked Hans whether he needed any help, and he told her that he was here with his wife and that we were looking for a white dress. Sasha smiled at Hans and looked at the different dresses the clerk showed her. She needed a size fourteen; and the dresses were few but pretty. Sasha found a beautiful white dress laced with white beads and luckily it was a size fourteen. Sasha wanted to try it on, and the clerk showed her the fitting room. Sasha gave Hans the baby and went to try it on. Hans sat on the chair with Natalia and the woman asked him about his leg. Hans told her that he had been hit by a bomb in Munich when the Russians had attacked his unit. She was quite impressed that Hans was a commander in the war. Hearing this information led her to explain to Hans that her husband, also an officer, was missing in action. She told Hans that he never came home again. As she was telling the story, she was dabbing her eyes.

Hans asked her his name just in case he might know who he was, and Hans was shocked to find out that his name was Lieutenant Captain Goetz. "Goetz?" Hans asked. The clerk asked Hans whether he knew him, and she begged him for any information he could give. As Hans was about to answer her question, Sasha came out showing Hans how beautiful the dress looked on her. She looked gorgeous in the dress, and Hans asked Sasha whether to buy it for her. Sasha shook her head no, but she wouldn't tell why not. Hans asked her whether she wanted to buy anything else, and she said, "No, thank you." Hans thanked the clerk and told her that they would come back again.

ASHAMED OF THE PAST

Outside, Hans asked Sasha what happened inside of the store with the dress. She held tight to Natalia and choking on her tears. "It is my arm," she said. Hans asked her "What was wrong with your arm?" Hans asked. Sasha pointed to the numbers tattooed on her left arm from the concentration camp. Hans stopped short and felt an egg in his throat. The number given at the camp was engraved into her skin and it showed when she did not wear a long sleeve. Hans told Sasha how deeply sorry he was and that the best solution was to wear something long. "The war in over with, and you are saved; so please don't cry anymore about this problem. I love you," said Hans. He did not want to press the issue there, but they could talk about it that night. Finally back home, Hans helped Sasha with her bags and found his father was sitting in the living room when they opened the front door. Hans was happy to see his father laughing again with the rest of the crew. It would be nice to see Sasha smiling again and forgetting what had happened at the shop.

DISCUSSION

That night, they had a light dinner, and then Hans went upstairs because the baby had to have a bath. Sasha got the small tub ready with water for Natalia. She did not like the water at all, so they tried to make it as fun as we could for her by putting little toys in the water. Sasha washed Natalia and did her hair, took her out, and put her on the towel to dry her. Natalia was still crying and fussing, and Sasha knew that she was hungry. She dressed her and wrapped her in a warm blanket and Sasha nursed her. Within thirty minutes, Natalia had fallen asleep, so Sasha wrapped her in the blanket and laid her down in her crib. Hans now found the time to discuss what had happened at the store today. He told Sasha that what happened about that dress was irrelevant and not to worry about it. "I wish that you never had to go through this," said Hans. "You just need a dress with long sleeves." Sasha agreed and began to feel better. Hans also told her that the number now gave her love and freedom. "I know that you lost your family," Hans said, "but look what you have gained. I saved you and that is all that counts now." Hans wanted to go back to Berlin and surprise Sasha with a long-sleeved dress. He determined to make the trip the next day. Sasha kissed Hans good night and thanked him for the years that they had been together. Hans answered her that they would have many more. Sasha told Hans that she would be lost without him. Hans looked at her and said, "So would I. Good-night, my love."

SATURDAY

Hans woke up early. He asked Otto whether if he would like to go to Berlin with him to pick out a dress for Sasha. He said that would be fine, and Hans asked him whether he wanted to drive; he did. Hans said that he wanted to surprise Sasha with a dress and that she needed something as beautiful as she was. Hans also told Otto about how he had met Goetz's wife at the shop in which she was the clerk. "She asked me whether I knew her husband; and as I was about to answer her, Sasha came out of the dressing room. She also told me that her husband had never come home from the war nor had she any word about him. How can I tell her that we buried him at the camp because of the bombing?" asked Hans. "I really do not know how to approach her about this matter, yet I must do so; it is only right. Then I ran into another problem, what if Frau Goetz would like her husband's body returned? Otto didn't know what to say except to be honest with her. Hans and Otto arrived in Berlin and discovered many cars on the streets. Hans assumed that many people had come to shop. Hans went over to the dress shop, but Frau Goetz wasn't there. He asked the clerk whether Frau Goetz was in today. The clerk said, "No, she is off today." She then wanted to know if Hans needed anything. He told her that he needed a size fourteen dress in any color and with long sleeves. The clerk showed Hans four dresses: black, white, navy and rose. Because Sasha had liked the white dress, Hans decided upon that one and the rose color dress as well. Hans asked the clerk to gift wrap the dresses. Hans was happy, and he knew that Sasha would be too. The clerk finished wrapping; Hans paid her and left. He decided to have a quick beer with Otto, so they stopped at the pub. They ordered two beers. The pub was getting crowded. Actually it was nice to see locals coming alive again since the war.

Hans told Otto that he had to see Frau Goetz again so that he could tell her the truth about her husband. He wanted to go back to the shop to ask the clerk when Frau Goetz would be in again. They finished their beer and went back to the shop. The clerk told Hans that Frau Goetz would be in on Monday from 10:00 am-6:00 pm. Hans asked her for the telephone number of the shop so that he could call her on Monday. She gave it to Hans and he thanked her. When Hans and Otto began their homeward journey, the weather looked like rain, and it was getting dark outside. By the time we reached home, the rain was pouring and thundering had begun. Hans protected his box from the rain and went as fast as he could to go inside. He looked for Sasha and found her upstairs taking a bath. Hans asked her how long she would be. She wanted to know whether he needed anything, but he first said, "No," come out when you are finished. Hans checked on Natalia. She looked so cute sucking her thumb. She was almost two months old, and so was his son.

IN LOVE, AGAIN

Sasha got out of the tub and put on her long robe with a towel wrapped around her hair. She dried her hair letting it fall in front of her face while she combed her hair. Her face was shining from the soap, and she put her hair into a bun. She was beautiful. Sasha asked Hans where he had gone. He said, "Close your eyes." Hans held the box in his hands and sang, "Surprise!" Sasha was so overwhelmed about how pretty the box was wrapped and about the fact that Hans had bought her something. She was anxious to open the package, and she admired how Hans could think of her by giving her a gift. As Sasha opened the box, she gave Hans a smile. "Oh my, what is this beauty?" She pulled out two beautiful dresses, one white and the other rose, size fourteen, and long sleeves. She started to cry, and she told Hans how beautiful that they were. She thanked Hans practically all night and promised to try them on in the morning. I love you Hans! Thank you for making me feel better! "I love you so much and I wish my family was alive again, because if they were, Mama would love you!" Sasha exclaimed. "Mama always said that if someone loves me, then I must keep him forever." Hans asked, "I guess that she would love me?" "Yes, Hans, she would," replied Sasha softly. The baby was sleeping and they wanted to be with each other. Sasha had not lain in Hans's arms for a while. They lay there, and Hans kissed Sasha. His heart melted again as he saw Sasha happy and in love. She just let everything fall into place as they lay together. Their hearts became as one and Hans never felt peace as he did with Sasha. He felt what had been missing he had finally found, for awhile. So we just lay still as though we were looking at the stars in the sky. We talked, laughed and fell asleep in each others arms, again. "I love you, Sasha," whispered Hans. "I love you Hans," Sasha assured him.

MORNING BLISS

They both woke up early in the morning because the baby was fussing, and Sasha had to feed her. As Natalia grew older, she wasn't crying as much. Hans and Sasha got dressed. They were like a newlywed couple very much in love and feeling so much bliss. Last night they spent the time together, the first time in a long time. At night, they had usually been tired and busy. Hans's accident put them behind in a lot. Most of the time, Hans's leg bothered him, making him tired and not really feeling like doing anything. Hans was happy, wanted to do something special today, but what? After breakfast, Hans took a shower and dressed. The weather again was changing, but they still had some warm September days. Hans wanted to see his horse. Hymen was the one Hans had assigned to take care of him. Hans went into the shed to see how Zurich was doing and he gave him oats and water. Hans was determined to ride again in the spring. When he told Sasha about riding again, she was overwhelmed. Again, Sasha thanked Hans for a good life, for saving her, and for Natalia. Hans felt totally happy for a change, recognizing that nothing could change this feeling at this moment.

SASHA'S REACTION

(as told by Sasha)

That day I became so different, so much in love and I wanted everyone to know how I truly feel. I really adored the dresses Hans bought for me. The colors are so nice, and Hans was so thoughtful! Hans so understood in how I felt about the numbers on my arm and he tried everything to make me feel better. When I tried on that dress that I really liked, I had forgotten that I had those numbers on my arm tattoo. I was embarrassed to let anyone see it because they would know that I had been in a concentration camp. They would not understand how I felt or what had happened. Hans has been my best friend for so long. I really don't know what I would do without him. For this reason, I worry about him at times and when something happens to him, I am very devastated. Sometimes when he rides his horse, I fear that he is going over to that camp, trying to relive his past again. The last time he did, he was hurt. If we had not gone there, he could have been really hurt. I know that he is upset at times the way things are, but I know things will get better. I always tell Hans to have faith and believe. He usually does. I know I love Hans, but I am not sure if he loves me the way he says that he does. I never told him that I really believe that he loves Mela, but I could see in his eyes how he reacted to her getting married. I remember that time that Mela visited Hans alone in his den. I said nothing, but am almost sure my husband is in love with Mela. I let the matter go because I trust that someday all of uncertainly will be resolved; but how it would be, I am not sure. I thank you Hans again for those dresses, and I do hope we get to go somewhere special before Natalia gets older. I love you Hans and Natalia, she is beautiful like you.

TELEPHONE CALL

Hans asked Sasha about Frau Goetz and for her ideas about what he should say about her husband. She told me to tell the truth as I always do, and not lie to Frau Goetz because she needs to know about her husband. Around 11:30 AM, Hans went into his den to make the call to Frau Goetz at the dress shop without any interruptions. Frau Goetz answered the phone. Hans reminded her that he had come in with his wife and baby. Immediately she knew who Hans was and asked, "How are those dresses that you bought?" Hans told her that his wife loved them and thanked her. Hans cleared his voice as he began to answer her unfinished question about her husband. Hans told her that he had known her husband when he was stationed at Camp Kassel. Her voice was getting louder; She knew what Hans was saying was true. Hans told her that her husband had been under my command at Camp Kassel. Hans also told her that at the end the camp was bombed. Sadly, that he had seen hurt and several of his officers were killed. "I am sorry to say that your husband was one of the officers who were killed," Hans said slowly. Frau Goetz asked where his body was, and Hans told her that since the army had to abandon the camp that his body was buried in the field. "He is still buried there," said Hans gently. Hans heard her crying, and his heart sank; it seemed that the camp still haunted him with something. Frau Goetz asked whether it was possible to bring his body back to her so that she could bury him properly. Hans told her that he could get someone to find him and asked her to give him her address so that he could bring her husband's body to her. Hans told Frau Goetz that he would build a box to contain her husband's remains. She broke down again and thanked Hans once more. Hans told her that there were no more headquarters or any communications when we were bombed, leaving him to make the right choice; she understood. Frau Goetz asked whether Hans could start on the box for her husband's remains as soon as possible. He told her, "Yes, he could, today." Hans also promised her that he would call her when he had finished it and had picked up her husband's remains. Hans also confirmed that he would deliver her husband's remains to her. Frau Goetz thanked Hans. As soon as he hung up, Hans dabbed his eyes and called Hymen.

BUILDING THE BOX

Hans asked Hymen to help build the box for Goetz's remains from the camp and told him that they needed to return him back to his family, properly. Hymen got out the wood, a chisel, wood screws, and sandpaper. Hans told Hymen that Goetz had been about 5'10, so they would need to make the box at least 6ft long and 3 feet wide. Hymen started to measure the wood, and Hans helped to cut it. They then put the wood screws in place and sanded down the edges until the box was perfect. They put the shiner on it and then let it dry. Hans went inside to call Frau Goetz so she would know that the box was finished but had to dry overnight. She was pleased and thanked Hans again. Hans informed her that several men would go to the camp to dig up her husband's body and bring the box to her the next day before 4:00PM. Frau Goetz asked Hans whether he could deliver the box to the back of the store because her son would be there with his truck to to take the box. "That will be no trouble," Hans assured her.

Hans asked Hymen, Otto and Peter and the Rabbi to come with him to the camp tomorrow to find Goetz's body. Hans explained the reason, and Otto suggested taking the truck to the camp and then to Berlin. We still had the Bedford MJ from the camp.

PICKING UP GOETZ

At 6:00 AM, Hans had some breakfast and asked Hymen and Otto to put the box into the Bedford ready to go. Hans kissed his family good-bye until later and reminded Sasha that he would be expecting a call from the hospital for an appointment. Sasha reassured Hans that she would take care of everything. The men left at 6:30 AM with the Bedford MJ. The truck had some shovels, gas masks and gloves that they would need. They needed at least two hours to arrive at the camp again, then two hours back and five more hours for Berlin, then another five hours to return to home. They would be on the road for fourteen hours and decided to change drivers every four hours so that no one would become too tired. At 8:24AM they arrived at the main gate, Peter drove the truck to where the kitchen had been located. Hans knew that he had ordered Goetz to be buried in the field behind the kitchen. Peter parked the Bedford. The men got out and walked slowly with shovels in their hands. Hans looked over at the side and there was Goetz's grave. Hans started to dig, and so did everyone else. Hans told them to put on their masks because of the stench. They dug almost five feet down. Presently they felt the body which made them aware that they we had to be careful so that the body would not fall apart. They moved the dirt away and saw Goetz with his uniform torn and partially burned. The men put on gloves to pick up the remains and then laid Goetz in the box. They closed it securely and loaded it into the Bedford. They threw everything they had used into the back of the truck. Otto was to drive to Berlin. En route, they grew hungry and were glad that Sasha and Mela had packed them plenty of sandwiches and drinks. When they arrived around 1:30 PM, Otto pulled the Bedford into the back of the shop where Goetz's son met them. He asked whether we could please help him take the box out and load it into his truck. Hymen and Peter helped him; and when the box was loaded into the truck, we took a moment of silence. Everyone saluted Goetz for his bravery and service, and his son thanked them with tears in his eyes. He told them that he was happy that his father was finally home. Hans really felt that they accomplished something good even though they were exhausted. "I feel good because we made a family happier than they were before," Hans told his companions. Hans drove the Bedford home, arriving around 7:30PM.

BEST NEWS

Sasha greeted Hans at the door with baby Natalia, and she said that both of them had missed him. Hans took Sasha in his arms and kissed her then took baby Natalia and sat down to catch his breath. Hans was glad that dinner was ready because everyone was very hungry and mostly tired from the trip. Sasha told Hans that the hospital called and the appointment would be on September 30 at 11:00am. Hans thanked her and concentrated on eating. They had potato soup with dumplings, and plenty of roasted chicken, and of course, sweet bread. Hans was so hungry that he couldn't speak any more for awhile. Later, he asked Sasha for any mail? She then handed him two letters, one from the treasury and the other from the Colonel. Hans opened the letter from the treasury, which contained his check for 750 marks. Then he opened the letter from the Colonel, who had written: "Commander Hans, hoping this letter is finding you well, I did want you to know that we have increased your wages each month due to your injuries while on duty. Your pay takes care of the injuries, and if you have any question, please call me." Hans showed Sasha the letter and he was overwhelmed by this increase. Hans knew that the money would never replace his leg, but it would surely help his family. To celebrate, Sasha brought out a bottle of brandy and poured us each a glass. She then made a toast to Hans and his successful life. Hans took a warm shower, got into bed and played with Natalia for a while, then spent his remaining time with Sasha. Hans felt as though he had been neglecting her at times even though she understood. Hans asked her whether she wanted to go away for a few days, and of course she agreed. “How about Switzerland my love?” he asked. Hans told her that they could leave on Wednesday and stay until Sunday. Sasha nodded happily. They kissed good night, and kissed the baby, and wearily turned out the light.

TIME OFF

Hans shaved off his beard just because Sasha says that it tickled her face when she kissed him. Hans told Sasha that he would continue to grow one and then shave it every second day. He just liked the feeling of having a beard then getting rid of it. Hans then began to make reservations today at the "Chateau Hotel" in Switzerland for Sept 20-24th. "I guess we will go Frankfurt to get a plane out and I have to check that out also. I have a busy day ahead of me, and Sasha is excited about going away and I can't blame her for that," Hans said to himself. He knew that sometimes it works going away. Hans felt this trip would be able to clear out his mind. "Sasha and I need this trip to revive our marriage and to find out who we really are to one another. I have always told Sasha that I will love her in my own way, and that no matter what ever happens she would be special. The same was said to me from Sasha. Sasha is a wonderful wife and mother and I don't blame her for anything, it is me that has caused problems. Sometimes we think we really want something and when we get it, the love for it is no longer there. I am not sure about this, but I am sure that I am willing to try." Hans called the hotel and airport up and arranged everything. He and Sasha couldn't wait to go. Peter said that he would take them to the airport and would pick them up on the return. Hans realized that he and Sasha would be taking their first vacation together. He was also so happy that his daughter was part of their lives. "She gives me something more to love," said Hans to himself. They packed, and Sasha put her new pink dress into the suitcase just in case they decided to do something special, like dinner. Hans told her to pack plenty of diapers and formula and that pretty pink dress that he had bought for Natalia. Hans packed some shirts, trousers, his coat, and extra shoes and socks. They were so excited for this trip that they wished they were there already. Their plane would leave Frankfurt at 7:30 AM, so they had to be up early. For the rest of the remaining day Hans left instructions for Hymen concerning Zurich, the house, and his father. We all took our baths including Natalia. They all went to sleep early so that they could get up earlier than they normally did.

ARRIVING IN SWITZERLAND

They awoke at 5:00AM and had a light breakfast because they wanted to eat something at the airport if they had the time. We dressed the baby warmly because it was a little chilly outside. When Hans had finished dressing, Sasha asked whether he could take Natalia while she got dressed, so Hans held the baby and gave her a bottle. Natalia looked so cute in her pajamas. Hans just sat there admiring his daughter. "No father could ever deny that he does not love his children because if he does, that man is not worthy of the blessing that God gave him," thought Hans. They went downstairs to meet Peter and left in Hans's car once again. It was still chilly outside when they arrived at Frankfurt airport after two hours or so. Hans thanked Peter, who reminded Hans to call when about their pick-up. Hans told Peter around 2:00PM on Sunday but that he would call him to confirm the time. Hans showed the tickets at the check-in counter and checked in their baggage. Shortly thereafter, they boarded the plane. Many people were on the plane, and Hans was amazed that it was full. Hans and Sasha couldn't wait to start their vacation together. Two hours later they arrived in Switzerland. From the distance, they could see the Alps. Sasha bundled Natalia with double blankets so that only her small face stuck out. They got into a taxi and Hans asked the driver to take them to the Chateau Hotel. When Hans and Sasha arrived at the hotel, they had someone open the door for them and took their baggage to the front lobby. Hans checked in and received the key for room 214. The desk clerk said that the bell boy would take them up and let us into our room. The clerk wished them a good stay. The bell boy took them up in the elevator, and there they met the peace that they longed for in Room 214. Hans gave the boy a tip and thanked him. Hans could hardly believe how beautiful the room was, especially when they opened the curtains and there were the Alps in front of them in the distance. The bed was soft, and Natalia had her crib on the side with cuddly blankets. Hans went into the bathroom where he saw a double tub and plenty of towels. "This is remarkable," exclaimed Hans. "I am so pleased that we came here!" Sasha was just as overwhelmed in what she was seeing and loved every minute of it. Hans told her that there would be no distractions, noise, phone calls or anything that would disturb them. Hans could actually hear himself think. They noticed on one table a complimentary bottle of red wine "imported from Switzerland." They put their coats down, and Hans called the front desk for some lunch. He ordered some crackers with cheese, ham and whatever else the hotel could recommended. Sasha was feeding Natalia oatmeal and a bottle of milk. Natalia fell asleep in Sasha's arms as she reached over to the crib to lay her down and cover her. Hans and Sasha stood there looking at one one another, Sasha rushed over to Hans, hugged him for this trip and asked whether he truly loved her. Hans told her that he loved her very much, and that he just wanted to live for today and not plan for tomorrow. Sasha respected what Hans had said. She knew that Hans cared for her so much and especially their daughter. Hans vowed to be a good husband and father because he realized how very important to him his family was, no matter what might happen.

BEAUTY IN ITSELF

The hotel was beautiful. Hans felt so good not to see any damaged or bombed buildings. "I really wish that Germany looked like this again," he said. Hans then went downstairs to ask at the front desk whether there were any trips or events for this week. The manager told Hans that the hotel had a sleigh ride at 11:00 this morning to tour the area. Hans wasn't sure because of Natalia, and he did not want her to be cold or Sasha. So he asked what else they had. The manager told Hans that they had a tour going out by bus that afternoon to local places and a tour around the Alps the next day. Hans wanted to pay for both tours, himself and for his wife and baby. The desk clerk said that Hans would not have to pay for the baby and reminded him that the bus would be leaving from the hotel at 11:00AM on both days. Hans thanked the clerk, who wished him a good day. Hans went upstairs to tell Sasha to be ready by 11:00AM because they were going on a tour that should be fun. He also told her that if she finds anything she wants, to buy it. They went downstairs to have breakfast and then to wait for 11:00AM to arrive. Shortly before, the front desk announced the bus leaving for town and asked all who had tickets to board the bus. Hans, Sasha, and Natalia went to the bus. Hans handed the driver the tickets and saw fourteen people on the bus. The scenery was beautiful, and Hans told Sasha as they rode that it would be nice and peaceful to live here. She looked at him and agreed without hesitation. In town, they saw so many shops and restaurants to eat. The driver announced that he would pick them up at the same spot at 4:00PM and wished them an enjoyable day. Hans and Sasha were overwhelmed as they looked at the shops.

They saw one shop that sold nothing but souvenirs. When they went inside, a nice woman greeted them and welcomed them to her shop. She asked where Hans and Sasha lived. Hans told her that they were from Cologne, Germany, and that they were on tour. She also asked them whether they liked the area: "Yes!" they said in unison. The shopkeeper said, "Feel free to look at what we have, and if I could help you, do let me know." Hans and Sasha saw key chains and selected some that they liked as well as postcards, cups and anything else they like. They even bought Natalia a blanket with "Switzerland" embroidered on it. The shopkeeper was happy to see that Hans had found what he was looking for. Hans told her that they had many at home and that he was bringing these gifts for them and maybe a key chain or two for himself and Sasha. The shopkeeper laughed and thanked them for coming to Switzerland.

SHOPPING IS FOR SASHA

Sasha and Hans went over to the ladies' shop where Hans bought Sasha two cashmere sweaters that had been made locally. She loved them and the colors were very pretty: pink and light blue. Hans told her they would be nice for her and that her hair would complement them nicely. She agreed and said, "Well, Hans buy something for yourself instead of me always." Hans went over to a man's shop where he saw everything that he liked. He bought four long-sleeved shirts and some socks. Sasha looked at Hans and asked, "Could you shop better?" Hans replied, "All right." He reached for three pairs of trousers. Sasha smiled and said, "Better Hans." Sasha looked at the time. It was 2:25PM. They had time left, so they went to have lunch and then to see whether they could find a baby shop so that Sasha could buy Natalia something to wear. Hans and Sasha went into a cafe where they saw so many desserts and sandwiches piled high with Swiss cheese. Natalia was sleeping, so Hans and Sasha sat down. A waitress asked whether they wanted to see a menu. Hans told her that would be fine. We ordered sandwiches and desserts. For drinks, Hans had a beer and some water for Sasha. Everything was delicious, and they were so filled that they could not move. Hans paid the man, and they went over to the baby shop. They still had enough time to shop for the babies. They went in, and Sasha was looking around while Hans held on to Natalia. Sasha found a beautiful pink outfit for the winter for Natalia, and Hans told her to buy four of them. Sasha also asked about a small jacket for Natalia and socks. Hans told her to buy whatever she feels their daughter would need. Hans also asked Sasha to buy Danderick something. Hans paid the clerk and they left with so many bags that Hans didn't know how to carry them anymore. We went up to the bus, and the driver asked whether we were having a good time. Hans answered, "Look at all the bags: does that tell you something?" The driver laughed, and we got on the bus once the last tourist was on. The bus left. Hans and Sasha were so pleased that they talked about coming back again. This was a moment in their lives that we were so happy together. Sasha was worried about money, but Hans told her that they had enough money, especially with his increase. Hans didn't want his family to be without anything, and he would do his best to keep it that way.

BACK AT THE HOTEL

They arrived at the hotel and went upstairs to put all their bags on the bed. Sasha changed Natalia and Hans ordered dinner but not until 7:00PM, giving them enough time to get Natalia settled in and for them to take a bath. Hans and Sasha played some music as they felt so much peace in their room. The food came around 7:10PM. Hans had ordered Sauerbraten, pork and dumplings, and a bottle of red wine. Natalia was now asleep, as Sasha and Hans had a chance to eat and relax after a busy day. The dinner he ordered was German food. It was excellent, especially the fresh bread. After finishing dinner, Hans put the cart outside of their door. The time had gone by so fast. Tomorrow would be Friday. They would have another busy day with touring. Hans dressed in his night pants. As always, he left his shirt off. Hans had to take his artificial leg off. Usually he did not take his artificial leg off, but tonight his leg hurt. Hans excused himself to Sasha. She asked whether he was all right. Hans always appreciated her asking. Sasha came out of the bathroom combing her long dark hair. Then she climbed into the bed. Hans turned the light off, and as always, they discussed their day and their future. Sasha had her head on Hans's chest. He looked at her told her that he loved her. She told him the same.

MORE SIGHTSEEING

Shortly after dawn, they took a quick shower then went downstairs to have breakfast. Sasha fed Natalia some oatmeal and milk. It was almost 10:00 AM when they went back upstairs. To be downstairs at 11:00AM for their tour guide. They left their room at 10:45AM and met our tour guide and other tourist waiting. The guide announced that anyone who had tickets for the Alps tour and luncheon, should now come to the front desk. He directed the group to the bus. We waited for five minutes and then we were off on our journey. After the bus started to move, the guide welcomed everyone and announced the itinerary. The first stop would be the brewery and after that, to the Swiss cheese factory. We watched the workers from both of the factories performing their jobs in making beer and cheese and both were interesting. The factory manager gave everyone a sample of beer and the cheese. The beer tasted different from German beer, but still it was good. The Swiss cheese was so good that Hans bought some cheese for us to take back to Germany. Hans and Sasha bought some more interesting souvenirs. One of them was little cheeses on a key chain. Hans thought his friends back home would like one of the key chains. After this tour finished, the group re-boarded the bus. This time, Hans and Sasha sat next to another couple,who asked Hans where he lived, and he said, "Cologne, Germany." They began to speak to Hans and Sasha in German. Both Sasha and Hans spoke German to them, pleased that they had another couple speaking their language. They said that their names were Heinrich and Helga Rosenheim from Hamburg. They also said that they had just been married and that they were on their honeymoon.

Hans and Sasha wished them the best. Hans remembered his own wedding done in secret at the camp. Hans could never tell Sasha that he believed that they should have waited because then she would feel that he didn't love her. Hans dropped the thought. Their final tour before lunch would be to have a meal at Swiss Chateau Restaurant. So we got off the bus and went inside where they found a lot of customers waiting. The waiter told them that they that would need to wait at least ten minutes for seating. Once they were seated, the waiter asked whether they needed anything for the baby and handed them the menu. Sasha refused politely, anything for the baby. She and Hans looked over the menus and saw so much to choose, making their decisions even harder. Hans found a sandwich with melted Swiss cheese and ham on fresh bread and ordered it with a beer. Sasha finally ordered roast beef with melted Swiss cheese and seltzer water. Sasha leaned over to Hans and asked whether they were financially all right, and he told her that they were fine. He mentioned that when he was Commander, he had saved every paycheck for all those years at the camp and in Munich. He also mentioned that he had his disability—veteran check each month. Sasha then asked Hans whether they could move here in Switzerland. Hans told her to wait and see what happens and then they could consider. "Plan it out carefully," Hans told her. She replied, "Just as you had planned it out in the past?" Hans nodded his head and smiled to her, "Yes." The time went by fast so fast that they could hardly believe that they were going back to the hotel. It was around 4:00PM when they went upstairs and ordered dinner for around 7:00 PM. Natalia was fussing somewhat and it was because of her teething. The next day they would be going back home. Hans knew that he would surely miss this area because he and Sasha had a wonderful time. Hans remembered to call Peter. Mela answered, and Hans asked her whether Peter was around? She said he wasn't but that she would give him a message. Hans told her to tell him to pick them up at the airport around 1:30 PM. "If the plane is late, to wait." She said to me, "Anything for you, Hans." Mela told Hans to take care until she would see him again. He hung up the phone. Hans's leg was aching him today as he sat in the chair. Hans had to make an appointment for next week to see the doctor, and he planned on mentioning this occurrence. Hans disliked walking with his cane because it slows him down. “Oh well, we’ll see,” said Hans under his breath. Hans wanted to take a short walk just to smell the fresh crisp air; but he couldn’t, so he relaxed for the rest of the evening playing with Natalia and being with his wife.

GOING HOME

The next morning, Hans and Sasha packed their suitcases and went downstairs so that Hans could pay. The desk clerk asked whether they had a good time. Hans told him that they did and were planning to return. The desk clerk was pleased with our comments and wished us a safe trip back to Germany. We took a taxi to the airport. The journey took only 25 minutes, so they arrived earlier than expected. Hans went to the boarding desk to show the tickets, and the staff directed them to the rest area. With about an hour before boarding, Hans asked Sasha if whether she would want to go to the store and pick up anything. She said, "No." Hans played with Natalia hoping she would feel better. He really loved his little Natalia; even when she grow older, Natalia would always be his little girl. Hans heard the announcement that Flight 104 was boarding for Frankfurt,Germany, and those who are holding tickets should come to Gate 3. Hans had to take his time because he couldn't walk as fast. Sasha knew that when Hans couldn't walk, he had to stop to catch his breath from the pain and strain. Hans was happy board the plane. He was tired and couldn't wait to get home. In between, the crew gave them a drink and a small snack. Hans put on the earphone to listen to music and he fell asleep. Before he knew it, he felt a nudge from Sasha. "Wake up," she said. "We're landing in Frankfurt." Hans was still groggy when they landed. The pilot announced that the plane had to wait for clearance to land. Finally they got off the plane and walked down the path to the waiting room where they saw Mela and Peter. Hans and Sasha saw them and rushed right to them. Peter and Mela both grabbed them and hugged them and told them that they missed them. Hans told Peter that he and Sasha had a wonderful time and that Switzerland was breathtaking.

Mela kept her eyes on Hans as he spoke to Peter but never said anything, except hello. Danderick was so cute, and Hans wanted to hold him so badly; but he didn't dare to ask. Peter told me that everything was fine at home. He also said that the three former prisoners had found family and left. Hans was happy for them, happy that they had found family, a huge surprise. Hans asked about any other news for him or Sasha; and Peter said, "Oh yes, there was a call from Colonel Buchwalter, he would like you to call him."

JOB OFFER

Hans spoke to the Colonel. He Hans whether he would be interested in working for the Treasury Department. He said that Hans would be in charge and would work a few hours per day. Hans told the Colonel that he would not be interested at this time because of his leg, but he suggested Peter or Otto for the position. The Colonel asked Hans to have Peter call him as soon as possible and promised that when another position comes in, he would call. Hans thanked the Colonel, who said that he would be in touch with Hans. Later that day, Hans spoke with Otto, his first choice for that position, but Otto refused because of the distance. Hans then went to Peter and explained about the position that the Colonel had offered to him and said that he had suggested either Peter or Otto. "Unfortunately, Otto refused the position because of the distance, so you are the only one left to decide," said Hans. Peter thanked Hans for recommending him and said that he would like to speak to the Colonel about the position. Hans gave Peter the telephone number. "Call today and speak directly to him." Peter called the Colonel. Then he came to Hans to report that he had accepted the position. "Now I can think about getting my own place to live with Mela," exclaimed Peter. Hans congratulated him, not for wanting to move with Mela, but for taking the position. Hans now felt disturbed that his offer to recommend Peter would make it easier for him to move with Mela. Hans stood there again, as foolish as he could be and wondering where this will ever lead him. Peter told me that tomorrow he would be going down to Berlin to start his new position.

MELA

Peter left for work early because of the distance and time. He asked Hans to tell Mela that he would not be home until after 6:00 PM because of the distance.

When Hans went into the kitchen to get some breakfast, he ran into Mela and told her that Peter said that he would not be home until 6:00 PM or after. Mela thanked Hans and asked whether he wanted breakfast. Hans shook his head "Yes," and asked her whether he could please hold his son for a while. Mela handed baby Danderick to Hans, who held him as though he was an angel sitting on a bed of clouds. Danderick was so handsome; he resembled Hans and Hans was proud of him. When Hans told Mela that Danderick resembled him, she assured Hans that she knew that. "Every time I look at Danderick, I am looking at you, Hans." Hans continued to hold Danderick, kissing him and playing with him. Mela told Hans that Peter wanted to be the father to Danderick and to keep him out of the relationship. Hans understood and asked Mela whether she agreed with him on the decision. She told Hans that she was against Peter's decision but did not care because she would find a way for Danderick to be with Hans. Mela then told Hans that she wished that he would have married her so that they could be together as they had been at the camp. As she talking, Sasha walked into the kitchen and looked as though she was disturbing something going on. She saw that Hans was holding his own. She wasn't upset, but she was concerned about their relationship. Sasha asked Hans whether he had breakfast, and Hans told her that Mela made him some eggs and toast. Sasha looked as though she was upset but left the matter at that. Hans sat there and said, "Peter will find a place to live and then take my son away; then he will not know who his true father would be." Mela disagreed with Hans. She said, "There would always be a way that you would be there for me and Danderick." Hans knew what she meant. Hans was glad that Sasha was not there when Mela told him this because he would have to explain himself to her. Mela promised to do what she could for Hans. Because he had given Mela the gift of life, she would do the same for Hans. Mela came up to Hans secretly and kissed him. Hans then reached over to Danderick, and kissed him, and gave him back to his mother. As Hans was leaving, he turned around to Mela thanked her, and went to the den. Mela smiled because she knew about Hans's feelings for her and how they both carried those feelings for each other trying to cover them with something or someone else. She felt that surely the situation would change someday.

"TRUTHFULLY, YOURS"

Hans went to his den to think about his love for Mela. In Hans's silence, he kept saying to Mela, "Truthfully, Yours." He knew in his heart that someday he would be with Mela. "Someday, I will be united with Mela, my dearest love," Hans said to himself silently. "I have made a mistake with Sasha and I will correct that someday," Hans said. Hans sat in his den alone. He had thoughts of love for Mela, and he fought within his heart the feelings he carried for her. Hans secretly gave his words to Mela, "Truthfully, Yours, my only true love." "I'm sorry Sasha for the mistake that I have made," said Hans to himself. Hans sat in his den for awhile, thinking, and hoping that his heart someday will be united with "Truthfully, Yours."

CONFRONTATION

Hans continued to sit in his den, though he poured himself a glass of brandy. He still had the old habits from when he was commander of the camp where a drink was not too early or a cigarette to blow away his worries. Although he never wanted to drink this early, Hans knew what was next in his life and wanted to drink that worry down. He finished his brandy, and because it was nice outside he went to sit on the porch and have a cigarette. As he was sitting there, sighing to every thought he had about Mela, he was confronted by Sasha. She came out asking about the conversation that he had with Mela. Hans looked at her hoping to hide his true feelings and told her that he did not know what she was talking about. He became upset, and now Sasha had to make his life worse than what it was. He replied very harshly to Sasha, asking her what she was referring to and not to hide it. He then got up as the argument became a little louder. To avoid any more of it, he went to the den and closed the door. Sasha went upstairs, and Hans did not move for some time. As he was sitting there, he found a book with pictures on the shelf. He opened it and to found pictures of himself. Hans didn't remember anyone taking them, but he did remember that Sasha would take secret pictures of him. These pictures were from the camp with him outside during roll call on his horse and dressed in his full black uniform. Hans saw so many pictures that he just gave up looking at them and closed the book. As he was closing the book, a picture of Mela fell out and landed on the floor. He picked up the picture only to recognize Mela from the camp. His feelings were now in trouble. Hans put Mela's picture it in his pocket so Sasha would not know. Hans then went upstairs and found Sasha at the door. She was upset about what happened outside. Sasha said that she wanted to know about his feelings for Mela. Hans told her to quit the questions because all that he and Mela had discussed was about his son. "My son is very important to me and I wanted to see him, to hold him, and to be friends with Mela. "Is that all right with you?" Hans asked harshly. Whatever his feelings were for Mela, Sasha felt she could never change them or ask Hans to give his love up for her. Sasha didn't mention the subject anymore and was prepared for the future in what might happen. Hans went into the shower and decided to stay there to think and to be alone. When he had finished, he put on cologne, slicking his blond hair back, and dressed in a shirt and black trousers. He went over to his daughter and kissed her then walked downstairs. He went into the kitchen where Mela was still feeding Danderick. Hans waved good-bye and said the he'd see her later. Mela knew that Hans was upset, but she couldn't do anything about his problem.

A NEW PROJECT

Hans sat outside while he smoked another cigarette, then went into the shed to see his horse. He pat him on the head and told Zurich that he would be there all day building. Then he gave Zurich a carrot to eat. Hans gathered some wood to build two small chairs for the babies. Hans cut the wood as he measured the size of the chair where he started to cut out the pattern. He made the holes with his chisel and fit in everything as the chairs began to take a special feature. Hans stood there trying to get all his feelings out of his mind. He was sorry for his mistakes; but he could tell Sasha the truth, she would walk out on him. "Sasha did nothing to him; it is something I did to her," Hans said as he started to bang the pieces into the holes and pushed in wood screws to keep the wood in place. Hans went back to his feelings about Mela, and how he truly loved her, but he knew that he had now no purpose ever to love her because she married Peter. "I have no right to her anymore because I gave her up," Hans berated himself. "I was selfish and I should have never married during the war because it tore Sasha and me apart. I married her because I didn't want to hurt her feelings in what I promised," Hans said sadly. "Oh God, help me through this agony that I have each day," Hans pleaded. Hans then took the two small chairs and sandpapered the edges making them smoother. Needing a break, Hans took Zurich outside and tied him to the pole. Hans was standing outside to get some fresh air when Sasha came outside. She looked at Hans and saw how dirty his clothes were. She asked whether he was working in the shop. Hans nodded. Sasha then apologized for what she had said to him. "Whatever happens to us, I will always be there for you," she promised. Hans remained silent. He didn't want to pursue any more of the conversation. Then he kissed her and went back to the shed. There he found his peace as he finished sanding the chairs and painted the shiner on the wood. He then put the chairs on the working table to dry.

HANS'S ENCOUNTER

Around 1:00PM, Hans saddled Zurich, noticing that he still had his rifle from the camp strapped on, but he really didn't care. He mounted Zurich and saw Mela through the window watching him. Hans acknowledged that he saw her by looking right at her waving good-bye. As he was riding slowly out to the road, he decided to go to town for awhile. He noticed the birds were singing so sweetly, and the thoughts of hearing them reminded him how he used to hear the birds when he was in the camp. The sun beat down on Hans, but he did not seem to notice because he was in deep thinking about what had happened earlier that day. Hans was convinced that Sasha was trying to tell him something, yet he didn't want to hear that something. For that reason, he had decided to quit the argument and just let Sasha say she was sorry. He could never let her know the truth in his feelings for Mela, so he decided to let this feeling go and not hold on to it anymore. He just wanted to get away for a while and try to regain his feelings for Sasha. Han arrived in town shortly after, tied Zurich to a pole and went into a store that sold practically everything. He came across a lot of different objects as he searched for something special for Sasha. Hans wasn't sure what he wanted until he found one item that he thought Sasha would find interesting. It was a pin with these beautiful multicolor rhinestones, practically new. Hans asked the clerk to wrap it up in a small box. Hans thanked the clerk, paid her, and went to the pub for some lunch. It felt good to sit by himself capturing his thoughts and feelings. The waiter came over, and Hans asked him for a beer and pork with Sauerbraten. Nobody was around except Hans and a woman sitting at the bar. She looked to be around 25, and Hans assumed that she was having a cup of coffee by herself. Hans went up to her and asked whether she wanted to join him at the table. He noticed that she looked distraught. Hans introduced himself to her, and she did the same by calling herself, Mari. Hans asked her whether she was from around Cologne, and she told him that she lived down the road. She came here often. By the time she finished her sentence, Hans received his food and offered to buy her some lunch. She said that she didn't want to impose upon him or take his money. Hans told her that he saw no problem and called over the waiter to ask him to bring Mari some food. She ordered the same food that Hans was eating and asked for another cup of coffee. Before long, Mari was telling Hans about her life. As she was reaching over to pick up some salt, her blouse sleeve displayed something familiar to Hans, numbers tattooed on her arm. Hans knew exactly where she had come from. Hans was very cautious in what he had to say to her because he knew that he would not see her again. Hans asked her whether she had been in this area during the war, and she said, "Yes." Mari returned the question. Hans nodded his head. Hans looked at her. Mari looked at Hans deeply as though she was trying to dig into her past and remember where she had seen him. She asked Hans whether he had been in the war perhaps. Hans was stuffing the food into his mouth so he didn't have to answer so quickly. Mari excused herself for asking while he was eating. Hans then swallowed his food and I said, "Yes, I was." She asked whether he had been stationed somewhere close to here. Again I answered, "Yes." Suddenly, Mari pointed her fork toward him and said that she had known Hans from the camp. Hans asked her what she meant, and she said that she knew him as the Commander of the Slave Camp in Kassel. Hans looked at her dismayed, not knowing how to answer her. Hans couldn't deny it, so he said, "Yes, that is who I am." Mari looked at Hans as she grabbed his hand and kissed it and said, "I was hoping that I would run into you again and thank you for setting me free from death." Hans smiled and said that she was welcome.

After they finished eating, Hans told Mari that he had to go home to his family. Mari wished him the best, thanked him and said, “Someday we’ll meet again.” She thanked him again and disappeared into the distance.

CONFRONTING SASHA

Hans hadn't realize how long he had been, when he looked at his watch. It was half past four already. Hans was not home to find out how everyone was doing after the argument. Hans came home and put Zurich into the shed. He went into the house where he found Sasha lying on the bed. Natalia was in her crib playing with her stuffed animals. I picked her up and told her that Daddy was home; and as he did, he saw Sasha crying. Sasha was upset and told Hans that she was sorry for what happened today with the argument. Hans came over to her and handed Natalia to her while he sat on the bed next to Sasha. Hans told her not to worry about the conversation that they had, because he already forgotten about it. Sasha reminded Hans that they had an appointment at the clinic the next day and that they would have to leave around 6:00 AM to arrive there on time. Sasha tried to change the subject, but still Hans asked her, "What happened today?" She was upset because of Mela, and the rest she could not explain to Hans. I told her that Mela was just a good friend to him and that it all points to his son because Peter doesn't want Hans to see the baby much. She understood, and again apologized, and kissed Hans.

HOSPITAL VISIT

Hans and his family prepared to leave at 6:00 AM, and Sasha was feeding Natalia in the car. Because his leg was aching today, Hans went inside again to see whether Hymen was available. Hans found him in the kitchen and asked him whether he could drive them to the clinic. Hymen nodded. Hymen sat behind the wheel as Sasha and Hans went into the back seat with Natalia. Hans was very restless today, but by the time they had arrived at the clinic, his restlessness was over. They took the elevator to the waiting room and signed in. Hans had a separate appointment from Sasha and Natalia and was called in first. The nurse took him into the small examination room where she asked Hans in how he felt. Hans told her that his leg was aching but otherwise he was doing well. He told the nurse that often his leg ached sometimes it slowed him down. She wrote down this information all down and took his temperature and blood pressure. Everything checked out normal. "The doctor will be in as soon as possible," she said. As Hans was sitting there he heard a baby crying and knew Natalia was getting her shots. As soon as Natalia was finished, Sasha would be checked also. Hans had to wait for the women to be finished before the doctor would be visiting him. He did not have long to wait. Within five minutes the doctor came in and said to me, "Hans, your daughter is beautiful. She is doing just fine, and your wife, well congratulations on your second child; your wife is pregnant." "What did you say?" Hans asked. "Your daughter is fine and your wife is pregnant, again." Hans was speechless; he couldn't move, and all of a sudden he became dizzy. Hans was overwhelmed. He said to himself, "That is the reason Sasha came with me today, yet she said nothing." The doctor checked Hans's leg and told him that his leg was aching because it needed minor adjustments, which he then made. Hans thanked the doctor, who told Hans if any other problems please call him. Hans went to the waiting room where he met Sasha and Natalia waiting for him. Sasha kissed Hans and he was waiting for her to tell me the news. Still she said nothing. They met Hymen downstairs and left for home. While they were in the car, Sasha was looking at Hans as though she wanted to say something to him. Her face spoke a thousand words, and he knew that she was pregnant but he hadn't expected this pregnancy so early. Hans wasn't sure how to handle this one, and he wished that she would say something to him and get it over with so she could rest in peace about the baby.

TELL ME, SASHA

Hans kept saying this to himself, "Tell me, Sasha; and tell me." Hans assumed she was upset and scared of what I would say, or perhaps the doctor had made a mistake. To make his anxiety not obvious, Hans did his usual work around the house and chopping wood for the fireplace. It was chilly outside and everybody was asleep. Hans made the house cozy by starting all the fireplaces with wood. Hans felt ashamed of himself for not sleeping later because he was used to getting up early in the camp. Hans decided to put a pot of water on the stove for tea and coffee. Hans heard someone coming down the stairs. He waited for the door to open hoping it was Sasha all ready to tell him the truth. It wasn't Sasha, but his father. He looked at Hans and asked if he was doing all right. Hans said, "Fine, thank you." Hans told his father that he was actually waiting for Sasha to get up. He didn't want to tell father or anyone because he wasn't sure whether Sasha really was pregnant. Hans then had a cup of tea and some toast with his Father, and then he excused himself and went upstairs. There he found Sasha with Natalia combing her hair and putting some kind of cream through her hair. Natalia smelled so nice and her skin was soft like her mother's. Sasha asked Hans to hold Natalia and feed her a bottle while she went downstairs. She went downstairs for something and then came back. Hans asked her if everything was all right. Sasha told Hans that she was fine while he kept saying to himself, "Tell me, Sasha; tell me Sasha." Nothing still. Now Hans began seriously to doubt that the doctor was wrong about the pregnancy, so he gave up waiting. Sasha knew what to do and when to say something. Obviously, Hans did not.

WINTER AGAIN

December had now come; Natalia was already four months old and wanted to talk but couldn't. Sasha and Hans made a bet what she would call first, "Mama" or "Dada," and the prize would be a five minute kiss. Hans asked Sasha whether she wanted to go to the stores in Cologne and do some Christmas shopping. She was quite happy about the idea, and they went upstairs to dress before they had a bite to eat. Then they wrapped Natalia in a warm blanket and left in Hans's car headed for the city of Cologne. As we arrived, the shops already decorated with lights and trees. Pretty red, green, yellow, and blue lights were twinkling in the windows of the shops. The city looked beautiful. Sasha loved the colors and little Natalia just stared at the twinkling lights. Hans was hoping that Sasha would break down today and tell him about her pregnancy, but he waited it out. It was cold again, and they walked around town holding on to one another looking to find the first store for shopping. They looked at the list to see whose name was there to buy gifts. Hans had Sasha, Natalia, Otto, my father, Mela, Peter, Danderick, Elda, and Hymen and of course, Rabbi Jacob. Hans was hoping it would be easier to shop for everyone if he asked Sasha to help him with some of the gifts. Hans wanted to go to the novelty shop. The shop had so many gift ideas in the shop that Hans did not know what to buy. He spotted leather wallet for Peter, socks and shirts for his father, a watch for Otto, and a beautiful yellow dress with matching booties for Natalia. Hans paid the clerk and asked whether she had any wrapping paper and bows. She showed me so many colors that Hans wasn't sure what to buy. Hans asked her to give him some of the red and blue paper and a bag of bows. Hans wished her a "Merry Christmas" and left for the next shop. He went to the candle shop where he bought a beautiful candle for Mela and Elda. Next, he went into the antique shop and found some more nice gifts. He even found a Star of David and was surprised that there were any left in Germany because of the war. Hans bought that gift for Rabbi Jacob. When Sasha saw it, she said, "Hans, you are special." Hans laughed and continued his shopping. He bought more gifts which included toys and cards to put money in. After hours of looking, they had finally finished. Hans asked Sasha whether she wanted to go over to the restaurant. At the restaurant, Hans gave Sasha money to do some shopping herself, for he knew she wanted to shop. Hans told her to take the baby to the shops and look around while he did some more looking. Hans was looking for a fur coat for Sasha and went over to the woman's boutique. He found a fur coat, just what he wanted for Sasha and asked the clerk what kind of fur it was. She said, "Rabbit." "Yuck," Hans said, "Rabbit." Hans asked for size 14, and the clerk said that she had one in the back if Hans wanted to see it. She brought it out and it was beautiful inside and out. Hans told her that he would take it and asked her to wrap it for him. She wrapped it, and Hans paid her a little extra for doing that for him. He wished the clerk a wonderful Christmas, and he left to find Sasha. She and Natalia were in the next store as Sasha was looking around. Sasha said that she was not finished shopping, and Hans said, "There is tomorrow." Sasha looked at the big box that was wrapped in blue and silver paper and a big white bow. She asked, "Hans Schweitzer, what on earth is in that box?" He told her that she would find out on Christmas morning. Finally Sasha said to me, "Hans may I speak to you before we leave?" Hans told her it would all right, and said to himself, "The truth will finally be told." So he rushed to the car as fast as his leg could carry him, so sure the moment that he had wanted so badly had finally come.

"I LOVE YOU, HANS"

Sasha got into the car while Hans put all of the gifts in the trunk and Natalia was sleeping in Sasha's arms. Hans started the car, and they waited for the heat to come on so the car would be warm for them. They had to wait ten minutes before they could leave because the car was so cold. Hans finally left, driving slowly so Sasha would have the opportunity to tell him what she wanted to say. She did, finally. "I love you Hans, you know that I do." Then she said, "Hans, I found at the doctors that I am pregnant again." Hans laughed so hard that his tears ran down his cheeks. Sasha asked why he was laughing at something at something so serious. He replied, "It's fine. Don't worry about another baby. I am happy about that." Hans paused, then said, "Eventually we must find a place to live." The children will need a bigger place to play and grow up. Hans told Sasha that he loved her, and he thanked her for good news that he waited so long to hear. He didn't tell her that he knew already from the doctor because that would have ruined her surprise.

HERE WE GO AGAIN

Hans wasn't sure really how to accept the fact that his wife was pregnant again. Hans wanted to spend time with Natalia, at least play with her and help her to learn; but now his time would be limited to another child. He had to adapt to another child, and he could not show Sasha how he felt about this pregnancy. "I do know that I will support her with this baby no matter what," Hans promised. "So here we go again," he commented to Sasha. Hans told her that he wanted to get through this new situation with Natalia and the new baby. Hans told her that they could not spend time with each child if more are going to be born. Hans also mentioned the fact that they needed to wait after the second child before having any more because Sasha would have to heal and rest. They were still young. Hans said, "Let's take the time together and enjoy our lives together." Sasha agreed.

HOLIDAY DISCUSSION

Hans had a discussion today with Sasha about the holidays. Hans told her that although she was Jewish she could celebrate Christmas with him, as before. He also offered to celebrate her holiday with her as something different for them. Sasha was shy, about her heritage, and because of the war and the feelings toward Jews. She had decided not to celebrate her heritage. Hans told her not to be embarrassed because we had Rabbi Jacob among us. Sasha agreed and asked whether Hans would like to celebrate next year. Hans told her that would be fine and he dropped the subject because he could see that she didn't want to discuss the subject any longer. Sasha said that she still had to do her shopping as Hans went to my hidden safe and took money out for her to buy everyone a gift including her. Sasha turned around to tell me that she wanted to celebrate Hanukkah, which was her Jewish holiday near Christmas. She told Hans that it would be different and he asked her why she changed her mind. She told me that she would be doing it for her family in remembrance. She said that everyone would be getting one gift in honor of her parents and brother. She appreciated Hans so much for great understanding. She told him that he was an angel and that she would always love him no matter what might happen between them in the future. Hans kissed her and thanked her for being a wonderful wife and mother.

"FRITZ, MEIN FREUND"

Fritz had been born in Frankfurt, Germany. There he became part of Hitler's Youth where he was trained in the Nazi way of life. There was one problem, however he did not approve any of the rules. He was trained very hard to be perfect in all he did. Headquarters made him a soldier and guard at the camp. His job was to protect the Commander of Kassel Camp, and that was the only job to which he had been assigned. Rather than heed to the ideas of the Reich, Fritz wanted to become a man that his family raised him to be, regardless. Fritz spoke very little English and obeyed Hans in everything he asked. Fritz left the camp, and at the end, went to live at Hans's father's house. Quiet as he seemed, Fritz became a good friend to Hans and Sasha, and at one point Fritz swore his friendship to them. Hans treasured his friendship because Fritz had protected him and his quarters. "Good friends should be treasured and not destroyed," said Hans. Fritz agreed. Fritz was a gentleman. He stood almost 6 ft 1. He had very blue eyes and dirty blond hair. He was thin and weighed no more than 180 pounds, and he had no girlfriend at this time. He said he had no girlfriends in his life because he knew that he would be leaving them behind when he signed up for the war. He kept to his word about his life and was pleased that his family had escaped the brutality of the Gestapo. However, tragically his family disappeared somewhere in Germany, and he didn't know where to look for them. He swore that someday he would find them with great determination. Hans said that he would help him. Fritz had a talent for building and wanted to find a job as a builder. He thought that because Germany would need men to build what was destroyed, he was going to apply. This prospect gave him dreams to hold onto even though most of them were shattered from the war. Sometimes Fritz would sit in the living room reading a book talking to Elda. He had known her from the camp but never had spoken a word to her until he came to Hans's father's house. Elda enjoyed speaking with Fritz. One day when Fritz was in the living room with Hans, Elda came to see how everyone was doing. She was dressed in a very pretty flower-print dress with a pair of peasant shoes and wore her long blond hair tied back. Like Fritz, Elda's eyes were blue. As shy as Fritz was, Fritz asked Elda how she was doing and then turned to speak to Hans. Hans knew the story about them and got up and excused himself and left. Once they were both alone, Fritz stayed quiet. Elda knew that she would need to be the one to say something. She asked Fritz how he was doing today and about Christmas. Fritz's voice was low, but he manage to answer her by saying that he really didn't have any family to buy a gift. She pursued the conversation by asking whether he had any family still in Germany, and he said that he wasn't sure. Elda knew right there that she would make Fritz her priority to buy him a gift for Christmas. However, Elda did not know what to buy him because she didn't know much about Fritz. Still Elda knew it would be better to give than to receive, soon Fritz would find that out from her.

THE TREE, PLEASE

It was now December 15. Hans remembered the previous December and how the Colonel planned to have all his prisoners moved to another death camp. One year later, Hans was already bored from all of relative guest and was looking for any change that would make his life more bearable. As he was thinking, he suddenly realize that he had forgotten his wedding anniversary on November 18. Sasha never mentioned anything about it to him, so he thought that maybe she had forgotten about the date too. He felt so stupid that he forgotten his own wedding anniversary and wanted to do something to make it up to Sasha. To celebrate, Hans suggested buying a tree and having everyone decorate it. He drove Sasha and Natalia to town to find someone selling a Christmas tree. Just before they reached town, they saw a man on the side of the road selling trees. Hans wanted a special tree tall with lots of branches. Unfortunately, this man had only small trees and skinny ones, but none that Hans liked. He asked Sasha which tree, if any, she found attractive to buy. As he was asking Sasha, Natalia kept pointing to the trees, "Dat, Dat." Sasha took her over to the trees and asked Natalia which one she liked. Natalia grabbed one tree which Hans seemed to have missed, and Natalia held onto it while Hans bought the tree. Hans gave Natalia a kiss on her cheek thanking her for what she found. In matter of fact, Hans also adored the tree and he waited for the man to tie it up. Before you knew it, they were off. On the way home, Hans thought how blessed he was to have a wonderful family and friends at this time of the year.

He apologized to Sasha for forgetting his anniversary, but he thanked her for their first year together and for a wonderful daughter. He leaned over to kiss Sasha.

"Happy Anniversary," he said.

WE ARE FAMILY

Hans, Sasha, and Natalia brought the tree home and put it in the living room ready to be decorated by everybody including Natalia and Danderick. Hans went into the basement and he brought up the balls, lights, and the stand for the tree. There were so many decorations from when Hans was a young boy, and they brought back so many memories of the days when he had helped his parents. Hans put the tree onto the stand and made sure that the tree stood straight. He then went to get some water to put into the stand so the tree could remain wet. Everyone came down and grabbed decorations and happily put put them on the tree. Hans picked up Natalia and asked Mela to bring Danderick over to grab a decoration and give it to him as Hans had done for Natalia. The babies were brought closer to the tree, and then they threw the balls into the tree and we all laughed. Hans told Mela that wherever they had thrown the balls, he would hang them on that spot. Sasha produced her camera and started to take pictures of the children and all of us decorating. We had such fun, something to always remember by all of them. Hans couldn't believe that all of them who suffered so much during the war were now good friends and accepted each other as family. Rabbi Jacob was sitting with Hans's father talking about family. Fritz with Elda were laughing over something that no one else knew about. Otto was sitting back with Hymen and Hans. Hans was holding his daughter, Natalia who was enjoying the lights that twinkled on the tree. Indeed, this was a special Christmas season in which all of us are grateful for being alive and together as a family.

MY DEEPEST THOUGHTS

After trimming the tree, Hans excused himself and let Sasha take Natalia while he went into his den and had a glass of brandy. He sat in the chair to regain his thoughts think about how far he had become since the war. He knew that he had been tough on many, that he has forced work and changed the rules. As he sat there, he wondered what had became of many of the prisoners whom he had let go? The refugee camp had moved from Munich, and Hans had learned at that time that headquarters had moved the camp, but where? My secret, that I ponder in my heart, went with that refugee camp. Sometimes Hans found his mind deeply haunted by his past and the way he had lived his life from early age to now. He remembered when he first joined Hitler's Youth at the age of seventeen and then had gone to officer's school. Hans also remembered when his mother died and how she waited for him to come home and then passed away. Being upset as he was, now Hans only had his father, and even though he is not that old, Hans still worried about him. Hans knew that death does not care how old anyone is, that it could happen to any of us including his father. Hans loved his father and wanted to stay at the house to help him. Hans even promised his father that eventually he would want to restart his business in the building. Hans's father had told Hans that the business would be his and suggested now would be a good time to start it. That opportunity left the way open to make money for his family. Hans promised always to be there for his father and grateful for what he had done for everyone here. Without him, they would have never survived. Hans was so overwhelmed by his feelings, and I was not sure whether the feelings were as strong because of the holidays or just Hans himself. He knew that he had been very scared at times, especially with what my past had been at the camp. Hans ponder a very special secret in his heart that no one knows about, except God. Someday, Hans will reveal to everyone that secret. Today, he missed his mother, dearly.

SASHA GOES SHOPPING

Hans drove Sasha and Natalia into town so that Sasha could have some time for shopping. Hans really wanted his wife to celebrate her Jewish holiday in which she hadn't mentioned any more about it. Hans was hoping that next year she would continue celebrating so their children could learn about it also. Hans dropped Sasha off and she told me to pick her up in about an hour or so. Hans took Natalia and put her into her stroller. Hans held on to the stroller for support and strolled down the street looking at the Christmas lights. Natalia kept saying "Dat, Dat, mama, Dat." She had just begun calling Sasha "mama" and calling Hans "Dat." Natalia was just like her mother, quiet at times and fussy once in awhile. Hans loved her just as he loved Sasha. Hans felt lucky to have two beautiful women in his life. Hans went over to the cafe for some tea and to give Natalia a bottle. The cafe was somewhat crowded, so he had his tea and then decided to go over to the other restaurant where there was much more room to sit and eat. Hans always enjoyed his tea and ordered another cup with some pastry. He gave Natalia a small piece to eat. Hans was weary but happy from all the excitement that the holiday always brings. We sat there as Natalia ate her pastry, getting crumbs all over her face and stroller. Hans hoped that Sasha wouldn't yell at him because he gave Natalia some sweets. As Hans and Natalia left the restaurant, Hans saw Sasha walking with many bags and boxes. Hans called to her and went to help her to the car. Hans asked whether she had finished shopping because the weather turned very cold outside and snowy. However, they decided to stay out a little longer and bundled Natalia up in her blankets. Sasha said that the snow was cold, but Hans told her that he will hold on to her to keep her warm. The lights were very bright. Hans enjoyed looking at them and they walked around admiring the decorations. Hans asked Sasha whether she wanted some lunch. "If you are buying, I will." Hans said, "Sure, for the special girl in my life!" Hans took her to the restaurant where he had gone for tea and pastry and saw that it had some good food. Hans ordered for himself some dumplings with gravy, and Sasha had a ham sandwich with a salad. As Hans finished, he noticed a man eating at a table near them. Hans knew him from officer's school, and he approached the man to ask whether he had been at officer's school in Berlin. He looked at Hans as though he knew Hans and he said, "Hans Schweitzer, how are you doing?" I knew his name was Paul Müller from class. Müller asked Hans how he was doing after the war. Hans told him that he was fine and introduced Sasha as his wife and Natalia, his daughter. Müller shook Sasha's hand and tickled Natalia on the face. He told Hans that he had been stationed at the front line in infantry and that he been in Normandy for a long time. Hans then mentioned the fact that he had been commander in one of the local camps then transferred to Munich with the 3rd Division. Hans told Paul that he had been seriously injured in Munich when the bombs fell and that he had lost his leg in the war. Paul looked at Hans and apologized for all hardships that he had endured. Hans then had to excuse himself and his family because they had to leave before the snow comes down any heavier. Hans wished Paul the best and hoped to see him again. Paul bid his farewell and gave his best wishes to Hans and his family.

SNOWSTORM

Hans had to drive slowly because the snow was coming down heavier than before. They had only fifteen minutes left before they would reach home but the snow made it harder to drive, as the journey took longer. Finally they reached the front of the house. Hans told Sasha to wait until he could get out to help her and the baby to the door. The snow was falling harder than before making it harder to see. Hans helped Sasha to the door and then went back to the car to unload the bags and boxes in the trunk. As Hans was taking out the packages, he turned and slipped on ice and fell very hard hitting his face. The blow knocked him out for a few seconds and he lay there freezing to death. Sasha didn't know about his fall. Hans was trying to move but couldn't. Hans kept saying to himself, "Someone, please come out and help me." Then he lost consciousness again. When Hans still had not come in, she asked Hymen to go outside, he saw Hans was lying on the ground bleeding and unconscious. He yelled for Otto and Peter to come outside to help Hans up. Hans was hurt badly. Blood covered his face. When he tried to wake up, he couldn't speak a word. Hymen carried Hans into the house and laid him on the sofa. Sasha ran over crying and asking what had happened. Hans's father came running, saw Hans's wounds, and told Hymen that Hans needed to be seen by a doctor immediately. Hymen and Peter carried Hans to the car for yet another visit to the hospital. Sasha asked Mela whether she could watch Natalia until she returns. She was very emotional as she thought that Hans was going to die. The snow was rapidly turning into a snowstorm. The nearest hospital was in Cologne. The journey took a while to get there because of the snow falling. When they arrived, Peter ran inside for assistance because Hans was unconscious and bleeding. A doctor and a nurse came out with a stretcher and wheeled Hans into the emergency room. The several doctors and nurses on duty and nurses looked at Hans's head and face and ordered x-rays. Sasha was outside giving all the information to the nurse so that the doctor's would know what had happened. Sasha knew nothing about Hans's insurance, but she did say that it was through the Republic of Germany because Hans was in the war. The nurse told Sasha that she didn't have to worry; the hospital would take care of all of the details. Sasha was concerned for her husband; she didn't want Hans to die. Peter tried to calm her while Hymen held on her. Meanwhile, Hans was in the emergency room when the x-rays came back. The doctor's aid that he had a concussion; and they wanted to keep him there overnight, especially because Hans had been knocked out. Slowly Hans regained consciousness and tried to catch his breath, hoping that he wasn't going to die. He couldn't die! He He had survived several falls, bombs, and accidents. The attendants put Hans in a ward with other men. All he could remember was that his face was hurting and that he had a nasty headache. Hans wanted to see his family, but the doctors wouldn't allow anyone to visit him. Sasha asked whether she could come up to Hans, but the doctors refused. One doctor said, "Tomorrow, if everything goes well, Hans could go home. If anything goes wrong during the night, someone will call you immediately." Sasha was very upset and worried and asked Peter to help her to the car. Hans lay there in the hospital hanging on to his life, injured again. He was fighting once again to be with his loved ones as he had done did in the war. Memories came back, again.

BACK IN THE WAR, AGAIN

Hans lay on the bed while his mind fell into a deep sleep, a sleep that went beyond his control. He traveled back to a familiar place, a camp where pain and suffering hung over everyone. Hans, the Commander, stood there tall, dressed in his black uniform riding his horse, Zurich. He was telling everyone to get ready for inspection and that they better have their uniforms pressed. He told them that their boots had to be shined or else they would be doing hard work. He was sitting in a room with Sasha, telling her that he was going to marry Mela instead because he loved her much more. His dream continued with other prisoners, yelling, beating and spitting on each other. "Stop it, stop it," Hans said to myself. "You are dreaming. Wake up, wake up Hans." But Hans couldn't wake up, so the dream continued. Hans was now in Munich commanding the forces to strike against the bombers. Bombs hit; his leg was blown off. "Shoot them!" Hans commanded." He was hurt, wounded. What would he do after this war? Hans's mind was racing. "Sasha, where are you? Help me!" Hans continued his dream, riding his horse around the camp. His memories were bursting. "Get me out, now!" Hans jumped up! Finally, Hans woke up. The nurses came running to Hans as he awoke, and he asked them whether he was still in the camp. "The bombs: help me!" Hans cried. The nurses told him to lie down, assuring him that he was safe and nothing would hurt him anymore. He fell back to sleep and quietly he dreamed about Sasha and his daughter. He was happy that the camp dream was over.

GOING HOME

Hans woke up and found himself in a room with so many people. The patient next to him had a bandage around his head, and others had broken legs. Hans had a bandage covering his left eye and he asked whether his eye was all right. The doctor said, "Yes, it is slightly cut open so we had to put in a few stitches." Hans asked if whether he would be going home today, and the doctor said, "why not?" If Hans had been a child again, he would have clapped and jumped up and down because he was so happy. Hans learned that his family was downstairs waiting to take him home. A nurse helped Hans to dress and then wheeled him downstairs. Hans went into the elevator ready to see Sasha and his friends. Unfortunately, he had these same clothes on that he had wore when he came into the hospital. All Hans wanted was a warm bath, and clean clothes, and a kiss from Sasha. His hair had some spots of dried blood on it. Hans was annoyed that he looked dirty. His hair hung on the sides; and he kept pushing it back, but still he looked a mess. As the nurse wheeled Hans into the waiting room, he saw Sasha and Peter. Sasha ran up to Hans putting her hands around his neck, "Hans, you're going home and I can take care of you." I looked at her and said, "Let's go Sasha; I am ready."

SASHA'S THOUGHTS ALONE

{as told by Sasha}

I never realized how lonely I was without my husband, Hans. I missed him very much and I prayed that he would come home. I was very upset that this accident that happened to him, and I blame myself that I should have helped him that night. I am alone tonight with thoughts of what it would be like without Hans. I had been with him at the camp for almost five years. Hans was almost twenty years old when I first met him. We have been married a little over a year, and already we are having our second child. Hans has been my support, my help and my hero. I loved Hans from the moment I met him all the way until now. I am so lost without him that I cannot explain. My life depends upon him; he is an angel to me. I do want Hans to know my deepest thoughts, for him to know how I feel. I have loved him for all these years, and I shall continue no matter what happens. I remember him for what he did for me and how he helped me from death. I was once a prisoner and Hans risked his life for me and others. I am here now for him until I die, and one day I shall tell our children about what their father did for me. "I love you Hans, no matter what happens."

DID I MISS CHRISTMAS?

When Hans went through the door, he saw the brightly lit tree and the presents under the tree. Hans asked, "I didn't miss Christmas, or did I?" Sasha replied, "Hans, you did, and I am sorry; but we waited for you to come home so we could celebrate." Hans was so surprised that they had waited for him and now they were going to celebrate Christmas together. Hans asked whether she could help him to take a warm bath and put on some clean clothes. I needed her to help me with my clothes. Hans went upstairs with Sasha. She drew him a nice warm bath. Hans had to remove his false limb because he was not supposed ever to get it wet. He stayed in the bath for almost an hour and washed his hair. Now he felt so much better. Sasha helped him out of the bath and wrapped a towel around him. Hans thanked Sasha. She kissed him and left. Hans took the towel rubbed his hair dry, and put on some light clothes. He was still drowsy from the medicine the hospital had given him, and he really wanted to lie down for a while. Hans pulled myself to his bed and lay down, and fell asleep. I woke up sometime later with a tug from Sasha, who announced that dinner was ready. Hans asked her how long he have been sleeping, and she said, "For about an hour or more." Hans felt somewhat better as Sasha helped him downstairs for dinner. Hans excused himself to everyone that he was not dressed, but they didn't pay any attention to that. What Hans wore was minor to them because all that counted was that he had come home for Christmas. Hans went into the kitchen and there he saw Mela and the babies. She she was putting a pot away and stopped to look at him. Hans said hello to her and asked how his son was doing. He reached for

Natalia and picked her up. She was saying "DA-DA." Hans kissed her on her cheek and said, "Daddy loves you, Natalia. I do love you." Mela said, "Hans, did you wish us a Merry Christmas?" I looked at her and said, "I wish you what? I almost forgot, oh yes, Christmas! I wish you all a Merry Christmas." Hans then went into his den to be alone for a while.

GIFTS

After awhile, Hans walked into the living room and put on music. As he looked at the tree, he told everyone that Natalia had picked out the tree, not him or Sasha. Everyone liked the tree, and indeed it was beautiful. Sasha announced that she was having another baby and that there was no way any of them would not recognize her changes. Mela just looked at Sasha. Hans went outside to see Zurich. It was so good to see him again! Hans rubbed Zurich's nose, and fed him a carrot, and put some oil on his hair to make him smooth. Hans even combed Zurich then covered him with a blanket before leaving. At least Hans knew that his horse was doing well: "After this winter passes, I am going to ride!" Hans promised himself. He wanted to buy Sasha a horse so that she could ride with him. "I may just do that eventually. I will wait until spring and then discuss it with her," Hans promised himself again. Hans went back inside. The women had dinner cooking, and the cookies coming out of the oven. They were chatting, but when they saw Hans they seem to stop. Hans knew that they had been talking about him because they stopped as soon as they saw him. Hans walked out and went back into the living room. The women came out of the kitchen. "Hans, we are going to open our gifts now," said Sasha. Mela called everyone into the living room. Sasha said, "We shall do something different this year. We shall go under the tree finding our own gifts." Of course, everyone but Hans went under the tree. Everyone then started to open their gifts, and soon the living room was filled with bows and paper. Sasha opened her big box and she stood still as she opened it. She said, "Hans, why did you buy me this? It is beautiful! I adore it very much." She tried it on, and it fit well except her stomach held it back from closing. Sasha said that after this baby comes, the dress will fit well on her. She told Hans that after the baby is born, she would like to go to dinner and dance. Hans said, "That sounds fine with me!" After everyone had collected the gifts and loved them, Sasha helped to distribute the cards with money inside, adding to the delight. Hans was very pleased with his gifts, and so was everyone else. Hans tried his best to be in the spirit of Christmas. Being in the hospital and wearing this bandage had made him feel sick and tired. He had to use only one eye to see, making him tired, so he excused himself to everyone and asked Sasha to bring him dinner upstairs. He had to rest because of his weakness. Hans said good-night and Merry Christmas to everyone. Hans noticed Mela looking at him with such sympathetic eyes. She looked at him as though she wanted to help him but couldn't. Hans looked at her with his one eye and said, "Goodnight."

"IT'S BACK; GO AWAY"

Hans realized as he lay on his bed looking at the ceiling that he still was in love with Mela. He wasn't sure whether this feeling would ever go away from him. He had tried so hard to fight his feelings. As soon as he had overcome them, they would return. Hans realized that no one could fight this feeling except himself. Hans was in the hospital dreaming about Mela. Hans realized how disturbing this feeling was for him, and he was determined to see Mela alone to tell her that he cannot carry this feeling any more for her. He had to find a day when Peter was not around so he could speak with her. Hans respected the fact that Mela was married to Peter, but Hans could not respect the fact that Peter did not want Hans to bother with his son. Hans felt torn between his wife and his love for Mela, but he had to make the choice; the choice had to be Sasha.

ANOTHER YEAR

It was now 1946. Hans swore that he had never seen years go by so fast as these last few years had been going. It was another cold and snowy day. Peter had to go to work early because of the snow. Hans saw his chance to speak with Mela. He had to tell her the truth or he would be burden by these feelings. It was early, and Mela was in the kitchen. Hans knew that this would be the best time to speak with her when no one else was up. She was preparing breakfast and asked Hans whether he wanted any, and Hans told her that he needed to speak to her. Hans looked at Mela hoping she would not see how much he was in love with her. He had to bring it out before anyone got up so he could explain myself without disturbances. Hans told Mela that he loved her very much ever since he had met her and that for all those years he had never stopped. "However," he said, "I have to respect our children and spouses." Mela agreed. "Can we be good friends, Hans?" Hans told her that she would always be his friend no matter what. Mela assured Hans that she felt the same way and would try not to love him in the wrong forbidden way. Hans reached over, gave her a warm hug, and left. Mela stood there with tears in her eyes saying to herself, "Hans, I will always love you, no matter what you say to me for I am "Truthfully, Yours."

MAKING AN APPOINTMENT

Hans made an appointment with the doctor on January 6, 1946, for his bandages to be removed. Hans prayed that his face wasn't scared from the fall. "I cannot wait for the bandages to be removed," Hans said. "Right now, I am miserable because I cannot see, and looking out of one eye is tiresome." Seeing out of one eye made Hans feel so helpless. Sasha said that she would go with him to the clinic. Hans hoped that there wasn't any snow on the ground at that time because the snow made walking harder. Hans hoped that Sasha or Otto would drive him. Peter had to work, and Hans prefer to have Hymen home with his father so he could help him with any chores. Hans asked Sasha whether she would like to visit the doctor for a checkup on that date, and she said that would be all right for her. She was now almost two months into her pregnancy, and Hans wanted her to have a follow up because she had become pregnant so fast. He called the clinic for her and asked whether she could come in when he had his appointment. The clinic told Hans that they would have 10:45AM for January 6. Hans gave all the information on Sasha that the clinic wanted. They asked her age, and Hans told them that she was twenty-five years old. To make matters easier, Hans gave them the insurance information also. They confirmed that they would see Sasha on January 6 at 10:45AM.

GOOD NEWS

Hans went outside for a while to smoke his pipe, and enjoying the fresh tobacco that he had purchased in town. Normally he didn't smoke a pipe; but when he had been in the war, most of the men did. When Hans tried it out once, he enjoyed the pipe. Sasha said that he looked like a chimney with smoke coming out. Hans laughed. He filled the pipe and took a deep breath; the taste was good, and the aroma was good for him. As Hans was sitting down, Fritz came over to see him. There was something different about him today. His eyes seem to be glowing with excitement or something like that. He hardly spoke English to me and said that he felt much more comfortable speaking German. Everything was German to him, and there were times that Hans had to translate English to German for Fritz. Fritz told Hans that Elda was very nice and great company for him. He told me with excitement that he had asked her out on a date and that she had admitted to him she cared for him. Hans was overwhelmed and happy for Fritz because Elda had grew up with Hans and he knew that she was a fantastic friend and woman. Fritz told Hans in German that she was decent and very good to him, never saying anything bad. Hans believed that Fritz was in love but refused to admit it to himself or anyone else. Fritz had crossed his youth into manhood and now was in love. "Yes, Fritz, you are in love, my friend, and you need to tell Elda." Hans asked him whether he had made any special plans. Fritz said, "Nothing as yet." Hans knew that nothing could turn into something for all of them. Hans had been there and was still there. Fritz asked Hans for a favor. He asked whether he could borrow Hans's Mercedes to go out with Elda. "Of course," Hans said, "Yes, just be safe." Hans laughed and congratulated Fritz. Fritz thanked Hans and went inside. Hans laughed to himself, and smoked his pipe. When Hans went into the house, Mela greeted him at the front door, asking, "Hans, can you please help me with Danderick upstairs?" Hans told her that he would be more than happy to help his son in any way that he possibly could. Hans went upstairs and found Danderick was sitting in his crib. Hans went over to pick him up and gave him the biggest kiss that he could ever give. Danderick returned the kiss and smiled for Hans. Mela had wanted Hans to hold Danderick until she did a few things in her bedroom, which she finished rapidly. Hans suspected Mela didn't really need his help; it was her excuse to see Hans. Hans handed her Danderick and told her that if she needed him again, to ask. They ended with a smile.

MEMORIES OF ME

Hans went into his bedroom and found Sasha feeding Natalia baby food. The food was all over Natalia's face. Hans told Sasha that it was her turn to clean up the baby, and Sasha knew that Natalia needed a bath after her feeding. Sasha told Hans that he needed to take a day to himself to relax and to stop helping everyone unless they really need it. Hans knew whom she was referring to, yet she never said who it was. Hans then went downstairs for a while and sat in his comfortable chair in the den. He still had his night clothes on, his night trousers and no shirt because the fireplace heated the entire house so well. Hans could not stand much heat; in fact, he preferred fresh air. Hans turned on a small light in the den which made it cozy for him. When he put on the radio to hear any news, he discovered a photo book of his family. Hans opened it up and saw memories of his mother and father and, of course, himself. Hans saw pictures of when they had gone on picnics, father building a barn, mother outside sitting in her lounge chair. Hans could remember when he first joined Hitler's Youth at age seventeen to be exact. As he was remembering all of these things, Sasha came down with Natalia in her arms. She asked whether Hans could use some company. "That would be lovely," he said. Sasha asked about the pictures, and Hans showed her all of them. There were even pictures of Hans in Hitler's Youth with his tan uniform. Sasha started to ask Hans a few questions this time, he wanted her to know all about him. He had nothing to hide then or now. She asked how old he was, when he went into the school for training, and about his mother. Hans told Sasha briefly, that he was seventeen when he had to join Hitler's Youth and nineteen when he attended officer's school. When he turned twenty, he had his first position as commander. Sasha asked whether Hans was twenty when she first met him, "Yes, I was," he answered. Sasha laughed and said, "How blessed I was to find you that day. Your mother, I know, was very sweet because you are also." Hans looked at her and said, "Mother was more than sweet; she was my angel." Sasha finished giving Natalia her bottle, and the baby fell asleep. After taking her upstairs to her crib, Hans looked at Sasha and said, "It must have been the bath that put her to sleep." Sasha agreed. Shortly after that, Hans became Sasha's baby when the lights were out.

COLOGNE

Cologne was a very beautiful city. Hans had been born here, so were both of his parents. Taking Sasha out in Cologne made her very happy and contented, and Hans enjoyed taking her in town even just to walk around. Sasha was Hans's delight, and on this day he decided to have Hymen drive them to Cologne and to have some dinner, to walk around, and maybe to shop. Hans told Hymen to pick them up around 4:00PM in the afternoon because they would be spending the day in the city. Sasha had Natalia's stroller which made it easier for both of us because at times she was heavy to hold. They had bundled the baby into her blankets on top of her snowsuit. Sasha and Hans wore warm coats with scarfs wrapped around their faces to prevent any cold air from hitting them while they walked. Hans was cautious because of his leg, and Sasha was pregnant, so they took their time walking. Hans and Sasha came across so many nice shops. They went into one place that sold paintings and antiques. The shop smelled of musty old items. The gentleman who owned the shop came up to Hans and asked whether he needed any help in finding something. Hans actually told the shopkeeper that he was just looking but if he finds anything, Hans would let him know. The man nodded his head and continued in what he was doing. Sasha had to stay in the front because the stroller was so big. The small shop had a lot of strange items. Hans found a beautiful painting that had an ocean as the background and seagulls flying through the water. Hans asked the clerk the price of that painting. The shopkeeper said it was a local German artist who had painted it, and that it was only 10 marks because he wanted to sell the painting. Hans asked him to wrap it up. Hans thanked him, left with Sasha. Sasha asked Hans what he had found, and he told her that it was a gift for her. She asked him why he would give her a colorful painting of an ocean with birds flying around. He replied, "Because that is you flying with everyone who was set free from the war, and now you are free to fly." Sasha kissed Hans and thanked him for such a pretty gift. They continued to walk around as snow started to fall lightly. People who were out were singing and cheering. Hans liked snow but not enough to cheer it on to continue. As they came around another corner, Hans saw a shop that he had never noticed before. It was an old relic of Germany. Hans told Sasha to go in; and as they entered, memories of the war hit Hans's mind as a flash of water had just hit him. The shop was covered with pictures, weapons and books on the war. Hans was amazed to see all of these things and asked the clerk what this shop was all about. The clerk asked Hans whether he had known anything about the war and anything else that went with it. Hans replied that he had been commander in the war. "Yes," he said, "I know plenty." The clerk said, "Well, a lot of these relics were found in the streets and the bomb shelters; instead of burning them, we kept them. Hans asked whether he could look around in the shop. The clerk said, "Go right ahead." So Hans and Sasha looked around and found pictures of officers, soldiers, and Hitler. Hans couldn't believe what he was seeing, yet the collection was very real. Hans asked whether he was still buying, and the clerk asked Hans whether he had anything to sell. Hans said, "Plenty." He said that he would be in touch later. For lunch, Hans and Sasha went into the café where they always went. Hans was delighted to sit down for a while and enjoy the fireplace and music. He helped Sasha with her coat. Natalia was sleeping. Sasha said that she would like to see the menu, and the waiter appeared to bring her one. Hans ordered a beer and Sasha, as always, a seltzer. The menu had some interesting items that day. Most of them were German, but some were Italian. Hans wanted Italian; he loved spaghetti, and as long as they gave him fresh bread, he was happy. Sasha, on the other hand, looked at the menu and said she would like to have dumplings with pork, gravy, and bread. The waiter came back with a tall glass of lager beer as the foam falling from the glass and a seltzer water. The waiter took the order and said that the food would be 15 minutes and that he would be back with our fresh bread. Hans looked around the café. It was so cozy, and the light were dim and romantic. Hans asked Sasha whether she would like to go out tonight alone with him to the banquet hall for dinner and dancing. Sasha said, "Yes, I would."

MAGICAL NIGHT TOGETHER

When they arrived at home, they brought all of their bags upstairs and Sasha helped Mela with dinner preparation. Sasha also asked Mela whether she would watch Natalia that evening. Mela never refused when the matter concerned Hans and always returned any favors that he or Sasha asked. Mela wanted to know what the occasion was, and Sasha told her that Hans was taking her out to dinner and dancing. Mela turned quiet and knew that she wanted to be in Sasha's place because Peter never took her anywhere. Mela could only hope that someday Peter would take her out. After dinner, Sasha told Mela that she was going upstairs to shower and dress. Sasha found that Hans had finished with showering, and now he was dressing. Sasha gave him a quick kiss and went into the warm shower where she is waiting for her delight tonight. Hans put on his new crisp white shirt that he had wore when he was commander and his black trousers and jacket. He even found a black tie to go with his suit and looked stunning enough to become a prince. He slicked his blond hair back so it wouldn't fall into his eyes and dabbed French cologne on his face to finish his dressing. Hans stood there looking as handsome as he could be, ready for his magical night. He was not even worried about his leg or that he couldn't dance. He made it a point to dance with Sasha. Sasha soon came out with a towel wrapped around her hair and partially dressed. She stopped when she saw how handsome her husband looked. He was handsome enough in his uniform, but nothing like this. She felt as though he was a knight in shining armor, ready to save her from the bad queen. She loved every moment of it. She then turned to her expensive lilac cologne that Hans bought for her when they were together in the camp and splashed it all over herself. She then put on her brand new rose-colored dress and a pair of black high heels. She wore her hair down and fixed it with a pretty sequent pin. Then she put on her make-up to make herself look like a movie star ready to be filmed. Yes, they were the perfect couple tonight; and when they left, they were ready for their magical night together. Hans pulled up in the Mercedes, his sharp-looking car from the war. He opened the door for Sasha, and then they were ready for their magical night. Hans and Sasha went to the finest restaurant in town. They had reservations for dinner at 7:00 PM and arrived right on time. The greeter outside opened the doors for both Hans and Sasha while they went into their enchanted night. He parked the car for them, and he admired the make and how expensive this car must have been. Meanwhile inside, Hans gave his name to the greeter, he showed them to the table where history would be made for the night. When they walked in, everyone admired Sasha's dress and how beautiful she looked and how handsome Hans looked in his perfect suit. Hans had taken his bandage off his eye for the evening and put a patch on it to make it less noticeable. They were seated near the fireplace and the musicians who were playing right next to them making the setting even even more special. The table was covered with a white tablecloth and a candle in a glass that made it very romantic for Hans and Sasha. Hans was satisfied because right next to their table was the dance floor where they could dance and make music together. The waiter came to welcome us and asked whether they were ready to order. Hans told him to give them his finest bottle of French wine. For dinner, Hans ordered the French crepes with wine sauce and pork. He also ordered shrimp as appetizers for both Sasha and himself. Sasha ordered the roast beef with brown gravy and French mashed potatoes. The waiter brought out the chilled bottle of French wine and poured it into the crystal glass. Hans and Sasha sat wondering about what to make a toast to, and then the idea came. They held up their glasses and toasted their love and years together, then they drank their first glass of happiness. As they finished the last drink, Hans asked his wife to dance with him. They went onto the floor to dance. For some reason, Hans's black patch on his eye made him quite distinguished and Sasha's heart melted with love. They danced and danced and danced until they couldn't dance anymore. Hans looked into Sasha's eyes and said, "I love you, Sasha." "I love you too, Hans," she replied. They sat down and held hands as their dinner arrived. Hans gave Sasha a kiss on her cheek and sat down to eat his meal while the candle burned with fragrance. They had discovered a love that everyone wanted, a love that forgave the past and united a forbidden love that everyone wishes to have. They found that forgiveness goes further than hate and that it creates peace and understanding. Hans and Sasha ate their delicious dinner, leaving them very full, but Hans wanted Sasha to enjoy dessert with him. So they ordered the restaurant's famous cheesecake and some coffee. Hans and Sasha sat there holding hands for a long time, wishing that night would never end. Finally, Hans asked his love whether she was ready to go home, and she said she was. Hans held out the chair for Sasha, then paid the manager and thanked him for a wonderful time. Hans and Sasha holding on to one another as though they were on their first date while the greeter drove Hans's car to the entrance. Hans tipped the greeter and helped Sasha get into the car so she wouldn't fall. As Hans drove into the night, he thought, "Where love over powers hate, we showed that love in the present and the future can prevail in all races. Throwing away hate can open the other side which is love. We finally proved to the world that yes, we can remember and never forget; but when we forgive, the memories would be less painful. It is all right to remember as long as we forgive because the memories would be less painful." When they arrived at home the snow was falling. Sasha thanked Hans for a wonderful night together and creating that magical love that they had waited to have. "I love you, my sweetheart, forever," she whispered.

THE HOSPITAL, AGAIN

Morning came early the next day because Hans and Sasha had an appointment at the hospital. Hans asked Mela whether she would watch Natalia again, while he and Sasha went over to the hospital. Hymen took Hans and Sasha to the clinic in Cologne where Hans had cheated on his bandages and put on a patch for their dinner date. The switch was worth it for Hans, who would not regret that night. The clinic was crowded with a lot of the men from the war, who had missing limbs or other injuries like Hans. Hans overheard one man telling another that he had lost an eye when they were bombed in Munich. Many were still here having their wounds attended; the pain still lingered. Hans gave the nurse at the desk my name and also Sasha's and any other information they needed. He then went over to the window where Sasha was sitting. Hans noticed that the sky was becoming darker than usual, and he had the feeling that it would snow again. As he leaned his head back and becoming comfortable, the nurse called his name. The nurse took Hans to a small room and did the normal routine. She asked whether anything was unusual, and Hans told her "no." She told Hans to wait, that Dr. Haas would be in shortly. Hans started to doze off when he heard the door open. Dr. Haas came in and shook his hand asking how he was feeling. Dr. Haas admired Hans's patch, and Hans told the doctor that he had taken the bandage off and put a patch on because of a dinner date with his wife. He understood, and took the patch off looking for any signs of an infection. He said that everything looked good and asked Hans how his head felt, any problems? Hans said that he felt fine. The doctor told Hans that he should continue with the patch until his eye adjusted to the lights. Dr. Haas said that Hans should take the patch off every two hours for three days and then remove it completely and to use the eye drops every four hours. He said that Hans should be fine and that if anything came up to call right away. Hans thanked Dr. Haas and went into the waiting room to wait for Sasha. Finally she came out with a bottle in her hand. She spoke to the nurse at the desk and came over to Hans. Hans asked Sasha what the bottle was for, and she told Hans that the doctor had given her vitamins. She also told Hans that she had to come back on February 4 at 10:00AM for another check-up. As Sasha and Hans were leaving a man in his twenties came up to Hans and asked whether he was Commander Hans Schweitzer. His name was Luther Sweiter, and operated the Panzer Faust and the machine guns. Hans said that he remembered him very vaguely but thanked him for what he did that day in Munich. Hans was grateful to Luther in what he did and how he risked his life for everyone. Luther shook Hans's hand and thanked him also.

DON'T TELL ME, PLEASE

When Hans and Sasha arrived at home, it must have been after 2:00PM and Mela had been watching their little girl, Natalia. She heard us coming into the house and told me that everything was fine and that she had fed Natalia and Danderick together. Peter, on the other hand, had come home early from work and said that he wanted to speak to Hans when Hans had the chance. Hans asked Mela where he was and she said, "In the kitchen." Hans went into the kitchen and asked Peter to come into the den for a chat. Peter came in and asked whether he could speak to him. Peter came out bluntly telling Hans that very soon he and Mela would be moving into a new apartment with Danderick. Hans looked at him as though he had pulled his heart out, but Hans promised himself to keep his mouth shut. Peter said that he wasn't sure what date; but as soon as he could find a decent place and not near any bombed-out area, he would let Hans know. He said that there was too much damage in Berlin and Munich, so probably they will live in Cologne somewhere, but not sure where. Hans replied, "That is fine Peter." Yet he said to himself, "No it wasn't." Hans didn't want to face this situation because the move would keep him away from his son and Mela. Mela told Hans that she would tell him where they would be moving so he could visit. Hans depended upon that promise. Hans thanked Peter for the news and asked Peter to keep him updated on it. Hans then went upstairs. In the back of his mind, he felt that he should have told Peter to wait until the spring when the weather would clear up, but he didn't. Again, he shut his mouth and said nothing.

MY FRIEND, ELDA

Hans had dinner and decided to listen to some television. He turned on stations and found nothing good on except news. He switched it off and said, "Now I know why no one listens to the television." He was sitting on his chair with his eyes closed when he felt someone sitting next to him. He opened his eyes and saw his friend, Elda. Hans was delighted to see her. He knew Elda for so many years. She had been the best friend that anyone could ever ask for in childhood. Hans had always been there for Elda. She wanted to have a talk with Hans as he did with her. Hans asked her about Fritz and how they were both coming along in friendship. She admitted they have been secretly dating but nothing serious had developed yet as she hopes for. She sounded a bit upset that Fritz was not making a move towards her. Hans told Elda not to worry. "That is how Fritz is, and if he seems slow it is because he is cautious and that is fine. Don't worry Elda. It will all work out fine with Fritz; take your time and just take one day at a time with each other." Elda wanted to go out and do some shopping but only if Fritz went with her. Hans said, "Ask him; and if he agrees, then he can use my car. Elda got up, kissed Hans on his head and said, "Thank you, Hans; you had always been a good friend to me, and I will never forget all you have done for me and others." Hans was pleased, and so was Elda; but when Hans turned his head, he saw Sasha coming around the corner and stopping dead in her tracks.

"WHAT'S THIS HANS?"

Hans looked at Sasha and asked how she was doing. Sasha gave Hans a look that he had never seen from her before. She wanted to know why Elda had kissed him on his head and looked so happy. Sasha asked whether Elda was one of his lovers. Hans looked at her so puzzled and weak in his words. Yet he pressed on the best he could and told her that he had known Elda since they were children, and that they had grown up together. "She is only a friend and not some secret lover. As a matter of fact, Elda was discussing her relationship with Fritz," said Hans. "Why did she kiss you?" "I don't know." Hans told Sasha again and again that it was only friendship and nothing else. "This conversation is ridiculous," Hans said. Finally, he took his car into town and stayed there for some time. Hans took his pipe out, filled it with tobacco, and smoked it until he was tired of smoking. Hans looked at his watch and saw that the time was 2:30PM, as he went over to the café for lunch. He was terribly hungry and he ordered a beer and a roast beef sandwich with cheese. Hans picked up his beer and moved to a table near the window so that he could look out. He read the newspaper and waited for his food to arrive. He enjoyed roast beef, and that's all he really wanted, especially on the fresh bread. Hans sat alone wondering how Sasha could accuse him and Elda of being lovers. An affair wasn't even on his mind. Sasha had actually cheapened his friendship with Elda, something that Hans had not appreciated. For this reason, Hans didn't want to go home because he realized if he did, Sasha would start it all over again with him. To avoid going home, Hans had another beer and streusel with cream on top. He pulled out his pipe and smoked it until he ran out of tobacco. After lunch, Hans went over to the tobacco store to buy some smokers for himself with a few cigars and a pack of cigarettes. He even purchased a new lighter and some new aroma for his pipe. Then he went over to the bookstore and looked around for a while. By that time, he saw that his watch registered 5:30PM. Hans really didn't' care whether Sasha was worrying or not. He walked around wondering whether his marriage to her would end. "I know for a fact I married too young; and since Sasha was my girlfriend, I went into it too fast. I could have just saved her and dated her afterward, but I didn't. I ruined my life, my hopes, and my dreams as a man and now look what is happening with my marriage!" Hans said to himself. "I know eventually that I am going to leave Sasha and move on, maybe not now, but soon," said Hans silently. Hans continued to stay out going through every shop in town and not wanting to go home. He then decided to go have dinner and didn't return home until after 10:00 PM. He was sure that Sasha would accuse him of hiding another woman lover somewhere in town, that would be next. "If she does, then I am packing my suitcase and leaving," Hans said spitefully. Finally, Hans went home. It was cold outside and he was freezing from walking around. When he pulled in, there was Sasha as always, outside waiting for him.

"I'M SORRY, HANS!"

Sasha met him at the car. She looked really upset, and to be honest, she was the one who had caused her upsets, not me. She told me to come upstairs where she started to cry. Sasha told me that she didn't want anyone to know they were fighting, Hans asked, "Why not? We are human, aren't we, Sasha?" She said that she was hoping that Hans would come home and that Natalia missed her daddy. She kept saying she was sorry and asked Hans to forgive her. By then, Sasha was hysterical and her body was shaking from yelling so much. Several minutes later, Sasha was lying on the floor and not moving. Mela came running to find out what was going on with Sasha, and Hans told her that she was accusing him with other lovers after which she became hysterical. When Mela tried getting Sasha up, there was no response which had Mela screaming for help. By then, everyone came running to find Sasha on the floor, not moving. Hans was praying to God that no one was thinking he had did something to her, because he didn't. Peter and Hymen carried Sasha to the car, and Hans drove Sasha to the hospital not knowing what happened to her. As they were riding, Peter asked, "What happened to Sasha?" Hans explained what happened when he came home. He said that Sasha had become hysterical, and had fallen down on the ground. Hans told Peter that he was concerned for the baby and that he didn't want the baby to die because of this ridiculous argument. Sasha got up slowly and kept repeating the same sentence, "Hans, please forgive me; please forgive me." They reached the hospital and the emergency nurse came out to bring a wheelchair so that Sasha could go into the emergency room. Mela went with her into the emergency room while Elda gave the nurses all the information about Sasha. The doctor asked me what happened and Hans told him the truth. The doctor said that he would check her over and the baby. Hans kept saying, "The baby, the baby." Hans was out in the waiting room crying, when the nurse came out to him and asked whether he was Hans Schweitzer. Hans told the nurse that he was her husband and asked how she was she doing. Hans felt a knot in his throat not knowing what to expect. He had his share of hospitals; and this time he had really had it. Within minutes the doctor came out and asked whether he was Hans, Sasha's husband. The doctor told him that Sasha was fine but needed special attention. The doctor told Hans that she was suffering from lack of vitamins and wondered what she been taking. Hans told the doctor that he hadn't seen any. The doctor said, "It is for her welfare and the baby; if they do not get the vitamins they need, they will both die. She must eat right, take her vitamins, and rest." The doctor continued: "Once she eats correctly and takes vitamins, she will be stronger, and the baby will live." Hans could hardly believe what he had just heard. He was so overwhelmed that he just sat there with nothing to say. The doctor told Hans that they would be running tests to make sure that Sasha was not anemic and to be sure that the baby was doing well. The doctor also asked Hans whether Sasha had seen a doctor lately, and Hans said, "Yes, last week at the clinic here." The doctor wanted to know what happened, and Hans was honest and told him that he did not know because Sasha had said that everything was fine with her. "Well, I'll get those records from the clinic and look them over," the doctor promised. Hans asked the doctor whether he would be able to see Sasha. The doctor said, "I prefer that she rest, and I want to keep her overnight to run tests on her." The doctor told Hans that if everything goes well with the tests then Sasha could come home the next morning. Hans left for home with everyone. His heart was totally burdened because Sasha was either going live or die, and his child the same. Hans just sat there in the car feeling alone and upset at what happened over something so foolish, for he realized that Sasha could die any moment.

THIS IS FOOLISH

Hans's father had been watching the children for them. Once at home, Hans felt so guilty at this argument. But he kept telling himself that it was not his fault, that Sasha had taken it all wrong. Why would she accuse him of having another lover? Hans wasn't sure what to do with his unhappy life and tonight he had to decide. "I could stay here and pretend or leave," Hans said to himself. He went upstairs to see how Natalia was doing. She was sleeping and looked so happy. Hans went into the bathroom to take a warm shower and fell into the bed where he just lay. He really missed Sasha but he wasn't sure whether she was right or wrong about the argument. Hans felt that Elda was his best friend from childhood and just because she kissed me on my head meant nothing to him. She was my friend and only my friend. Hans kept asking himself why Sasha had acted that way. He was so tired that he couldn't sleep, so he went downstairs to his den and poured himself a glass of brandy. He sat there with his eyes closed, thinking. He felt that this time their trust to one another had failed, not on her part, but his own. Hans didn't know what to do at this time but prayed. He told God that he had made a wrong decision and that he should have waited before marrying Sasha. "I know, God, that I have sinned with Mela and I have to make my decision someday soon," Hans said. He asked God for His assistance in bringing Sasha back home and that she would be well. Hans ended the prayer and went upstairs to his room where he fell asleep.

THE CALL

Hans was sleeping with Natalia on his chest sound asleep. It was a picture in itself as both slept in peace. Downstairs, the phone rang at 5:30AM. It was the hospital wanting to speak to Hans. Peter ran upstairs and woke up Hans, took Natalia in his arms, and told Hans that the hospital was on the phone. Hans had to take some time getting down the steps because of his leg, and finally he picked up the phone. Dr. Nirenberg was on the phone telling Hans that his wife, Sasha, was doing well and that the baby was fine. He said that Hans could pick her up at 9:00 PM today. Hans thanked God and the doctor. He was relieved and crying inside for help but realized that Sasha was coming home and he was happy. Hans told everyone who wanted to go with him to the hospital that Sasha and the baby were fine and could come home that morning. Hans left Natalia with Mela as Peter was getting dressed while Hans went into the kitchen to make some coffee. They left for the hospital around 8:30AM and when we arrived, we parked in the lot near the waiting room. There was snow on the ground, and Hans had no idea how slippery it was outside. He walked slowly because of his leg, and the cane, and went into the front of the hospital. He told the woman at the front desk that he had come to pick up his wife who was being discharged this morning. The woman looked up Sasha's name and said she was in room 108. Hans walked as fast as he could to see her again. He reached 108, cleared his throat, and walked. There he saw Sasha smiling as he walked towards her.

INSTRUCTIONS

Hans was a little nervous going over to Sasha saying that he was sorry, but he really didn't feel that he had done anything to create her hysterical crying. He wanted in his heart to end this misery. He had to tell her that he was sorry. He said, "I am so sorry," and she said the same to him leading him that they were both forgiven. Hans kissed Sasha's head and said that he was happy that she and the baby were well. Hans thanked God for helping him through his pride for which Hans had to give up and humble himself. Hans was grateful to God for His help because he surely needed it from Him. The nurse came in to get Sasha so she could go home and to receive home instructions. The nurse went over everything for Sasha and stressed that she needs to eat more and rest. She must take her vitamins every day in the morning after breakfast and not to miss any. She must make an appointment with her doctor at the clinic for a follow up as soon as possible. "Any questions?" the nurse asked Hans. Hans said, "No" and thanked the nurse. She wheeled Sasha to the elevator to go downstairs while Peter got the car. Hans was happy that Sasha was coming home, so was Peter. They helped Sasha into the car and left to go home and for her have the proper care that she needed. In the car, Sasha was so happy to see Hans that she wrapped her arms around him and hugged him so tightly. Hans had not seen her so happy lately like this. The last time that he had seen Sasha so happy in this way was the day that he had taken her out of the labor camp. Hans was also greatly relieved, and he thanked the Lord again for what He has done.

FIRST WALK

The arrival of spring was close, and that meant a ride in the country with Zurich while Sasha enjoyed planting her flowers. She couldn't do much because of the baby, but she did promise that she would do more planting after the baby arrived. She anticipated that the baby should be due around May sometime, not many weeks left. Sasha had felt better since she had been taking her vitamins and now had more energy. Another doctor appointment would be coming up very soon. Hans was upstairs with Sasha and Natalia admiring how his little daughter had grown so much. She talked so much, and she had said, "Mama" first, meaning that their bet had been won, except that Sasha won an extra kiss. Natalia would soon begin to walk. Sometimes it seemed that she had much more energy that Hans did. Hans loved his daughter and told himself how important she was in his life. Natalia kept him breathing and moving on in life. Although he and Sasha had had their differences, Hans realized that they could not let any differences destroy them. Hans put Natalia down for a while because she was getting heavier, and she wanted to crawl around. Hans noticed that she had started to bring herself up to a table. Trying to walk should be soon. Hans sat playing with Natalia while Sasha had finished with her bath. Hans noticed that Natalia was grabbing the table and pulling herself up. She started to walk to Hans saying, "DA-DA." Hans was surprised that he couldn't wait to tell Sasha. Not only did she begin to walk, she said "DA-DA." He grabbed and kissed her. It felt good as a father to have her say his name. He couldn't wait to tell Sasha as soon as she came from the bathroom. Finally, Sasha came out, Hans told her that Natalia in how she called him

"DA-DA," and that she walked to him. Sasha was so happy that Natalia had called Hans "DA-DA." Sasha was excited but not as much as Hans. He looked at Sasha and said, "She is growing up." Indeed, their daughter was growing up before their eyes.

THE CLINIC AGAIN

Once again, they had to go to the clinic for Sasha's checkup. Hans woke early that he was still tired from the day before. He prepared breakfast and then went into the shed for the car. They left by 9:00AM. Sasha put Natalia's jacket on: then Hans helped them both into the car as they went on their way. Hans noticed that Natalia wasn't as fussy as she usually was, and that was fine with him. When they arrived, Hans parked the car in the back making it easier to get to the door where a nurse greeted them. They went upstairs to the clinic where Sasha signed her name and was told to wait. Within a half hour, the nurse called for Sasha to come into the room.

SASHA'S REFLECTIONS

Sasha went into a cold room where she had to put on a gown, and then she had to wait for the doctor. As she lay on the cold table, she felt the baby kicking, something that makes a mother's heart sing. Sasha thought of her mother and how she must have felt when she was inside her or even her brother. "If only my parents and brother were alive today! We would all have been saved by Hans and living a good life now." said Sasha to herself. As she was closing her thoughts about her parents, the doctor rushed in to see her. First, he asked how she was doing and whether she had been having any problems. Sasha told him that she felt better, but he still wanted to have a blood test just to make sure Sasha was all right. He called the nurse to take some blood and then he continued to check her more. Sasha lay there with blood taken out and the doctor checking her over. The nurse winked at me and told me that everything would be all right. Sasha knew that she had faith in God and that nothing could be worse than being in a slave camp. "Yes, I would be fine," said Sasha to herself. Sasha was happy that she was almost finished with this pregnancy, and she really wanted to wait before having any more children. Sasha needed to rest and let her body heal, and she was sure that Hans would agree with her. Sasha must tell Hans that she would like to wait for awhile to have anymore children. Minutes after this thought, the nurse came in with my results, and the doctor looked well pleased. He told me everything looked fine but to continue taking the vitamins even after she give birth. He gave her another bottle to keep in case she would run out of them. Sasha thanked him for helping her and he said that he wanted to see her in two weeks. She told him, “If God is willing.” He smiled and left for his next patient.

Sasha dressed and went to the front desk to make her next appointment. The nurse told Sasha that she would have February 28 at 10:00AM. Sasha walked over to Hans and Natalia. Hans was glad to see Sasha and wanted to know how everything went inside. Sasha told Hans that she was fine but that she needed to continue the vitamins for a while even after she gave birth. Sasha also told Hans that after their second child was born that she would like time to heal before any more. As always, Hans agreed with her. Sasha felt better, and Hans suggested lunch. He took her over to their favorite café where they had a hearty lunch together. Hans ordered enough food for all of us because Sasha had to eat; and if she didn’t, she would get weak. Hans ordered sandwiches, soup, and dessert. Natalia had her first piece of cake. She certainly liked it, and put it not only in her mouth, but all over her face. Everyone in the café was laughing, and I asked the waiter for a wet cloth to clean her face. Natalia enjoyed every minute of her cake, and everyone was pleased, although Hans wasn’t pleased about the fact that she had put her little hands on his clean white shirt, and left fingerprints on it, making his shirt look like as if it had dots all over it. We left after our lunch. Sasha did not need anything in the town, so they began their return journey.

MONTHS HAVE PASSED

Two months had already passed them by, and now they were well into the spring. Hans tried to convince himself that he could get on Zurich and ride, but it still was somewhat cold outside. The snow was melting, and Hans noticed some flowers were starting to come up. Beautiful as they were, he wished that the baby was already born so that they could do more as a family. Hans wanted to go places outside of Germany because the war had damaged his country so badly. "We cannot go to many places without seeing buildings down. Sometimes it is a sad sight to look at because I remember how it did look at one time, very beautiful," Hans said to himself.

The hospital reported that Sasha was due around May18 or later. Either way, Hans wanted to get through this experience fast. He tried to imagine how Sasha felt about having another baby without taking time off from Natalia. Hans remembered that he had agreed with her to take time off from having babies, that is if they even wanted any more. Hans hadn't gone through any names for the baby as yet, and he wasn't sure whether Sasha had come up with any, either. Hans knew that one time Sasha teased him about calling him Hans Jr. Han laughed for reasons and said, "No Sasha, not at this time." Hans had his reasons and purposes why no boy of his would be called, Hans Jr. "That is my secret and remains that way," said Hans to himself. She did say if it is a girl, she would like to call the baby Ilda, after my mother but that was not sure either.

Sasha remembered when Hans wanted to name the baby after my mother and she knew right there that Hans was ever so happy because it made her feel that her mother was closer to her than ever. That is a reason she loved Hans so much. No one could ever tell her that Hans had not been good to her and their daughter. Sasha always told Hans that no matter what might happen to them as a couple that she would always love him and be at his side if he needed her. Before Sasha had met Hans, her life in the Ghetto was so unbearable that words could not describe it. As a human being and being Jewish, Sasha had felt pain that she had lived with before she met Hans. The Nazis had shattered her life, especially when they took everything away from her family and left them with nothing but pain and horror. They were ruthless and inhumane. Later, Hans told her that many of the Germans found out that Hitler was not what he said he was at that time. They had to be quiet about their feelings because of the danger of being murdered or going into a concentration camp. Hans, on the other hand, had taken a great chance in setting Sasha and others free. Hans loved his country and served as best he could, but only the best so that the world could know that there were good Germans around. Sasha kept saying how much she loved Hans because so many people needed to know how he treated Sasha and so many others. Hans never challenge their beliefs as Jews or even questioned them. He accepted as many others should have. He respected her faith as being Jewish and never put her down about what she believed in. For that reason, Hans had captured her heart. Sasha knew that if she believed in God, and Hans did also, they could be a couple regardless of what faith they were. Sasha remembered staying with Hans in the camp where she had watched him as he performed as Commander. Hans never knew how Sasha watched him when he would be outside with his duties, and she had never told him that, either. Sasha had always admired Hans as being the most handsome officer she had seen. Sometimes Hans would go around in just his uniform trousers and his white crisp shirt with his blond hair sometimes falling down into his face. Sasha thanked God for Hans and for answered prayer. She was ready to live many years with Hans. Sasha often wondered whether any other officers rescued prisoners as Hans had done. If there are some out there, Sasha hoped that she could thank them for being as brave and helping so many.

DESTRUCTION

Today Hans bought a newspaper and the news was not good about Germany because there was so much destruction from the war. It would take years to rebuild what was destroyed. Cologne had so much damage that the stores they shopped in were the only buildings left. Hans was happy that his father's house was not destroyed or even touched by a bomb. Perhaps it was because we lived in the country and have only houses around. Hans wanted to take a trip to Berlin to see how things were progressing with the demolition. He was glad for nice weather because he could do much more than what he did in the winter. He remembered that he wanted to get Sasha a horse so she could ride with him. Hans wanted to surprise her. He liked surprising Sasha with things because she became all giggly and shy. Hans decided to take Zurich out and ride to town to see beyond the stores. Hans had seen the damage from afar, but he wanted to see it closely now. Hans heard that it would take years to build Germany again. He wasn't too pleased about how Germany's enemies had bombed his country; but most of all he was not pleased that Germany's leaders had built the country, and then tore it down to pieces. Hans saddled his horse, and told Sasha that he loved her, and rode to town, It was a beautiful day, and Hans wanted to make it the best that he could. Sasha told him that she would be in the yard doing what she could do with Natalia outside. Hans rode his horse to town although he really wanted to go to the old camp again and see whether it still stood; but that journey could be for another ride someday. "Maybe when I get Sasha her own horse, we could take a ride to the camp and just look around," Hans said. Hans stopped at the bakery where he bought some fresh bread, streusel, and cookies for Natalia. Hans thought the baked goods would be a good idea for dinner that night. He mounted back on Zurich and rode outside of the town. There, his eyes saw a disastrous sight. The damaged buildings gave him a flashback to his time in Munich. The buildings looked like what he was seeing now, and he knew that it would take years to clean up the mess and build again. Hans was so distraught that his hometown had been destroyed by ruthless people. When he had gone into Berlin some months before, he had seen that the buildings were down and pitiful to look at. Hans described the buildings as, "crumbled with nothing left." Furniture that once belong to families are now on the streets with nobody to claim them. Dead horses were still on the ground while the wild birds were eating the remains. Many of my people were crying and holding on to their dreams ahead. They had nothing left. Hans saw destruction many times, and it destroyed his mind causing him to have great depression. Hans loved his country; he was born here, raised and then served his country. He stood up for freedom but in the right way, not putting innocent people into camps. Germany must face the facts: our leaders failed us and the world. They have passed this mass destruction onto our children to see and bear memories of their fathers. "If my people had not voted for Hitler, we would have never been in war. Then again, if we hadn't been at war, what would have been my chances of meeting Sasha?" Hans asked himself. Hans put all his thoughts away and rode back into town and then headed home with his bakery goods for everyone. He rode slowly and enjoyed smelling the fresh air and listening to the birds singing to their mates. He had loved this day and like it. He also hoped that the baby would be born soon.

SURPRISE MYSELF

Hans was out, and Sasha was lying on this bed feeling strange in her stomach area. She was also building a strange sweat on my body. Sasha called for Mela to help her. Mela was always there to assist Sasha with whatever she needed. Sasha thanked God for Mela no matter what her differences had been with Mela and Hans. Sasha told Mela how she felt inside, and Mela suggested that the baby might be coming sooner than expected. If Mela were right, then the baby would be coming almost five weeks earlier than expected. Sasha grew worse by mid-day and wished that Hans was home from his ride to town. She needed him to help her so that she could call the hospital and ask what to do. Mela laid Sasha down, put my feet up, and got some rags and hot water just in case the baby came, She brought big bowls of hot water with rags, and then she called Elda. Mela told Elda what was happening, and they were now both prepared for what could come any minute. Elda was looking me over to see whether Sasha's water had broken; sure enough, it had. Elda told Mela to get ready because the baby was coming faster than expected. Sasha had wanted Hans here to see his baby being born and to assist, but he wasn't. Sasha became very warm. Finally, she couldn't take the pain anymore. Mela and Elda saw how Sasha was starting to bleed. They told her to push as hard as she could. They were screaming more than Sasha because they saw the crown of the baby's head. Mela told Sasha to push very hard. At this point, Sasha gave one hard final push, and there was her bundle of joy crying. She asked whether it was a boy or girl. "A boy," said Elda and Mela. They cleaned him off and cut his cord from me then wrapped him in a blanket while Sasha nursed him. Sasha named him, "Franz Luther Schweitzer" because Hans didn't want him to be "Jr." Sasha used Hans's middle name instead. The baby was so cute, so red, he had blue eyes with light brown hair, and he looked like Hans. Sasha couldn't wait for Hans to come home to see his new son. Sasha thanked Mela and Elda for all of their help and asked them to wait for Hans and to send him up as soon as he came home. They told Sasha they would.

RETURNED HOME

When Hans came home, he put Zurich into the barn shed where then brushed him from the dust and gave him a new carrot as a treat. Hans also fed Zurich a new bowl of oats and water. When he went into the house, Mela and Elda met him, saying that he needed to go upstairs to Sasha because she needed to see him right away. Hans went upstairs to their room, opened the door, and found Sasha sitting in the bed nursing their baby wrapped in a blanket. Hans fell down on the ground next to the bed and asked whether the baby was a boy or a girl. Sasha looked at Hans and said, "Meet your son, Franz Luther Schweitzer." Hans looked at Sasha with so much delight and asked whether he could hold the baby for awhile. Flashbacks of someone in Hans's life came to his thoughts as he looked at his son. A feeling of remorse fell upon Hans. He then took the baby in his arms where he just looked at him with so much love. Hans was so relieved to see the baby and knew that God had answered his prayer when he had asked Him to let the baby be born soon. Hans told Sasha that he was satisfied that they now had a boy and a girl. Hans really wasn't sure whether he wanted any more children. He told Sasha that if any more were to come, let them be from the Lord. Hans was thankful for two children and a wonderful wife. "All my gratitude goes to Sasha," he said.

BUNDLE OF JOY

asha showed Natalia her little brother. She couldn't understand, but she smiled at Franz and that touched Hans's heart. He knew that when she became older that she would have her brother to fall back and that they could help one another as family. "No one knows what could happen in the future," said Hans. He continued, "I can look at my son knowing that he will be raised correctly so that he will not hate or murder anyone because of their beliefs and difference. I see Franz as my son, growing older and me playing ball with him. Yes, he is my bundle of joy. Today, I shall go into town to buy him something."

UNEXPECTED CALL

As Hans was ready to leave for town, the telephone rang. Hans answered it. A stern voice asked for him. Hans told the gentleman that he was Hans and asked how he might help. The caller's name was Ammon Heisman from Berlin. He wanted to speak to Hans immediately about his position as Company Commander at Kassel camp. Hans's heart stood still. He didn't know what this call was all about, but he had a feeling what it might lead into. Hans asked him his location in Berlin and said that he could meet him this afternoon. Ammon told Hans for 1:00PM, and told Hans to bring his military identification card. Hans asked him his location. He did not want to tell Hans much about his location but he did indicate to meet him where the SS headquarters had once stood. Hans knew nobody by the name of Ammon Heisman. He asked Hymen to drive him to Berlin because he had some business to attend to. Hans went to Sasha and kissed her telling her that he would see her later because he had to go to Berlin for business. Sasha looked at Hans with weary eyes and told him to be careful. Hans did not like her "Be careful" words because it made him wonder for awhile who this Ammon was. Hans went with Hymen to the car, and they left for the unknown. During that five hour to Berlin, Hans wondered what this matter could possibly be about. Every thought raced through his mind leaving him still blank about this call. He closed his eyes and prayed that he would be safe in Berlin. Hans asked Hymen to park in the the front of the dilapidated building. Hans told Hymen that he would see him shortly and to sit tight. Hymen was gracious to Hans because he felt that since Hans had saved his life, he owed

Hans his. Hans had thanked Hymen every day for being a friend. This day, Hans would need that friendship. Hans got out of the car and saw a tall man standing near the debris that lay next the burned-out building. Hans went up to him, asking whether he was Ammon Heisman. He told Hans that he was and directed Hans to follow him. Hans looked at Hymen from the car and said, "It is fine; just wait for me." Not too far from the old headquarters stood part of a building Ammon brought Hans into it. Hans had a nasty feeling in his gut, knowing something was about to unfold, something nasty. This room that they entered was dark and cold. There stood another man with a leather coat on telling Hans to sit down. He asked Hans whether he was Hans Schweitzer, former company commander of Camp Kassel. Hans answered, "Yes." The man in the leather coat then took Hans upstairs to another room where he met Paul Greisen, another man in a leather coat, who asked Hans more questions but more detailed. He told Hans to sit down. Hans did as he was asked because he felt if he answered correctly, then he could be released. So Hans waited this scenario out answering any question with honesty but in the back of his mind, praying. The second man asked very sternly whether Hans was Lt. Colonel Commander Hans Franz Schweitzer. Hans said, "Yes, I am." "Were you the Commander of a Slave Camp in Kassel, Germany?" asked the man. Again, Hans answered, "Yes." The man became more intense asking Hans whether he had sent thousands to death. Hans replied, "No, I never killed anyone in the camp." The man looked at Hans with an ugly face that seemed to want to chew Hans up right there. He continued, "You, Hans Schweitzer are accused of murdering thousands of Jews and other prisoners at your camp." Hans kept telling him that he never had done so. The man looked at Hans with disbelief then punched Hans in the face until he bled. Hans wiped away the blood from his eye and told the man that he had witnesses who knew that he had never killed anyone in the camp. The man then laughed in Hans's face and told him that he was lying because there weren't any witnesses. The man then accused Hans of serious war crimes and said that he would be tried shortly for these murders and put to death. Hans told him that he was married to one of the prisoners who happened to be Jewish and that his driver downstairs was one of the former prisoners whom he had saved. Again, the man laughed and told Hans to shut up, or he would kill Hans without a trial. This ugly man told Ammon to lock Hans up in the cell until he went to trial. I kept telling him as he led me away that I was innocent, but still he didn't listen, although he asked Hans as he was being locked up in the cell, "Do you have these witnesses?" Hans answered, "Yes, my wife and others." "Your trial will be next week for two days and in those days you must prove your innocence," said Ammon. He then closed the door and left Hans in that dark, cold, musty, cell.

Hans only had thoughts of Hymen and his family and what could happen to them at this time. Now Hans was the prisoner just like those who had been at his camp. "But those I helped, I have no one now to help me." said Hans. He called on God, "Please send me help because I never killed anyone in or around the camp." "No one," Hans repeated. He was frightened and he had to lie down on the boards that had only a cover on top. Hans lay there and did not move, wondering what Hymen was thinking. Hans needed help and a miracle so he could get out of there. He was really afraid for once in his life, for he feared that his life was going to be over and that he would leave his wife and family behind.

BRIEF CALL

Hans had fallen asleep for a few hours and woke up to voices and laughing. He looked at his watch and saw that the time was after 4:00PM. Hymen had been outside for hours worrying where Hans was in a dark, derelict building. Hymen came into the building searching for Hans, and Hans could hear the man outside telling him to get out and go home. Hymen left, and Hans was happy that he did because Hans did not want anything to happen to Hymen because him. Hans tried to figure this situation out rationally because recently he had heard in the news that some intelligence group was rounding up war criminals. What this group did with them Hans could only imagine. Hans couldn't believe that they had imprisoned him, and right now Hans needed to ask God for all his help. As Hans prayed, he felt a calm feeling come upon him telling him not to worry.

Hans sat in the cell for days, eating nothing but some pastry with disgusting water, except for a few times that he had a meal with some salted pork and boiled potatoes. Hans couldn't wait to go home and taste Sasha's homemade cooking. How he missed her! As he was thinking about Sasha, he heard footsteps coming towards his cell. Heisman came to tell Hans that his trial would begin the next day. Heisman had a suitcase with so many papers in it, and took out a file on Hans. He also mentioned to Hans that notice of this trial had been posted in the newspapers. Heisman told Hans that he had better gather his witnesses before it was too late. Hans asked Heisman whether he could please call home. Heisman nodded his head to "Yes," and Hans called home.

"HELP ME, SASHA!"

Hans was allowed only two minutes on the phone; and when he called, Hans thanked God Sasha answered. She was so happy to hear from Hans and asked what she could do to help him. Hans asked Sasha quickly to gather enough witnesses for his trial the next day at Berlin courthouse. He needed everyone whom he had helped to escape from the prison. "Please be at the courthouse tomorrow at 10:00 AM and buy a newspaper. I am on the front page. I love you Sasha." Hans said as fast as Heisman took the phone out of his hand, hung it up, and released Hans back to his cell. Heisman slapped and punched Hans while he closed the cell door behind him. Hans sat there thanking God that he had reached Sasha.

NEWSPAPER

Sasha called the newspaper company in Berlin, and wanted to speak to anyone in charge. They transfer her to a Heinz Burggarten, who was the editor. She asked him about the article concerning Hans, and Burggarten was familiar with the story. She asked whether he could put it into the evening news that Hans needed witnesses and to call any former prisoners who had been in Hans's camp, to come to his assistance tomorrow at his trial. The editor doubted that Sasha's idea would work but told her that he would do his best. Sasha thanked him and hung up the phone. Everything was now in God's hands.

CALLING HELP

When Sasha hung up the phone, she went into the kitchen to tell Mela telling her Hans would be on trial for his involvement with the camp. "We must go as witnesses; my husband's life is on trial. He could be put to death after tomorrow." Sasha urged Mela to tell Peter that they were all needed at the courthouse for Hans's trial. Peter, Otto, Hymen, Mela, Sasha, Rabbi Jacobs, Elda, Fritz, and Hans's father all began working to help Hans. They were Hans's witnesses and would stand for Hans in what he did for them and others. Sasha told them again how much Hans needed them, and she broke down crying again. Desperately, she held on to her faith in God. She kept saying, "I have to save him from death, just like he did for me. Tomorrow we will leave to save Hans and together we will fight for his return."

MORNING PAPER

Sasha woke up early, got the children dressed and asked Elda and Fritz to please hold Natalia so that she could attend to Franz. Sasha fed them all including Danderick, and left them with Hans's father while everyone else went to Berlin. When they were leaving, Sasha asked Hymen to stop and buy a newspaper. There it was on the front page of the paper: "Save former Commander Hans Schweitzer." Sasha was so relieved and prayed that Hans's former prisoners would read this article in time to come to his rescue. Sasha read the story; it was fabulous. She prayed over this article that it would help her husband and prove his innocence. Sasha just kept her hand over her face, burying her tears within, until they reached Berlin. Just like that day in the Ghetto which marked the beginning of her freedom, she prayed that this day would be the beginning for Hans. "Together we will march into that courthouse with faith and belief that my husband would be home soon," Sasha said to her companions.

THE CELL

Hans had been in that musty cell for over a week living which his captors fed him water, tea, and nasty soup. Today, they gave him clean clothes and had Hans shave and take a shower. In honesty, they really had not treated Hans badly as far as beating or anything like that. They had just yelled at him. When Hans had finished dressing, Heisman came in and told Hans that he had better have enough witnesses, or he would be put to death by hanging or firing squad. For once, Hans felt like the prisoners with death hanging over their lives. He was scared, very scared. At 7:30AM, Hans had breakfast which consisted of tea and a piece of bread, after which Hans stayed in his cell until the time to go for the trial. Hans wore a white shirt and black trousers that his captors had given him to wear, and his hair which he had combed back, was still wet from the shower. Hans was ready to get this trial going, hoping that it would come to a halt. He sat there thinking, praying, and looking at his watch. As the time got closer to 9:00 AM, several of his captors came in to get him and transported Hans to the courthouse cell. There he waited until almost 10:00 AM for this trial to begin so he could finally know where his destiny lay. Hans kept his tears to himself, showing that he was innocent and not upset about this accusation. It was almost ten when Heisman came and two other men telling Hans that it was time to go. They led him in handcuffs into the courthouse. As Hans walked in, he saw Sasha and everyone from his house sitting calmly. Hans now realized that his friends had come to assist him and to save his life from death, just as he had saved theirs.

"SAVING LT. COLONEL HANS"

The court started at 10:00 AM, and Hans was sworn in to tell the truth. Loudly, he said, "Yes." Heisman was presenting Hans's case as a Nazi war criminal. Hans sat there biting his tongue at every word. Heisman told the court that Hans had been assigned as Company Commander of the Kassel Camp from 1940-1945, and while there he helped to murder prisoners that were there. The judge was about to say something when the door swung open widely and a huge crowd with around 60 people came rushing into the room. The judge banged his mallet asking who these people were. One man out of the group answered, "We are all former prisoners of Camp Kassel." Hans's mouth parted with shock, and the judge told them to find a place to sit and wait. As they sat down, one of the men looked at Hans and smiled. Hans knew who some of them were. In any case, these were Hans's former prisoners whom he had released on that day in December of 1944. Now, they had come to his rescue. Hans felt deeply honored. He was now reaping what he had sown, and realized that he had sown their new lives on that day that he had released them, and now he was reaping the same from them. The judge asked Hans to take the stand as Heisman came up to Hans asking him questions. Heisman first asked Hans his name. He then proceeded by asking what Hans had done in the camp and how he did it. I told him everything, from saving Sasha, to abandoning the camp because of the bombs. He wanted to know whether Hans had punished any of the prisoners by beating or shooting them. Hans told them, "No, that he never did." Then he turned it around asking whether Hans had let any of his officers do the beating and shooting of the prisoners. Hans answered with another "No." Heisman went on to ask Hans whether he believed in Nazism. Finally, Hans answered, "No, and I did not. I was against all those killings and rules in other camps but I had to follow some rules." "The rules that I followed did not affect the prisoners." Heisman then wanted to know why Hans had joined the army. Hans told him that he was seventeen, and that he had no choice but to join. "I was part of Hitler's Youth and then I became an officer." said Hans. Heisman insisted that Hans knew about the Nazis, but Hans replied that he had to join because of his family. "If I didn't join, the Nazis would have had them tortured. Heisman told the judge that he rested his case against Hans. Then another man came up with glasses falling down his nose and went on with other questions. He asked Hans how he could possibly prove his innocence to the jury. Hans told him that he had his wife who is Jewish and that he had helped to save her from the camp. The questioner asked whether she was in the courtroom. Hans said, "Yes, she is sitting there," as he pointed to Sasha. The judge asked Sasha to take the stand. The questioner asked Sasha who she was. She told him that she was Hans's wife and that she was a Jew from Camp Kassel. She also told him the entire story of how they had met and what happened, after that. The second interrogator rested his case and sat down. The judge finally asked the court about the witnesses to speak up about Hans. He asked Hans whether he was guilty of war crimes. Again, Hans replied, "No." Then the judge had the the witnesses all come up; and to his amazement, he saw over 60 of them standing before him. Hans had more than enough witnesses to save him, provided that the trial would be a fair one. Mostly all of the witnesses were interviewed, and they told the court about what Hans had done for them and how Hans had saved them. They also mentioned that Hans never hurt any of them nor shot anyone. They only remembered Hans as helping them but still following the rules. One man told the judge that Hans had risked his life in order to save him and everyone else now gathered here. The court rested its case and presented it to the jury for whether Hans Schweitzer was guilty or not guilty. So Hans had to wait for a while until they came back from their final decision. While the court had a brief intermission, Hans went outside to meet Sasha.

He was so happy to see her they kissed until the officers of the court called them back into the courtroom. An hour or so later they returned and Hans was happy to get back into that room to hear his destiny. After the jury returned, the judge asked whether they had come to a final decision about Hans. The jury foreman said that they had. The judge then told Hans to stand to hear his verdict. Hans's knees were shaking, and his mouth became so dry as he stood there waiting for what the jury had decided. The judge then asked the foreman to read the verdict. The foreman rose to read the paper out loud:

"We, the jury, find Lt. Colonel Commander Hans Franz Schweitzer "not guilty" of any war crimes at Camp Kassel." Hans then fell down in his chair while the guard came over to remove the handcuffs. The judge smacked down his mallet, saying, "This case is dismissed, and the court is adjourned." Hans was so happy that he screamed with joy, thanking God and his former prisoners. They all saluted Hans again as though he was standing before them the day they left him. Hans made it a point to return the salute to them and shook all 60 of their hands. Now he was free to go home with his family. Hans told everyone that he would like to have them over to his home at any time for dinner. Sasha gave them their address. They all nodded and thanked Hans for all that he had done for them. As they said good-bye, Hans walked with them out to freedom again, and Hans was so grateful to God that He had kept his word. Hans realized now when a person does something good: the good will come back to you. Hans had done his job, and the former prisoners rewarded him and saved his life.

THE ROAD TO A NEW BEGINNING

It was a long, drawn-out trial, and Hans never thought that such a thing would ever have happened to him, but it did. It was a good thing thing that he was innocent and the court was a fair one, or else Hans would have been put to death. Hans continued to be amazed that these former prisoners had come to his rescue. So many from Camp Kassel had come to Hans's trust, and he was grateful to all of them, including his family and friends at home. Hans thanked Sasha for being there for him and doing what she did. Contacting the newspapers meant a lot in terms of the trial's outcome. Hans was so overwhelmed at the reality that he was sitting in his own den again. "Now I realize how we need to appreciate something, because any time it could be taken away," he said to himself. Hans continued his reflections:

"I am twenty-seven years old now; ten years ago I became a victim of one of the most powerful regimes in the entire world. I fought for my country, not to show the world that I stood for innocent blood to be shed, but to show them that Germany did have good people. I fought for bravery, dignity, and pride. I still believe in a new world to come, but I want answers as to the reason that this war had happened. I also believe in the possibility of a new world to come where this is no hate but only love. As to the reason that this war had those prisoners who came to my rescue, they did it out of love for me, where love overcame all hate. Love does conquer all, even to the point of our own personal ghosts. I am grateful now, putting this all behind me. I am ready to live my life with my family and friends. I know I will not go through again what I have gone through these past years. I do know that I shall go with hope and faith for a better life. I am ready for my new life to begin as I journey through this new beginning. I am ready for my Truthfully Yours, forever."

The End for now and a new beginning to come, soon.

FINAL WORD

I hope that everyone who read my book enjoyed it and is looking forward to the second sequel: "Truthfully Yours," A New Beginning. In my final words, I am not sure whether there was a Hans or a Sasha during the war, but I can only hope that there were many. Let us all learn from Hans and Sasha that love comes in many ways by forgiving and putting away our differences. It is only then, we could live a better life. I hope all of my readers will live the Hans and Sasha legacy and pass it on to everyone. I look forward to the second book coming out in 2012. This book will continue from where Hans left off only to have a new beginning in his life. My final word: let everyone become a Hans and a Sasha so we could live our own legacy in the world today. Happy Reading to everyone and pass it on.